Bank Asset-Liability Management

Fidelio Tata

Bank Asset-Liability Management

A Guide to Managing Interest Rate Risk in the Banking Book for Practitioners, Regulators, and Supervisors in the EU

palgrave
macmillan

Fidelio Tata
International School of Management
Berlin, Germany

ISBN 978-3-031-80204-1 ISBN 978-3-031-80205-8 (eBook)
https://doi.org/10.1007/978-3-031-80205-8

This Palgrave Macmillan imprint is published by the registered company Springer Nature Switzerland AG
The registered company address is: Gewerbestrasse 11, 6330 Cham, Switzerland

Preface

3, 6 and 3.

Banking used to be so easy! Sabine Lautenschläger, former member of the ECB's Executive Board and Vice-Chair of the ECB's Supervisory Board, put it this way at a conference of the National Association of German Cooperative Banks in Berlin on May 31, 2017: "Once upon a time, there were bankers whose lives were marked by three numbers. Do you know those numbers? They were 3, 6 and 3. Bankers paid 3% interest on deposits, earned 6% on loans, and at 3 in the afternoon they drove to the golf course."

Many of the interest rate risk and asset liability management (ALM) techniques used by banks date back to those "once upon a time" days. Some have since been modified to reflect changes in the market or to reflect new market regulations; some are still in use conceptually unchanged, albeit calibrated to fit the current market environment; and in some cases, historical models are still being applied in an unchanged fashion. To assess the usefulness of various ALM techniques and models from today's perspective, it is important to critically review their purpose, their assumptions, their shortcomings and their role in modern risk management. As the old aphorism attributed to George Box suggests, all models are wrong, but some are useful. I wrote this book to help assess the usefulness of various ALM techniques and models from today's perspective.

The purpose of this book is threefold. First, it introduces the reader to the most common components of interest rate risk management within bank ALM. To this end, the book emphasizes the communication of risk concepts at an intuitive level. Analytical rigor and mathematical precision come later. This helps to avoid the illusion of scientific precision created by mathematical formulas. The book also aims to bridge the gap between widely used, general interest rate risk management techniques in the fixed income area and what is best practice in European banks on a daily basis.

The second objective of this book is to provide an update on the most recent changes in the regulatory framework for European banks' management of interest rate risk in the banking book (IRRBB), including new EBA guidelines.

Finally, the book covers the latest developments in interest rate risk management, such as behavioral modeling of bank customers, and the implications of the rapidly changing interest rate environment beyond 2022.

The book contains no advanced mathematics and assumes no knowledge of standard financial theory. However, a basic understanding of banking would be a plus.

I would also like to thank Tibor Dudás, Christos V. Gortsos, Dirk Holländer, Friedrich Penkner, André Tomfort and Burkhard P. Varnholt for kindly agreeing to review selected parts of this book and for providing critical comments and detailed subject matter suggestions. Any remaining errors are, of course, mine.

Many thanks to Tibor Dudás for allowing me to use some of his own illustrative examples and simulations.

Finally, I would like to thank my editor at Palgrave Macmillan, Tula Weis.

Berlin, Germany — Fidelio Tata

About This Book

The origin of this book can be traced back to material I have used when conducting training seminars for banking supervisors (micro-prudential) or staff members from the financial stability staff (macro-prudential) from central banks or national competent authorities (NCAs) in Europe. These training seminars are organized by the European Supervisor Education Initiative (ESE), an alliance of central banks and supervisory authorities in Europe with the aim of qualifying financial supervisors in Europe, and I have had the honor of teaching more than twenty of them since 2014. Over time, it evolved into a broader set of training materials for various academic courses on risk management that I have taught in recent years at the Berlin School of Economics and Law, the International School of Management, and the Frankfurt School of Finance & Management.

Other publications cover various aspects discussed in this book, and the aim is not to replace them, but rather than to develop a framework within which they can be used to complement and enhance the analysis. There are excellent books that provide an overview of asset-liability management and financial risk management in banks. *Asset-Liability and Liquidity Management* by Pooya Farahvash (2020), *Asset Liability Management (ALM) in Banken* by Martin Spillmann et al. (2019), *Handbook of Financial Risk Management* by Thierry Roncalli (2020), *Asset-liability management with ultra-low interest rates* by Ernest Gnan and Christian Beer (eds.) (2015), and *Bewertung und Steuerung von variablen Produkten bei Kreditinstituten* by Gennadij Seel (2023) belong to this class of literature. Then there are books devoted to the modeling, pricing and risk management of fixed-income instruments, such as *Fixed Income Securities* by Tuckman (2022), or of derivative instruments, such as *Options, Futures, and Other Derivatives* by Hull (2021). Finally, there are some very good working papers by bank regulators and supervisors that contribute to the topic of risk management and ALM, such as *Rising interest rates and implications for banking supervision* by Rodrigo Coelho et al. (2023).

The book is aimed at three different audiences. First, it is tailored for entry-level interest rate risk managers and risk controllers in European banks, including ALM professionals, treasurers, chief risk officers, accounting and finance managers, and liquidity managers. Second, it is aimed at European banking supervisors or financial stability staff (central banks and national competent authorities) who are new to the area of interest rate risk in the banking book (IRRBB). Third, it complements the academic literature for students of risk management in undergraduate and graduate programs in finance or central banking.

The book is organized as follows. After introducing the basics of ALM in Chapter 1, Chapter 2 describes the most widely used ALM techniques, including funds transfer pricing, net interest income calculations, and the so-called replicating model. Chapter 3 then discusses aspects of ALM from a practitioner's point of view. Chapter 4 presents a case study of the demise of Silicon Valley Bank and what can be learned from it. Chapter 5 takes an in-depth look at the regular treatment of interest rate risk and recent developments on the regulatory front. Finally, Chapter 6 presents a vision for ALM in the future.

References

Coelho, Rodrigo. 2023. Rising interest rates and implications for banking supervision. Financial Stability Institute (FSI) of the Bank for International Settlements (BIS), Brief No. 19 (May 2023). https://www.bis.org/fsi/fsibriefs19.htm. Accessed on January 18, 2025.

Farahvash, Pooya. 2020. *Asset-Liability and Liquidity Management*. Newark, NJ: Wiley.

Gnan, Ernest, and Beer, Christian (eds.) (2015). *Asset-liability management with ultra-low interest rates*. Vienna, Austria: SUERF.

Hull, John C. 2021. *Options, Futures, and Other Derivatives*. Boston, MA: Pearson Prentice Hall.

Roncalli, Thierry. 2020. *Handbook of Financial Risk Management*. Boca Raton, FL: CRC Press.

Seel, Gennadij. 2023. *Bewertung und Steuerung von variablen Produkten bei Kreditinstituten*. Wiesbaden, Germany: Springer Gabler.

Spillmann, Martin, Karsten Döhnert, and Roger Rissi. 2019. *Asset Liability Management (ALM) in Banken*. Wiesbaden, Germany: Springer Gabler.

Tuckman, Bruce. 2022. *Fixed Income Securities: Tools for Today's Markets*. Hoboken, NJ: Wiley.

Contents

About the Author

Fidelio Tata is a senior financial markets professional with some 30 years of leadership experience in derivatives marketing, institutional sales, risk management and global fixed income research. He is a veteran of top Wall Street firms including JPMorgan, Credit Suisse, HSBC and Societe Generale. His extensive teaching experience includes serving as a frequent guest speaker at conferences and training central banks in asset-liability management for over 10 years. He is currently a professor of Finance at the International School of Management in Germany. Previously, he held positions at the Berlin School of Economics and Law in Germany, the University of St. Gallen in Switzerland, the London School of Economics and Political Science in the United Kingdom, New York University's Stern School of Business, and Harvard University in the United States.

Abbreviations

$\sum$	The sum of
AFS	Available For Sale
AI	Artificial Intelligence
ALCO	Asset and Liability [management] Committee
ALM	Asset-Liability Management
BCBS	Basel Committee on Banking Supervision
BD&AA	Big Data and Advanced Analytics
BIS	Bank for International Settlements
bn	billion
bp	Basis point (0.01%), or Basis points
CASP	Crypto-Asset Service Provider
CEBS	Committee of European Banking Supervisors
CET1	Common Equity Tier 1
CRD	Capital Requirements Directive
CRR	Capital Requirements Regulation
CSRBB	Credit Spread Risk Arising from the Banking Book/Credit Spread Risk Arising from Non-Trading Book Activities
DCM	Debt Capital Markets
DeFi	Decentralized Finance
DLT	Distributed Ledger Technology
DV01	Dollar Value of One Basis Point (pronounced dee-vee-ohh-one)
e.g.	Exempli gratia (for example)
EaR	Earnings at Risk
EBA	European Banking Authority
ECB	European Central Bank

ECM	Equity Capital Markets
eds.	Editors
ELI	European Legislator Identifier
EoY	End of Year
et al.	et alii (and others)
etc.	Et cetera (and others)
EU	European Union
EUR	Euro
EURIBOR	Euro Interbank Offered Rate
EV	Economic Value
EVE	Economic Value of Equity
FDIC	Federal Deposit Insurance Corporation (United States)
Fed	Federal Reserve
Fig.	Figure
FinTech	Financial Technology
FSB	Financial Stability Board
FTP	Funds Transfer Pricing
fwd.	Forward
GAAP	Generally Accepted Accounting Principles
GL	Guideline(s)
HTM	Held To Maturity
i.e.	Id est (in other words)
IE	Interest Expense
IFRS	International Financial Reporting Standards
II	Interest Income
IRRBB	Interest Rate Risk Arising from the Banking Book/Interest Rate Risk Arising from Non-Trading Book Activities
IT	Information Technology
LIBOR	London Interbank Offered Rate
M&A	Mergers and Acquisitions
MBS	Mortgage-Backed Securities
MFI	Monetary Financial Institution
mm	Million
MV	Market Value
NCA	National Competent Authority
NII	Net Interest Income
NIM	Net Interest Margin
NIRP	Negative Interest Rate Policy
NMD	Non-Maturity Deposit(s)
NMP	Non-Maturity Product(s)
No.	Number
NPV	Net Present Value
OCI	Other Comprehensive Income
OIS	Overnight Index Swap

OJ L	Official Journal of the European Union, L series
P&L	Profit and Loss
p. a.	Per Annum (per year)
PE	Private Equity
PV	Present Value
RFR	Risk-Free Rate
RTS	Regulatory Technical Standard
SA	Standardized Approach
Sect.	Section
SOT	Supervisory Outlier Test
SREP	Supervisory Review and Evaluation Process
S-SA	Simplified Standardized Approach
SVB	Silicon Valley Bank
US	United States (of America)
USD	US Dollar
VaR	Value at Risk
VC	Venture Capital
Vol.	Volume
vs.	Versus
ZIRP	Zero Interest Rate Policy

List of Figures

List of Tables

1

Introduction

Asset-liability management (ALM) refers to the processes that manage the mismatch risk between assets and liabilities. In this book, we focus on ALM risk in banks and, more specifically, ALM risk in the banking book.

ALM is neither *pure art*, nor *pure science*; rather, it combines the creative, realistic, and pragmatic style of art with the rigorous and quantitative mindset of science. In this way, ALM can be thought of as a *craft*.

This chapter is divided into two parts. In the first part, we begin by contextualizing ALM within the broader ecosystem of a bank. We then review some selected concepts and models of interest rate risk management that are fundamental to ALM.

1.1 ALM in Banks

Any institution with a assets and liabilities on a balance sheet can engage in ALM. In fact, ALM is commonly practiced by insurance companies, pension funds and even corporations. In this book, however, we focus on ALM in banks. Because the primary business model in banking is to convert interest-sensitive deposits (which are liabilities from the bank's perspective) into interest-sensitive loans (which are assets from the bank's perspective), ALM is particularly important for banks.

In this section, we will: review how the recent rise in interest rates creates interest rate risk; introduce the two most common perspectives used to assess a bank's interest rate risk exposure (the economic value perspective and the

F. Tata, *Bank Asset-Liability Management*, https://doi.org/10.1007/978-3-031-80205-8_1

earnings perspective); discuss the purpose of ALM and define interest rate risk in the banking book (IRRBB); take a look at the stakeholders in ALM; contrast a bank's banking book with its trading book; provide an overview of the financial instruments used in ALM; and finally, introduce the risk-return perspective.

1.1.1 How the Recent Rise in Interest Rates Creates Interest Rate Risk

Interest rate risk is the potential loss resulting from unexpected changes in interest rates that may adversely affect a bank. It is defined as follows in the current European Banking Authority (EBA) guidelines[1]:

> Interest rate risk arising from non-trading book activities: The current and prospective risk of a negative impact to the institution's economic value of equity, or to the institution's net interest income, taking market value changes into account as appropriate, which arise from adverse movements in interest rates affecting interest rate sensitive instruments, including gap risk, basis risk and option risk.[2]

Different types of assets are affected differently by changes in interest rates. For example, an increase in interest rates may cause the interest income on a floating rate instrument to increase, while the same increase in interest rates will not change the cash flows on a fixed rate instrument; at the same time, the increase in interest rates will not change the value of the floating rate instrument very much, while the value of the fixed rate instrument will decrease.

After a prolonged period of zero interest rate policy (ZIRP) by central banks around the world, the period from Q1 2022 to Q2 2023 has seen the largest, fastest, and broadest rise in interest rates since the 1980s, with 1-year euro yields rising by more than 400 bp (see Fig. 1.1). The recent market turmoil has exposed the heightened vulnerabilities of banks, particularly those with significant exposures to long-term, fixed income assets, fueled by shorter-term, less stable funding. This challenging interest rate environment reinforces the strategic importance of asset-liability management for banks.

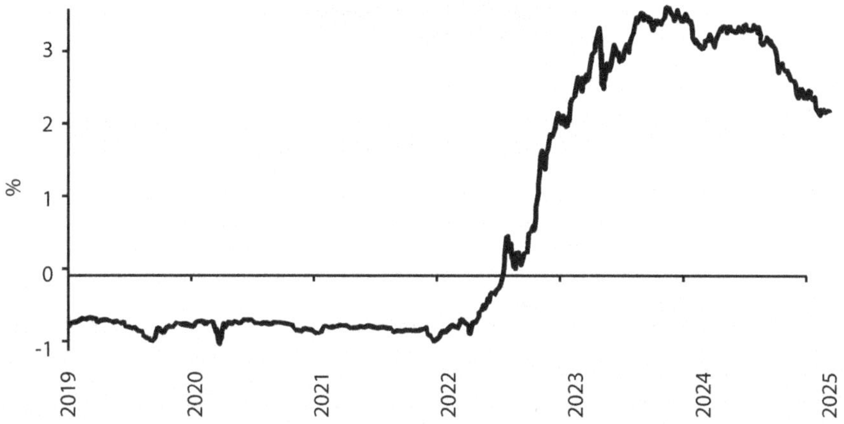

Fig. 1.1 1-Year maturity AAA-rated Government bond yield[3]

1.1.2 Economic Value vs. Earnings Perspective

There are two widely used perspectives for assessing a bank's interest rate risk exposure: the *economic value perspective* and the *earnings perspective*.[4]

The economic value of a bank is calculated as the sum of the economic value of a bank's assets, liabilities and off-balance sheet items. The economic value of a position is defined as the present value (PV) of all future cash flows expected to result from the position.

Earnings are accrued revenues and reported earnings that result in a profit or loss.

In interest rate risk management, the (primary) objective is not to provide an absolute estimate of a bank's economic value or its earnings, but how they *change* as the interest rate environment changes. In the context of ALM, what we are looking for from an economic value perspective is the *change* in economic value given a change in interest rates; from an earnings perspective, it is the *change* in earnings given a change in interest rates (see Fig. 1.2).

There are commercial reasons for a bank management to demonstrate to its shareholders (and stakeholders) that the bank is not facing imminent balance sheet deterioration or loss of earnings in the event of an adverse interest rate move. However, there are also regulatory requirements, set by the European Banking Authority (EBA) for banks to do this:

> Institutions should manage risks (…) that affect both their economic value and net interest income measures plus market value changes[5]

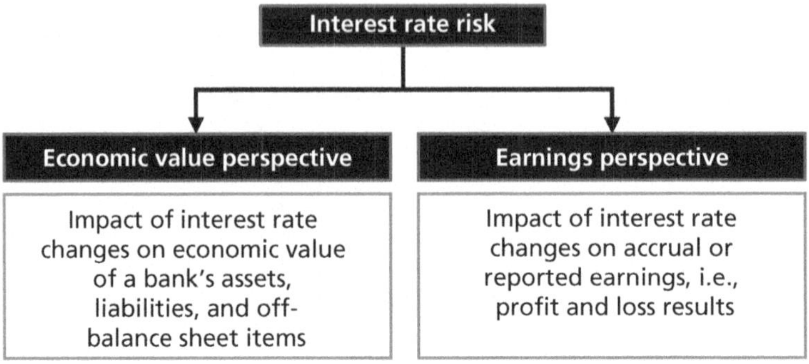

Fig. 1.2 Economic value vs. earnings perspective

It is important to recognize that it is not enough to focus on one or the other perspective; *both* approaches must be implemented!

The metrics for assessing economic value are detailed in Sect. 2.1 and those for assessing earnings are detailed in Sect. 2.2.

1.1.3 Purpose of ALM and IRRBB

The purpose of ALM in banks is to optimize profit and loss (P&L) and equity capital while maintaining adequate liquidity coverage and an adequate interest rate risk exposure. Typically, it is not possible to *simultaneously* maximize P&L, improve liquidity, and minimize interest rate risk and capital requirements. Instead, ALM aims to find some kind of optimal balance.[6]

The starting point for ALM analysis is the balance sheet. Expectations about the future development of the balance sheet and future interest rates also play a crucial role in ALM's proposals and actions.

ALM plays a critical role in the identification, measurement and management of the interest rate risk arising from the non-trading book activities, referred to as the interest rate risk arising from the banking book (IRRBB).

IRRBB refers to the current or prospective risk to a bank' capital and earnings arising from adverse interest rate movements affecting the bank's banking book positions.[7]

Managing IRRBB is not just a nice-to-have activity for a bank; it is a regulatory requirement:

> Institutions should treat IRRBB as an important risk and always assess it solely, explicitly, and comprehensively in their risk management processes and internal capital assessment processes. (…) Institutions should identify their

IRRBB exposures and ensure that they are adequately measured, monitored and controlled.[8]

Banks are even encouraged to go beyond the minimum regulatory requirements:

> Institutions should not rely on a single measure of risk but should instead use the range of quantitative tools and models that correspond to their specific risk exposure.[9]

1.1.4 Stakeholders of ALM

Top management bears the ultimate responsibility for prudent interest rate risk management in a bank. However, IRRBB is typically delegated to a bank-wide ALM department and an ALCO. ALCO (short for Asset and Liability Management Committee) is a risk management committee in a bank that assesses the risk associated with the bank's assets and liabilities. It manages interest rate risk while ensuring adequate returns and liquidity.

> Institutions should, in relation to IRRBB, ensure (…) that their management body bears the ultimate responsibility for the oversight of the IRRBB management framework, the institution's risk appetite framework and the amounts, types and distribution of internal capital to adequately cover the risks. The management body should determine the institution's overall IRRBB strategy and approve the corresponding policies and processes. The management body may, however, delegate the monitoring and management of IRRBB to senior management, expert individuals or an asset and liability management committee (…).[10]

Stakeholders in the ALM process also include Group Capital Markets (GCM), Controlling, Accounting, IT, Debt Capital Markets (DCM), Retail and Corporate Sales, and Market & Credit Risk Management. Thus, ALM can be seen as the heart of a bank, as it touches upon almost all corporate functions.

1.1.5 Banking Book vs. Trading Book

A sufficiently large and diversified bank includes activities that are not related to the typical customer-facing core banking business. Figure 1.3 shows a stylized balance sheet of such an institution. Separating the balance sheet items

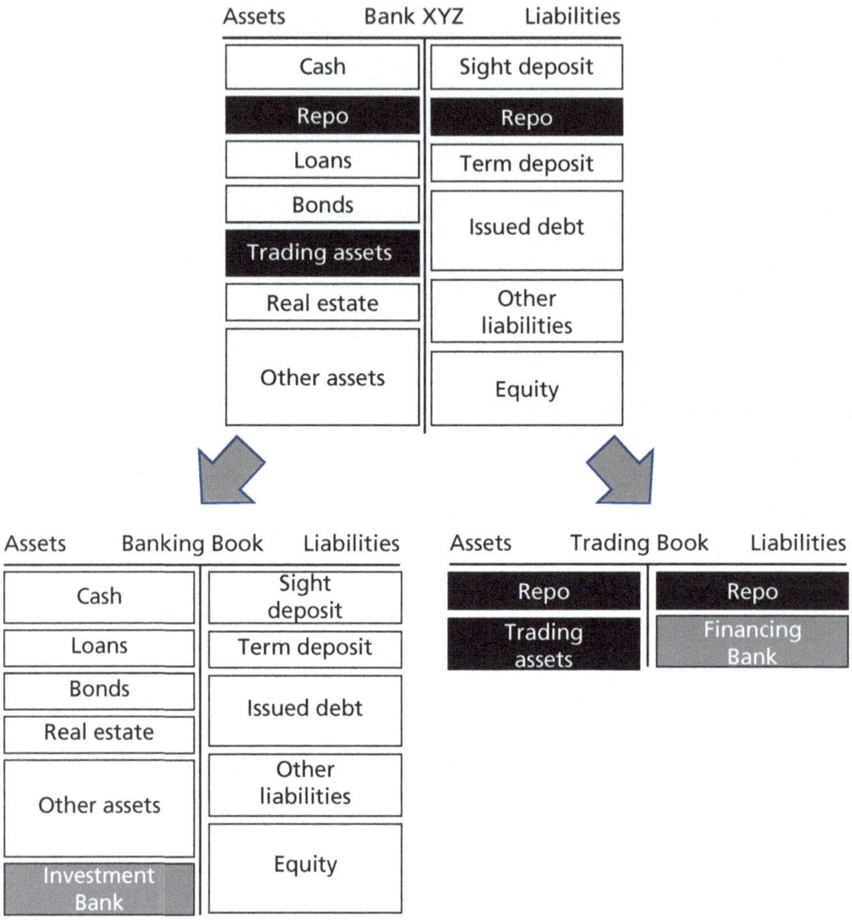

Fig. 1.3 Banking book vs. trading book

associated with the banking business and non-banking activities results in two sets of "books," the *banking book* and the *trading book*.[11]

The *banking book*, sometimes also referred to as the non-*regulatory trading book*, comprises all transactions and positions of a long-term nature that are related to the bank's client business and its financing. It includes the bank's equity capital.

The *trading book*, sometimes also referred to as the *regulatory trading book*, typically includes positions taken for the purpose of short-term resale, profiting from short-term price movements, generating arbitrage profits, or hedging risks.

One reason for splitting a bank's entire "book" into two books is that there are different regulatory requirements for each book. As mentioned

Table 1.1 Banking book vs. trading book

Classification of instruments and transactions according to their trading intent:	
Banking book	Trading book
Unlisted equities	Instruments in the correlation trading portfolio
Instruments designated for securitization warehousing	Instruments resulting from securities underwriting commitments
Real estate holdings	Instruments held as accounting trading assets or liabilities ("held for trading" assets and liabilities)
Retail credit and credit to small and medium-sized enterprises (SMEs)	Instruments resulting from market-making activities
Other types of credit	Listed equities (other than equity investment funds)
Equity investments in a fund for which the institution cannot obtain daily price quotes	Trading-related repo-style transactions (repo-style transactions that are (i) entered into for liquidity management purposes and are (ii) valued at accrual for accounting purposes, are not presumed to be trading-related
Derivative instruments that have any of the types of instruments mentioned above as an underlying asset	Instruments that would give rise to net short risk positions for equity risk or credit risk in the banking book
Instruments held for the purpose of hedging a particular risk of a position in any of the types of instruments listed above	Options including bifurcated embedded derivatives from instruments issued out of the banking book that relate to credit or equity risk

above, there are *specific* rules for managing interest rate risk in the banking book (IRRBB). Table 1.1 provides an overview of typical banking book and regulatory trading book positions as defined by the ECB.[12]

1.1.6 Instruments Used in ALM

ALM uses a variety of products to manage interest rate risk, including:

1. Internal positions from customer business
    i. Customer deposits
    ii. Customer loans
    iii. Customer credit lines
2. External positions to manage IRRBB

i. Financing vehicles (debt issuance, etc.)
ii. Interbank and repo transactions
iii. Fixed income instruments (bonds, etc.)
iv. Liquidity reserves

3. Off-balance sheet items, including derivatives

The initial step in determining the necessity of additional instruments utilized by ALM is the IRRBB created by the customer business. To some extent, a bank has limited influence over the customer business, as customer business often cannot be declined (without jeopardizing the bank's relationship with the customer). Furthermore, the pricing of customer products (e. g., the interest rate paid for customer deposits) is frequently determined by market forces.

Subsequently, ALM superimposes customer business with market transactions designed to alter the overall interest rate exposure of the bank. Such market transactions may encompass a vast array of liquid fixed-income instruments, including derivatives.

In the context of interest rate risk, only interest rate-sensitive instruments are taken into account in the calculation of IRRBB. This is a logical consequence of the fact that interest rate-insensitive instruments would not be expected to undergo a price change in the event of a change in interest rates. The EBA guidelines are explicit in this regard also:

> Interest rate sensitive instruments: Assets, liabilities and off-balance-sheet items in the non-trading book, which are sensitive to interest rate changes (excluding assets deducted from CET1 capital – e. g., real estate or intangible assets or equity exposures in the non-trading book).[13]

Derivatives may be employed for the purpose of implementing *micro hedges* with respect to an individual balance sheet position.[14] In this instance, the cash flows associated with the position are replicated by one side of a swap, with opposite direction, while the other side pays a floating rate, plus or minus a spread. Such a balance sheet position may be found on either the asset side or the liability side of the bank's balance sheet. Figure 1.4 provides

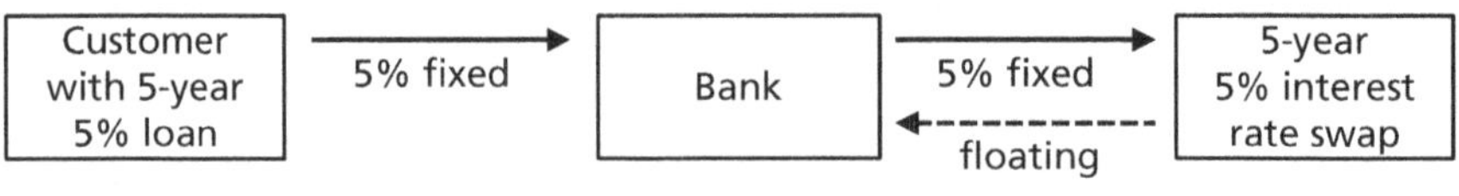

Fig. 1.4 Asset swap of a customer loan

an illustration of a customer-driven asset, namely a five-year fixed-rate loan, that is micro-hedged by a corresponding fixed-to-floating interest rate swap. Such a swap transaction is referred to as an asset swap.

It is somewhat surprising to note that the magnitudes of banks' net interest rate swap exposures are relatively insignificant in comparison to the scale of their operations and underlying exposures. In lieu of utilizing swaps, banks appear to offset potential duration mismatches through the deployment of on-balance-sheet positions.[15]

The implementation of an ALM strategy involving derivatives for hedging (or risk-taking) business necessitates a substantial degree of institutional expertise. In certain instances, an unsuccessful hedge can prove more detrimental than the absence of hedging altogether. In the context of derivative usage, it is incumbent upon the banking institution to demonstrate its possession of the requisite knowledge and expertise:

> Institutions using derivative instruments to mitigate IRRBB exposures should possess the necessary knowledge and expertise. Each institution should demonstrate that it understands the consequences of hedging with interest rate derivatives.[16]

1.1.7 Risk vs. Return

In general, when plotting the average expected margin contribution versus the volatility (σ) of the margin, a trade-off is typically observed. Margin businesses with higher volatility tend to be rewarded with higher expected margins. Please refer to Fig. 1.5.

The objective of ALM is to direct the bank towards an optimal risk-return profile. This may entail reducing risk if it can be done without compromising the expected margin, increasing the margin if this can be done without increasing risk, or a combination of both.

The ratio between return and risk, as illustrated by the slope of the dotted line in Fig. 1.5, represents the expected compensation per unit of risk. The objective of ALM is to maximize this ratio.

1.2 Interest Rate Risk

Interest rate risk is defined as the potential for adverse effects on an institution's activities resulting from fluctuations in interest rates.[17] The present analysis will be limited to activities related to a bank's core banking service,

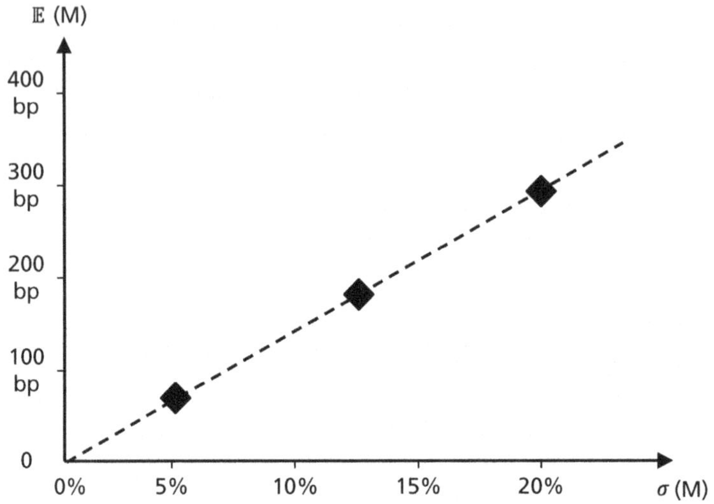

Fig. 1.5 Risk vs. return

that is to say, to interest rate risk arising from the banking book (IRRBB). The management of interest rate risk is a regulatory requirement:

> Institutions should regularly, at least quarterly and more frequently in times of increased interest rate volatility or increased IRRBB levels, measure their exposure to IRRBB in the context of the different IRRBB measures under various interest rate shock scenarios for potential changes in the level and shape of the interest rate yield curves, and to changes in the relationship between different interest rates (i. e., basis risk).[18]

This section will begin with an examination of the manner in which interest rates may fluctuate. Subsequently, the various types of interest rate risk will be examined. Afterwards, the concept of Duration, arguably the most prevalent interest rate risk measure, will be delineated. Then, we present the Duration Gap Analysis, which is founded upon the duration measure. Finally, we will examine two distinct risk measurement approaches, which previously introduced in Sect. 1.1.2. These approaches are centered around the Economic Value and the Earnings Measure.

1.2.1 Changes in Interest Rates

An *unchanged* interest rate environment is typically not considered to be the source of interest rate risk. Moreover, *anticipated* shifts in interest rates from the current rate to the forward rate[19] are also not the primary focus of interest rate risk management. A *sudden and unexpected* change in interest rates, however, causes concerns. *Sudden* means that there is no gradual shift of interest rates over a long period of time, say after most positions of a bank have matured already, rather than ad hoc shift that impacts existing positions; *unexpected* captures movements that go beyond a mere convergence from spot to fwd. rates.

In accordance with CRD IV (2013) and Commission Delegated Regulation (EU) 2024/856,[20] banks should calculate at least the six interest rate scenarios (illustrated in Fig. 1.6) for a sudden and unexpected change in interest rates as part of a *supervisory outlier test*:

a. parallel shock up, where there is a parallel upward shift of the yield curve with the same positive interest rate shock for all maturities;
b. parallel shock down, where there is a parallel downward shift of the yield curve with the same negative interest rate shock for all maturities;
c. steepener shock, where there is a steepening shift of the yield curve, with negative interest rate shocks for shorter maturities and positive interest rate shocks for longer maturities;
d. flattener shock, where there is a flattening shift of the yield curve, with positive interest rate shocks for shorter maturities and negative interest rate shocks for longer maturities;
e. short rates shock up, with larger positive interest rate shocks for shorter maturities to converge with the baseline for longer maturities;
f. short rates shock down, with larger negative interest rate shocks for shorter maturities to converge with the baseline for longer maturities.

As an early warning indicator and steering target, the Economic Value of Equity (EVE) should not fall by more than 15% of the bank's Tier 1 capital (to be discussed in Sect. 5.3.1) in any of the scenarios labeled "a" to "f" in Fig. 1.6, and the one-year Net Interest Income (NII) should not fall by more

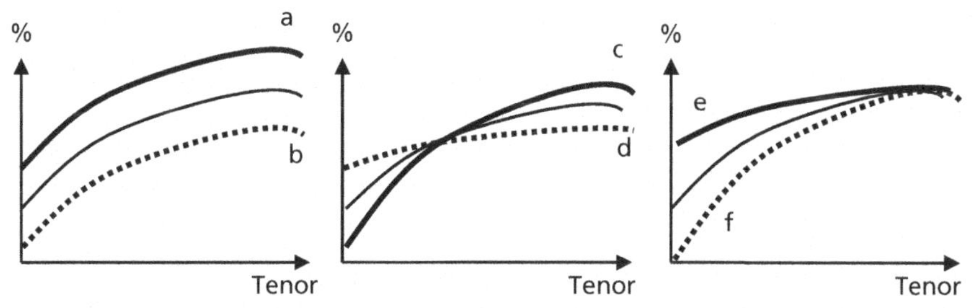

Fig. 1.6 Supervisory shock scenarios

than 5% of the bank's Tier 1 capital (to be discussed in Sect. 5.3.2) in either scenario "a" or "b".

In addition, floors are applied for shocked rates to avoid unrealistically low levels.

1.2.2 Types of Interest Rate Risk

Interest rate risk encompasses a multitude of discrete risks, which are typically classified into the following categories:

- *Interest rate gap risk*: The risk of changes in interest rates impacting balance sheet positions differently due to volume mismatches in different time bands.
- *Interest rate basis risk*: The risk of interest rate changes causing a change to relationships between interest rate indices (e. g., the 1-month 6-month EURIBOR basis).
- *Interest rate option risk*: The risk of interest rate changes causing (explicit and implicit) option executions, volume changes and behavioral changes.

Not considered to be pure interest rate risk and typically treated separately, but often closely related, are:

- *Credit spread risk*: The risk of interest rate changes causing changes to credit spreads (and market risk premia).
- *Liquidity risk*: The risk of interest rate changes affecting the capacity to liquidate and / or fund positions.

1.2.2.1 Interest Rate Gap Risk

Interest rate gap risk refers to the risk inherent in positions on the asset and liability sides of the bank's balance sheet that are subject to disparate settings and timing with respect to changes in the interest rate. This encompasses the risk that arises when a change in the shape of the yield curve (i. e., the curvature or slope of the yield curve) has an adverse impact on the earnings or the economic value of a bank. EBA defines interest rate gap risk as follows:

> Risk resulting from the term structure of interest rate sensitive instruments that arises from differences in the timing of their rate changes, covering changes to

Table 1.2 Interest rate gap risk

Month	6-month EURIBOR (%)	Asset (%)		Liability (%)
April	4	4	=	4
May	**5**	4	=	4
June	5	4	<	**5**
July	5	4	<	5
August	5	**5**	=	5
September	5	5	=	5
October	5	5	=	5

the term structure of interest rates occurring consistently across the yield curve (parallel risk) or differentially by period (non-parallel risk).[21]

EBA guidelines require institutions to identify gap risk as part of the IRRBB by focusing of mismatches in different time bands in a gap analysis (see Sect. 2.1.3) and / or to focus on the dispersion and concentration of mismatches in different time bands by calculating partial durations for yield curve risk (see Sect. 1.2.3).[22]

The following example illustrates the concept of interest rate spread risk. The situation may be described as follows: A particular asset is repriced based on the 6-month EURIBOR in *August*, while an otherwise comparable liability position is repriced based on the 6-month EURIBOR in *June*. The problem is that a rise in the EURIBOR in, say, May will have a disproportionate impact on both positions, even though they are linked to the same index. This is because the liability is repriced to the new 6-month LIBOR rate in June, while the asset continues to carry the old (and lower) LIBOR rate until August. See Table 1.2.

1.2.2.2 Interest Rate Basis Risk

Interest rate basis risk refers to the risk that can arise when different positions on the asset and liability sides of the balance sheet are based on different interest rate indexes. Examples of indexes are:

- IBOR-rates (LIBOR, EURIBOR, etc.)
- Risk-free Rates (RFR)
- Overnight index swap (OIS)
- Repo refinancing rates

EBA defines interest rate basis risk as follows:

Table 1.3 Interest rate basis risk

Month	1-Month EURIBOR (%)	6-Month EURIBOR (%)	Asset (%)		Liability (%)
April	4	4	4	=	4
May	**6**	**5**	4	=	4
June	6	5	**5**	<	**6**
July	6	5	5	<	6

> Risk arising from the impact of relative changes in interest rates on interest rate sensitive instruments that have similar tenors but are priced using different interest rate indices. Basis risk arises from the imperfect correlation in the adjustment of the rates earned and paid on different interest rate sensitive instruments with otherwise similar rate change characteristics.[23]

EBA guidelines require institutions to identify basis risk as part of the IRRBB by conducting an inventory of instrument groups based on different interest rates and by focusing on the use of derivatives and other hedging instruments in terms of different bases, convexity and timing differences neglected by the gap analysis.[24]

The following example serves to illustrate the concept of interest rate basis risk. The situation is as follows: A specific asset will reprice based on the *six-month* EURIBOR, whereas an otherwise comparable liability will be repriced based on the *one-month* EURIBOR, both in June. The issue is that a change in the EURIBOR in May could have a disproportionate impact on assets and liabilities (although the repricing date of both is the same) because the one-month and six-month EURIBORs do not necessarily move in lockstep. See Table 1.3.

1.2.2.3 Interest Rate Option Risk

Option risk refers to the risk that can arise when the amount and timing of cash flows of assets or liabilities can change due to optionality of on- and off-balance sheet items. EBA defines interest rate option risk as follows:

> Risk arising from options (embedded and explicit), where the institution or its customer can alter the level and timing of their cash flows, namely the risk arising from interest rate sensitive instruments where the holder will almost certainly exercise the option if it is in their financial interest to do so (embedded or explicit automatic options) and the risk arising from flexibility embedded implicitly or within the terms of interest rate sensitive instruments,

such that changes in interest rates may affect a change in the behaviour of the client (embedded behavioural option risk).[25]

Some options are *explicitly defined*, such as interest rate options (cap, floor, swaption, etc.) sold to corporate customers in conjunction with a loan transaction. Such options are typically straightforward to identify and to evaluate. Some other options are *implicit*, based on customer-specific behavior. Such options are frequently more challenging to discern, and their intrinsic value is often not amenable to estimation through conventional option pricing models. Alternatively, behavioral assumptions must be made in order to predict any deviations from contractual maturities, e. g., in the case of mortgages and for customer deposit and savings accounts.

An illustrative example of option risk can be shown with respect to a specific type of customer deposit called *sight deposit* (also referred to as *current account* or *overnight account*). The situation is as follows: The contractual maturity of sight deposits is zero, indicating that they can be withdrawn at any point in time. Nevertheless, ALM estimates a behavioral maturity of approximately two years. The issue arises from the possibility that behavioral changes may result in a more rapid withdrawal of funds.

In accordance with the guidelines set forth by EBA, banks are obliged to identify option risk as a component of the IRRBB. This entails conducting an inventory of all instruments that incorporate either implicit or explicit options, with a particular focus on two distinct categories: "automatic interest rate options," which execute rule-based, such as interest rate caps and floors, and "behavioral options," which influence the volume of mortgages, sight deposits, savings, and other deposits, where the customer has the option to deviate from the contractual maturity.[26]

1.2.2.4 Credit Spread Risk

Credit spread risk arising from the banking book (CSRBB), also referred to as or credit spread risk arising from non-trading book activities, measures the additional impact of changes to credit spreads. EBA defines credit spread risk as follows:

> Credit spread risk from non-trading book activities (CSRBB): Risk driven by changes of the market price for credit risk, for liquidity and for potentially other characteristics of credit-risky instruments, which is not captured by another existing prudential framework such as IRRBB or by expected credit / (jump-to-) default risk.[27]

The following example illustrates the concept of credit spread risk. The situation can be described as follows: The call schedule of callable assets is perfectly aligned with the call schedule of callable liabilities. The issue arises when liabilities are called by investors due to a deterioration in the credit quality of the bank, despite the absence of any change in general interest rates. In such a scenario, the bank is compelled to refund itself at a higher cost, due to the higher credit spreads that are currently being charged in the market.

1.2.2.5 Liquidity Risk

The term *liquidity risk* is used to quantify the impact of changes to liquidity. The concept of liquidity can be understood in different ways. For instance, liquidity can be defined as the ability to sell an asset at a reasonable price and with minimal impact on its market value, while also bearing reasonable transaction costs. Alternatively, liquidity can be seen as the ability to obtain funding for an asset. Additionally, liquidity can be understood as a change in the liquidity premium charged in the market, which is often part of the credit spread.

Interest rate simulations to determine gap, basis and option risk are typically conducted by shifting general yields that do not include instrument-specific or entity-specific liquidity spreads.

The following example illustrates the potential risks associated with liquidity. The situation is as follows: A bank's business model may include the practice of so-called *liquidity transformation*, whereby funding for *illiquid* mortgage loans is provided through *more liquid* savings account deposits. The issue arises when a crisis occurs, resulting in an increase in the illiquidity premium of mortgages. This subsequently leads to a mark-to-market loss on the assets in question and the inability to refinance them at attractive levels.

1.2.3 Duration

Duration is a summary measure of maturity, coupon, and yield effects that is used to approximate interest rate risk. Originally introduced by Macauley (1938), the concept approximates the percentage change in the economic value of a position that will occur given a small change in the level of interest rates.

The price-yield relationship of a typical interest-rate sensitive instrument is shown in Fig. 1.7. Such an instrument might be a bond, and its price is *inversely* related to changes in interest rates.

The relationship between price and yield is not linear, but *convex*.[28] Thus, the sensitivity of the bond price to changes in interest rates varies with the level of interest rates and can be approximated by the *slope* of the price-yield curve.

There are several ways to represent duration. One common measure is the *Macaulay duration*. It is the weighted average of the times until each payment is received, with the weights proportional to the present value of the payment.

Macaulay duration has a graphical interpretation in which discounted cash flows (i. e., the present values of cash flows at time t, denoted PV (CF_t)) are like proportional weights placed on a balance beam. The fulcrum (balanced center) of the beam would represent the weighted average distance (time to payment), which is the Macaulay duration. See Fig. 1.8.

Another widely used duration measure is the so-called *modified duration*. It is calculated as the Macaulay duration, multiplied by the 1-year discount factor, and can be viewed as the percentage change in price for a 1% (100 bps) change in yield.

For an illustrative example of a 5-year 5% coupon bond in a 3% interest rate environment, see Table 1.4.

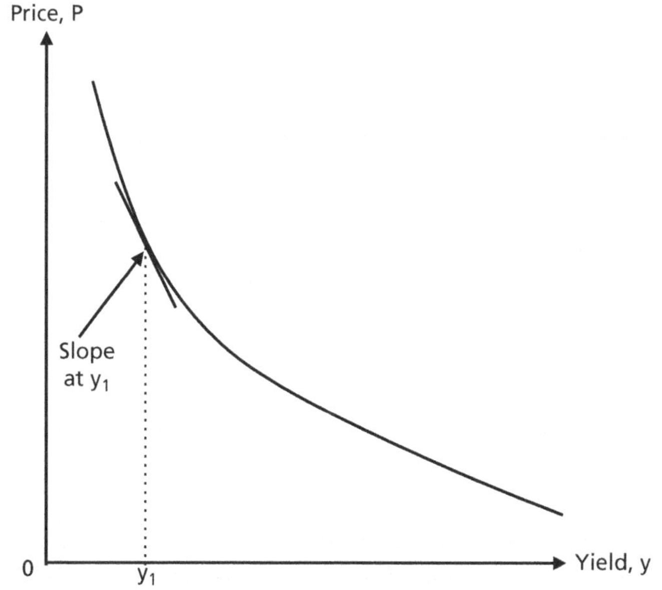

Fig. 1.7 Typical price-yield relationship of a bond

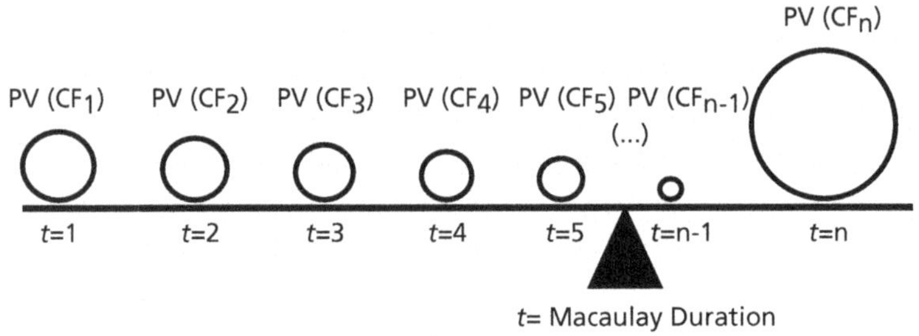

Fig. 1.8 Macaulay duration as weighted average of times

Table 1.4 Calculation of duration

(1) Time (years) t	(2) Cash flow (EUR)	(3) Discount factor (r = 3%) $= \frac{1}{1.03^t}$	(4) Present value = (2) × (3)	(5) Time × *present value* = (1) × (4)
1	5	0.9709	4.8545	4.8545
2	5	0.9426	4.7130	9.4260
3	5	0.9151	4.5755	13.7265
4	5	0.8885	4.4425	17.7700
5	105	0.8626	90.5730	452.8650
$\sum$ Total:			109.1585	498.6420
Macaulay duration		$= \sum (5) / \sum (4)$		**4.568**
Modified duration		$= \sum (5) / (\sum (4) \times 1.03)$		**4.434**

Finally, there is a concept of duration that does not assume a parallel shift of the yield curve in estimating the resulting price change, but rather an isolated shift of a particular key rate (while leaving other rates on the yield curve unchanged). This duration is called the *partial duration* or the *key rate duration*. Partial durations can be used to identify which part of the yield curve has the greatest impact on the price of a fixed income instrument, and also to estimate price changes resulting from non-parallel yield curve movements.

Notes

1. EBA/GL/2022/14 of October 20, 2022; see EBA (2022). The current guidelines are very similar with respect to interest rate risk to the previous guidelines EBA/GL/2018/02 of July 19, 2018; see EBA (2018). Both guidelines are issued on the basis of Article 84 of CRD IV (2013).

2. EBA (2022, 12–13).
3. Author's calculation based on ECB data.
4. Since the focus of this book is on interest rates, we'll define the economic value as that derived from a given interest rate environment (as opposed to, say, the strategic value in an M&A transaction) and the earnings as the net interest income (as opposed to, e. g., fee income).
5. EBA (2022, 17).
6. This book focuses on the interest rate risk aspects, while recognizing and incorporating some P&L, liquidity and capital optimization aspects where appropriate.
7. Article 84 of CRD IV (2013).
8. EBA (2022, 17).
9. EBA (2022, 34).
10. EBA (2022, 22).
11. Trading book instruments include instruments that are held as trading assets or liabilities for accounting purposes; instruments resulting from market-making activities; equity investments in a fund other than those assigned to the banking book; listed equities; trading-related repo-style transactions; options, including embedded derivatives from instruments issued by the institution from its own banking book, that relate to credit or equity risk. All other instruments must be included in the banking book. See BCBS (2020, 1).
12. See ECB (2024, 148–149).
13. EBA (2022, 13).
14. If certain conditions are met, international accounting standards allow a special treatment for micro hedges, known as hedge accounting. As explained in Kenyon and Stamm (2012, 89–90), "[t]he advantage of hedge accounting is that a derivative that is a proven hedge does not have to be recognized in the P&L as usual but can be attributed to the underlying. This is useful if the underlying itself is recognized at book value (e. g. if it is in a Loans and Receivables book). In order to be eligible for hedge accounting, the bank has to prove that the hedge is effective, which means that the value changes of the hedged item and of the hedging derivative due to changes in the hedged risk factors are highly correlated and have a regression between 80 and 125%."
15. E. g., McPhail et al. (2024), using regulatory data on individual swap positions for the largest 250 U.S. banks, conclude that swap positions are not economically significant in hedging the interest rate risk of bank assets.
16. EBA (2022, 22).

17. Article 84 of CRD IV (2013).
18. EBA (2022, 17).
19. Forward rates are interest rates derived from current spot interest rates and represent interest rates for transactions commencing in the future. Forward (fwd.) rates are considered by many to be the best estimate of rates to be expected in the future. In any case, fwd. rates can be "locked in" through certain market transactions including derivative instruments (such as forward or futures contracts), and thus any change in fwd. rates could be hedged. However, the change from spot to fwd. rates can no longer be hedged as it is already "baked in" to market prices.
20. Article 1(1) of Commission Delegated Regulation (EU) 2024/856; OJ L, 2024/856, 24.4.2024, ELI: http://data.europa.eu/eli/reg_del/2024/856/oj.
21. EBA (2022, 13).
22. EBA (2022, 34).
23. EBA (2022, 13).
24. EBA (2022, 34).
25. EBA (2022, 13).
26. EBA (2022, 34).
27. EBA (2022, 13–14).
28. The price-yield relationship is non-linear because the coupons paid to the bondholder are reinvested over the life of the bond, earning interest on interest. The amount of compounding depends positively on the size of the coupons and the period over which the coupons are reinvested.

References

BCBS. 2020. RBC: Risk-Based Capital Requirements, RBC25: Boundary Between the Banking Book and the Trading Book, Basel Committee on Banking Supervision, https://www.bis.org/basel_framework/chapter/RBC/25.htm. Accessed on January 18, 2025.

CRD IV. 2013. Directive 2013/36/EU of the European Parliament and of the Council of 26 June 2013 ("Capital Requirements Directive IV"). OJ L 176, 27.6.2013, pp. 338–436. ELI: http://data.europa.eu/eli/dir/2013/36/oj.

EBA. 2018. Guidelines on the Management of Interest Rate Risk Arising From Non-trading Book Activities, Final Report, EBA/GL/2018/02 From 18 July 2018, European Banking Authority, RBA 2018E. Accessed on January 18, 2025.

EBA. 2022. Guidelines on the Management of Interest Rate Risk and Credit Spread Risk Arising From Non-trading Book Activities, Final Report, EBA/GL/2022/14 From 20 October 2022, Mandated by Article 84 (6) of Directive 2013/36/EU (Capital Requirements Directive, CRD), European Banking Authority. https://www.eba.europa.eu/sites/default/files/document_library/Publications/Guidelines/2022/EBA-GL-2022-14%20GL%20on%20IRRBB%20and%20CSRBB/1041754/Guidelines%20on%20IRRBB%20and%20CSRBB.pdf. Accessed on January 18, 2025.

ECB. 2024. ECB Guide to Internal Models. European Central Bank, February 2024. https://www.bankingsupervision.europa.eu/ecb/pub/pdf/ssm.supervisory_guides202402_internalmodels.en.pdf. Accessed on January 18, 2025.

Kenyon, Chris, and Roland Stamm. 2012. *Discounting, LIBOR, CVA and Funding: Interest Rate and Credit Pricing*. Cham, CH: Palgrave Macmillan.

Macauley, Frederick R. 1938. Some Theoretical Problems Suggested by the Movements of Interest Rates, Bond Yields and Stock Prices in the United States since 1856. National Bureau of Economic Research (NBER). https://www.nber.org/books-and-chapters/some-theoretical-problems-suggested-movements-interest-rates-bond-yields-and-stock-prices-united. Accessed on January 18, 2025.

McPhail, Lihong, Philipp Schnabl, and Bruce Tuckman. 2024. Do Banks Hedge Using Interest Rate Swaps? Office of the Chief Economist, Commodity Futures Trading Commission, No. 2019-011. https://www.cftc.gov/sites/default/files/2024-04/Banks_and_Derivatives%20(11)%20-%20ada.pdf. Accessed on January 18, 2025.

2

ALM Techniques

With the basics out of the way, it is time to focus on the key ALM techniques. It would be nice if there were only one or two, but it turns out that there is quite a wide range of analytical frameworks being used to identify, measure and manage interest rate risk.

We begin by presenting two alternative measures for assessing a bank's interest rate risk exposure, the *economic value perspective* and the *earnings perspective.*

We then take an in-depth look at the most widely used method of pricing various banking products, known as *funds transfer pricing* (FTP).

We then devote a section to a class of products that causes the most headaches within ALM, the so-called *non-maturity products* (NMP).

Finally, the widely used *replication model* is described in detail.

2.1 Economic Value Measures

Economic value (EV) measures the value of a bank's existing positions, typically defined as the present value (PV) of their future cash flows. EBA defines economic value measures as follows:

The original version of the chapter has been revised. A correction to this chapter can be found at https://doi.org/10.1007/978-3-031-80205-8_7

F. Tata, *Bank Asset-Liability Management*, https://doi.org/10.1007/978-3-031-80205-8_2

> Measures of changes in the net present value of interest rate sensitive instruments over their remaining life resulting from interest rate movements, in case of IRRBB; (…) EV measures reflect changes in value over the remaining life of the interest rate sensitive instruments, in case of IRRBB (…) – i. e., until all positions have run off.[1]

The economic value of a balance sheet or an off-balance sheet position may differ from the reported accounting value. For example, a loan may be recorded on the balance sheet at par (100% of its notional amount), but may have a higher economic value if the interest rate payments on that loan are higher than the current prevailing interest rates.

2.1.1 Economic Value of Equity

In the past, there has often been controversy over how to treat equity capital in an economic value framework. Should equity be included in interest rate risk calculations, and if so, what interest rate sensitivity assumption would be appropriate for equity? One particular economic value measure is EVE, which stands for Economic Value (EV) of Equity (E).

EVE is defined as the difference between the economic value (EV) of a bank's assets (A) and the economic value of a bank's liabilities (L), including off-balance sheet (OBS) items, calculated at a given point in time: EVE = EV (A) − EV (L) + EV (OBS A) − EV (OBS L). It is clear that equity cannot be an input to the EVE calculation, otherwise it would affect its own economic value.[2] See Fig. 2.1.

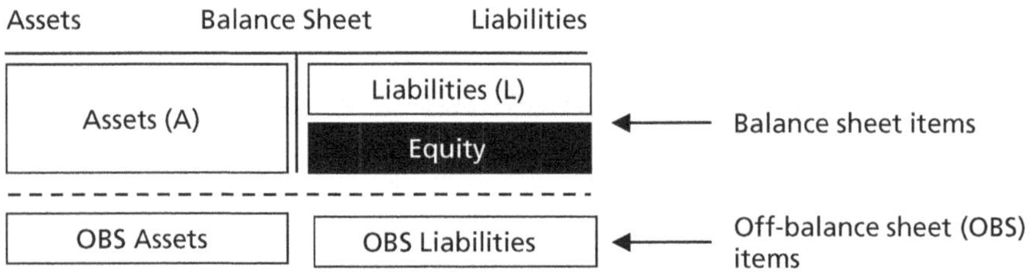

Fig. 2.1 Economic value of equity (EVE)

Table 2.1 provides a frame of reference for various economic value measures and a roadmap for how they will be addressed in different parts of the book.

Table 2.1 Reference frameworks for various economic value measures

Term	*Measure of*	*Calculated as*	*Detailed in Section*
PV	Present value of a cash flow	Discounted cash flow	
EV	Economic value of an existing positions	Present value of the position's expected cash flows	2.1.2
EVE	Economic value of equity	Difference between the economic value (EV) of a given asset and liability, including off-balance sheet positions	
ΔEV / ΔEVE	Change in EV / EVE	Difference between two EV / EVE calculations	
EVE risk	EVE interest rate sensitivity	Change in EVE (ΔEVE) for agiven change in interest rates (Δr)	2.1.3
SOT (EVE)	Supervisory outlier test with respect to EVE	Decrease in EVE of more than 15% of a bank's Tier 1 capital under certain assumptions	5.3.1

2.1.2 Economic Value Calculation

The economic value (EV) of a position is determined by the sum of the present value(s) (PV) of its (multiple) cash flow(s). To do this, the timing and amount of the future cash flows must be known. If not, the expected cash flows must be determined in a model. In addition, a discount rate, r, must be assumed that is consistent with the current interest rate environment. Then it is straightforward to calculate EV as the PV of future cash flows:

$$\mathrm{EV} = \sum_{t=1}^{T} \frac{CF_t}{(1+r)^t}$$

where T is the number of years until the final cash flow, CF_t is the cash flow in year t, and r is the annual discount rate (assumed to be constant over time). See Fig. 2.2.

By changing the discount rate from r to $(r + \Delta\, r)$, one can calculate the change in the previously calculated economic value, Δ EV, resulting from a change in interest rates, $\Delta\, r$. The change in economic value depends on the interest rate sensitivity of the asset. See Fig. 2.3.

Note that we have not changed the timing or amount of the expected cash flows following an increase in interest rates. If the cash flows depend on the level of interest rates (e. g., because of prepayment options or because the

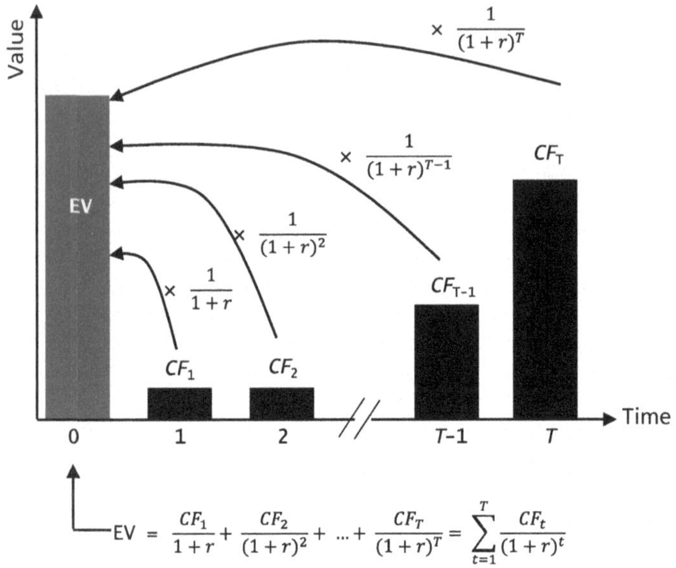

Fig. 2.2 Economic value (EV) calculation

cash flows are based on floating interest rates), the cash flow projections must be adjusted.

2.1.3 Repricing Gap Analysis

One of the simplest but most widely used techniques for measuring a bank's interest rate risk exposure to its economic value, or *EVE risk*, is the *repricing gap analysis*. It was described in detail by the BCBS more than 25 years ago.[3] It is based on a maturity / repricing schedule that allocates interest rate sensitive assets, liabilities and off-balance sheet items into a number of pre-defined time bands according to their maturity (if fixed rate) or time remaining until their next repricing (if floating rate). Those assets and liabilities that do not have fixed repricing intervals (e. g. sight deposits or savings accounts) or whose maturities may differ from the contractual maturities (e. g., mortgages with a prepayment option) are assigned to repricing time bands based on model assumptions.

To illustrate how a typical repricing gap analysis is performed, a simple 5-step analysis is presented.

Step 1: Aggregate balance sheet (and off-balance sheet) positions into a certain number of predefined product classes. Table 2.2 shows the balance sheet of a simple model bank.

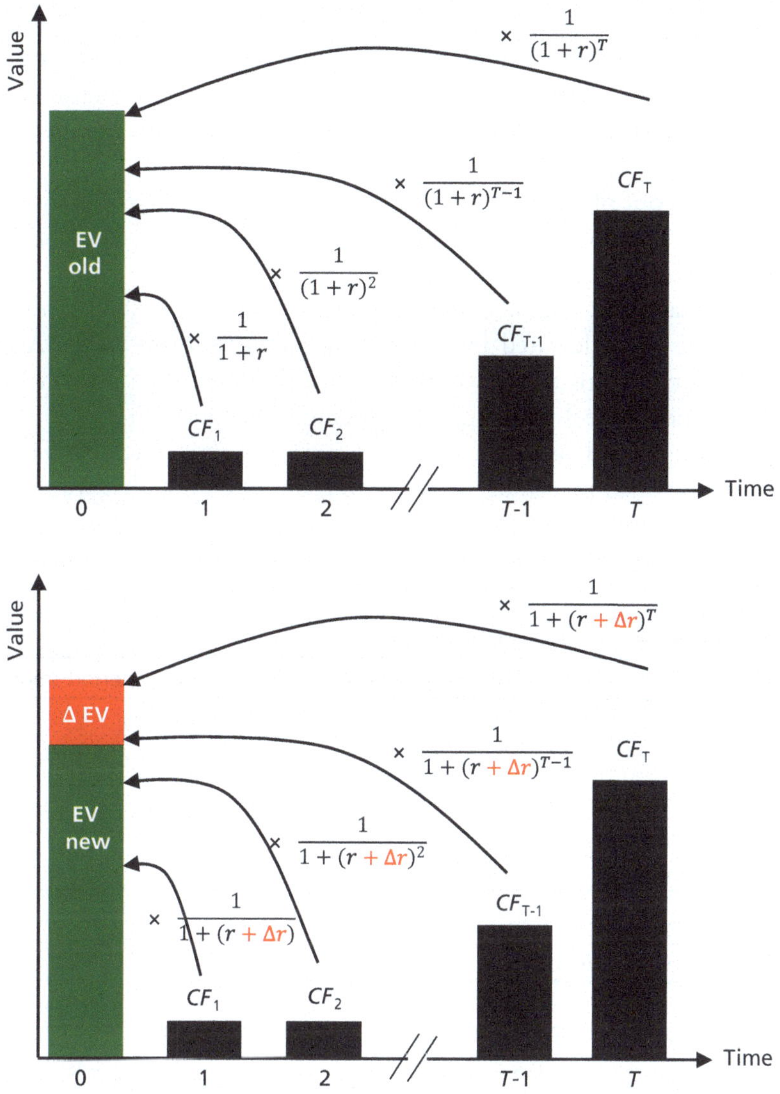

Fig. 2.3 Change in economic value (Δ EV) calculation

Table 2.2 Balance sheet of model bank

Assets		Liabilities	
Bonds	50	Term deposits	150
Loans	300	Savings accounts	200
Mortgages	150	Interbank deposits	100
		Equity capital	50
Total assets	**500**	**Total liabilities**	**500**

Step 2: Assign reset periods. Table 2.3 illustrates the (estimated average) reset periods for various banking book positions. Note that interest rate risk is only assumed to the next reset date, not to the contractual maturity date. This is because once a fixed-rate instrument is reset to market rates, it will trade at "par" again.[4]

Step 3: Roll out of balance sheet positions into appropriate repricing time bands. Table 2.4 shows the distribution of position volumes across different repricing periods.

Step 4: Calculate the net repricing gaps. Table 2.5 shows how net repricing gaps are calculated by subtracting liabilities from assets. A negative, or liability-sensitive, gap occurs when liabilities exceed assets (including off-balance sheet items) in any given repricing time band.

Step 5: Weight and aggregate the of net repricing gaps. Each gap is multiplied by an assumed percentage decrease in economic value that would result from a 1% increase in interest rates. Such a sensitivity measure would be based on estimates of the modified duration of the assets and liabilities that

Table 2.3 Reset periods for various products

Product	Maturity (months)	Reset period (months)
Bonds	60	60
Loans	6	6
Mortgages	60	12
Term deposits	3	3
Savings accounts	36	6
Interbank deposits	24	24

Table 2.4 Repricing time bands

Assets								
Time to repricing (in months)	<1	1–3	3–6	6–12	12–24	24–36	36–48	48–60
Bonds								50
Loans			300					
Mortgages				150				
∑ Assets	**0**	**0**	**300**	**150**	**0**	**0**	**0**	**50**
Liabilities								
Time to repricing (in months)	<1	1–3	3–6	6–12	12–24	24–36	36–48	48–60
Term deposits		150						
Savings accounts			200					
Interbank deposits					100			
Equity								
∑ Liabilities	**0**	**150**	**200**	**0**	**100**	**0**	**0**	**0**

Table 2.5 Net repricing gaps

Time to repricing (in months)	<1	1–3	3–6	6–12	12–24	24–36	36–48	48–60
∑ Assets	0	0	300	150	0	0	0	50
∑ Liabilities	0	150	200	0	100	0	0	0
Net repricing gaps	**0**	**-150**	**100**	**150**	**-100**	**0**	**0**	**50**

Table 2.6 Total repricing gap

Time to repricing (in months)	<1	1–3	3–6	6–12	12–24	24–36	36–48	48–60
Net repricing gaps	0	-150	100	150	-100	0	0	50
Mod. Duration (%)	0.04	0.16	0.36	0.72	1.39	2.25	3.07	3.86
Weighted gaps	**0**	**-0.24**	**0.36**	**1.08**	**-1.39**	**0**	**0**	**1.93**
Total repricing gap					**1.74**			

fall within each time band. The weighted gaps are then aggregated across time bands to produce an estimate of the change in economic value of the bank that would result from changes in interest rates, the *total* repricing gap. It estimates the *decline* in the economic value of the bank's equity for a 1% (parallel) *increase* in interest rates.[5] See Table 2.6.

A total repricing gap of 1.74 implies that the bank's economic value, or economic value of equity (EVE), declines by 1.74 for a 1% increase in interest rates (and vice versa) due to the lag in repricing various balance sheet items. Given that the bank's equity is 50, this corresponds to a 3.48% decline in equity for a 100 bp increase in interest rates.

Since the *supervisory outlier test*, or Basel interest rate shock, is defined for a 200 bp change in interest rates, the bank's Basel II-Ratio (relative risk of a ± 200 bp interest rate shock) would be twice as high, or 6.96%.

The standard repricing gap framework based on duration can be extended and refined in several ways.[6] First, one could estimate the effect of a change in interest rates by calculating the *precise* duration of each asset, liability, and off-balance sheet items and then derive the net position for the bank based on these more precise measures, rather than by applying an estimated average duration weight to all positions in each time band. This eliminates potential errors in aggregating positions or cash flows and is described in the following section. Second, basis risk could be incorporated into the analysis by making explicit assumptions about expected changes in the relationship between interest rates within a time band. Finally, the repricing gap analysis could incorporate expected changes in the timing of payments that could result from changes in the interest rate environment.

2.1.4 Duration Gap Analysis

The *duration gap analysis* model measures the direction and magnitude of the duration mismatch between assets and liabilities. The duration gap (also known as *funding gap* or *maturity gap*) is based on the concept of duration and is defined as the difference between the duration of assets and the duration of liabilities (excluding equity), scaled by their ratio. It can be used to explain how changes in interest rates affect the market value of the bank.

To calculate the duration gap of the model bank introduced in the previous section (see Table 2.2), we need to estimate the precise duration of each asset class. Interest rate sensitivities, as measured by duration, vary across balance sheet positions. Some positions, such as sight deposits (i. e., customer deposits that can be withdrawn at any time), may have short durations; other positions, such as loans or bonds, may have very long durations. Because of the different interest rate sensitivities, a uniform change in interest rates will result in a non-uniform change in the value of different balance sheet items. Table 2.7 shows the (estimated average) interest rate sensitivities, expressed as modified duration, for various banking book positions. Note that the modified duration estimate reflects the behavioral maturity, not to the contractual maturity, of the positions.

The duration gap would be calculated as the position-weighted sum of the modified duration of the bank's assets minus the position-weighted sum of the bank's liabilities:

$$\begin{aligned} &\left(\frac{50 \times 4.45}{500} + \frac{300 \times 0.5}{500} + \frac{150 \times 1}{500}\right) \\ &\quad - \left(\frac{150 \times 0.25}{500} + \frac{200 \times 0.5}{500} + \frac{100 \times 2}{500}\right) \\ &= 1.045 - 0.675 = 0.37 \end{aligned}$$

Table 2.7 Assumed durations for different products

Product	Modified duration
Bonds	4.45
Loans	0.50
Mortgages	1.00
Term deposits	0.25
Savings accounts	0.50
Interbank deposits	2.00

With a duration gap of 0.37, a 1% increase in interest rates results in a loss of 0.37% on 500, or 1.85. This represents 3.7% of the 50 equity, so the decline in the economic value of equity (EVE) is 3.7%.

Since the *supervisory outlier test*, or Basel interest rate shock, is defined for a 200 bp change in interest rates, the bank's Basel II-Ratio (relative risk of a ± 200 bp interest rate shock) would be twice as high, or 7.4%.

The economic value of equity risk is slightly different when calculated using the repricing gap method (6.96%) and with the duration gap method (7.4%).

2.2 Earnings Measures

Earnings measures look at the earnings generated by balance sheet items and how a change in interest rates causes them to change. A commonly used earnings measure is Net interest income (NII). NII is the difference between interest income on assets and the interest expense on liabilities during a given period.

NII typically changes over time due to various factors such as repricing, volume outflows, reinvestments, even if the interest rate environment remains unchanged.

Typically, the accounting department oversees the calculation and reporting of official figures for NII, which typically represents a large portion of a bank's total net income. The NII calculation is done for the *past* (retrospective view) and includes intra-month changes and movements.

While the accounting department has a *backward-looking* view, the ALM department aims to quantify net interest *exposure* on a *forward-looking basis* (prospective view). This is also required by the regulator:

> Net interest income measures: Measures of changes in expected future profitability within a given time horizon resulting from interest rate movements, in case of IRRBB.[7]

A simplified NII calculation for a caricatured "3-6-3" bank[8] is shown in Fig. 2.4.

Table 2.8 provides a frame of reference for various earnings measures and a roadmap for how they will be addressed in different parts of the book.

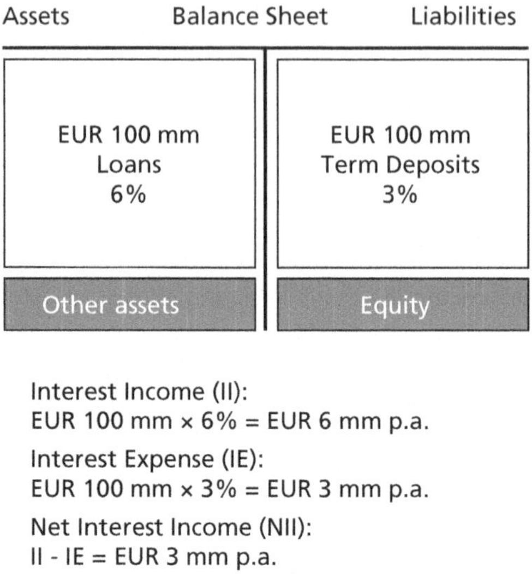

Fig. 2.4 Simplified NII of a caricatured "3-6-3" bank

Table 2.8 Reference frameworks for various earnings measures

Term	*Measure of*	*Calculated as*	*Detailed in Section*
Earnings	Net income	Expenditures minus expenses	
NII	Net interest income	Interest income minus interest expenses	2.2
NII forecast	Baseline for NII simulations	Projected NII under certain volume, spread and interest rate assumptions	2.2.1
ΔNII	Change in NII	Difference between two NII calculations	2.2.2 2.2.3 2.2.4
NII sensitivity	NII interest rate sensitivity	Change in NII (ΔNII) of the forecasted NII	
ΔMV	Change in market value	Impact of interest rate changes on the market value (MV) of instruments beyond the NII horizon	2.2.6
SOT (NII)	Supervisory outlier test on NII	Decrease in NII of more than 5% of a bank's Tier 1 capital under certain assumptions	5.3.2

2.2.1 NII Forecast

The net interest income forecast provides a *baseline* against which the impact of different interest rate scenarios is measured.

While the NII forecast is a very important metric by which senior bank management assesses the health and competitiveness of the bank, the accuracy of the NII forecast is less important to ALM when dealing with NII *sensitivities*. This is because any (incorrect) assumption made in the calculation of the NII forecast will be applied repeatedly in the calculation of the NII resulting from a changed interest rate environment. Since the NII sensitivity is calculated as the newly calculated NII minus the original NII forecast, a significant portion of the (incorrect) assumption is cancelled out.[9]

How an NII forecast is made in practice depends on bank-specific factors. Politics often plays a role, as well. For example, an organization may be reluctant to forecast an NII loss, even if that would be the most reasonable forecast. There would likely be some pressure (real or perceived) to change the underlying assumptions to arrive at a forecasted NII profit. Imagine the situation where ALM has to communicate to senior bank management that, after applying prudent risk management, NII sensitivities have been reduced to the point where the forecasted NII loss is now almost certain. No one likes to "lock in" an expected loss. In addition, an NII forecast is typically related to previous (historical) NII results, so that any major deviation will raise suspicions and cause discomfort.

The *time horizon* for NII forecasts is typically short- to medium term, often one to three years.[10] Extending the forecast period too far into the future would create a false sense of accuracy, as robust predictions of changes in customer business cannot be made over the long term. NII forecasts are calculated at different levels of granularity, such as monthly, quarterly, and annual.

As the objective is to calculate NII sensitivities to changes in interest rates, all positions that are not interest rate sensitive can be excluded from the analysis. These include positions in real estate, equity investments, intangible assets and the bank's own equity.

The starting point for the NII forecast is the *current balance sheet*. Ideally, the NII "forecast" for the presence would be the current NII as reported by the accounting department. If the forecast is not calibrated to current NII levels, projected changes in NII will reflect not only business performance but also, to a large extent, specific modeling assumptions. The current balance sheet reflects all on- and off-balance sheet positions resulting from existing customer business (including its volume, current margin, current fixed rates, their empirical duration, etc.) as well as market transactions (including capital market funding, derivative positions and other hedges).

In developing NII forecasts further into the future, the NII calculations must make assumptions about *future position sizes* and *future interest rates*.

2.2.1.1 Assumptions About the Future Balance Sheet

As business transactions mature over time (deposits are withdrawn, loans are repaid, swap transactions mature, etc.), it is necessary to have a view of the evolution of the size of the bank's various balance sheet positions. There are three commonly used model assumptions about the bank's future positions: the *run-off view*, the *static view*, and the *dynamic view*.

- The conceptually most trivial, but arguably the least realistic, view of a bank's future balance sheet assumes that all positions and transactions simply run off (mature) over time and are not replaced by new business. Since all past transactions are captured, the only significant effort in predicting future volumes is caused by transactions that have no (meaningful) contractual maturity or where volumes can change due to optionality. An NII analysis based on the so-called *run-off view* implies that the bank's balance sheet shrinks and that customer business eventually ceases to exist.
- More common than the run-off view is the projection of a structurally unchanged balance sheet. The implicit assumption is that all maturing positions, except ALM hedging positions[11] (such as derivatives), are replaced by new positions with comparable terms in terms of instrument type, volume, original maturity and margin. These new positions are established at the prevailing interest rate level (plus / minus the initial margin). The *static view* reflects a bank's earnings on a *going concern* basis. The bank's balance sheet is held constant. This is also the regulatory requirement for NII reporting.[12]
- The *dynamic view* reflects changes in customer business, debt issuance, and other activities based on the bank's forecast and business plan. It is the most complex modeling of the bank's future balance sheet and is discussed in more detail in Sect. 3.2, which deals with the planning of the NII.

2.2.1.2 Assumptions About Future Interest Rates

When positions mature, we assume that they will be replaced by comparable transactions (unless the run-off view is taken). For example, a maturing 6-month interbank loan (i. e., EURIBOR-based funding from another bank) is assumed to be replaced by another 6-month interbank loan. To roll over the interbank funding position, three assumptions must be made. First, it is assumed that the bank will be able to obtain comparable funding at all.

This may not be the case if the bank's perceived counterparty credit risk has deteriorated (as in the case of Lehman Brothers prior to its collapse). It may also not be the case if, for example, the interbank market freezes due to adverse market conditions (as in the 2007 / 2008 banking crisis). Second, it is assumed that the bank obtains funding at the same *spread* above or below the general interest rate level. We assume this spread (or *margin*) is constant, i. e. if the bank was able to borrow at 6-month EURIBOR plus 10 bp in the past, it will be able to borrow at the same spread in the future again. Finally, since EURIBOR is a floating interest rate that is reset daily, the actual interest rate reflected by EURIBOR on the maturing interbank loan is unlikely to be the same as the interest rate on the replacement interbank loan, which is based on a later EURIBOR setting. This example illustrates the need to make explicit assumptions about future interest rate levels when calculating NII in the future.

There is considerable (and often emotional) debate about how to make projections of future interest rates. One school of thought considers *forward rates* to be the best predictor of future interest rates. Forward rates are interest rates for a period in the future. They can be calculated either from prevailing (spot) interest rates or, often more easily, directly observed in the market from derivative instruments based on the forward rate (such as forward rate agreements, FRAs, or interest rate futures contracts). This school of thought is conceptually rooted in the so-called expectation theory, which assumes that long-term interest rates should reflect expected future short-term interest rates.[13] Using forward rates as the expected future interest rate has the additional advantage that this is then also the same rate that can be hedged in the market.

Another school of thought, often adopted by practitioners, views the *current* interest rate environment as the best predictor of the future. Forward rates are not considered to be truly unbiased predictors of future interest rates because they incorporate a (liquidity) risk premium that causes them to have a systematic upward bias. In fact, the idea that forward rates have the power to predict future interest rates has been tested and rejected by many academic studies.[14] Instead, an unchanged world is assumed to be one in which interest rates are unchanged from current market levels.

Finally, the assumed future interest rates could be based on a *combination* of current (spot) rates and market-implied forward rates, or they could be based on *forecasted* interest rates (established by quantitative forecasts, surveys or third-party projections). For simplicity's sake, ALM models for NII calculations should not be based on overly sophisticated, complex yield curve models, or else the calculated NII sensitivities will primarily reflect the model assumptions.

2.2.2 NII Sensitivity

Once an NII forecast has been established as a *baseline*, the *net exposure to interest rate changes* (i. e., the change in NII due to interest rate changes) can be calculated for various *shocked scenarios*. Different types of interest rate shocks are defined for the shocked scenarios. These include instantaneous vs. gradual interest rate changes, as well as parallel yield curve movements vs. a reshaping of the yield curve.

The change in NII for a given shock scenario relative to the *baseline* scenario NII is called *NII sensitivity* ALM cannot turn a failing bank into a successful one, but ALM can help *stabilize* expected NII by reducing deviations from the forecast. To meet current regulatory requirements, NII sensitivities for different shock scenarios should not exceed a certain level, defined as 15% of the bank's Tier 1 capital (discussed in Sect. 5.3.2). This means that in none of the predefined scenarios should the loss of net interest income (relative to the baseline NII) be greater than 15% of Tier 1 capital.

In order for a bank to have a proper insight into the net exposure to interest rate changes, the different shock scenarios should include the six interest rate scenarios based on CRD IV (2013) and Commission Delegated Regulation (EU) 2024/856,[15] discussed in Sect. 1.2.1. The objective is to have a clear picture of which scenarios would cause the most damage and about the level of vulnerability.

2.2.3 Earning Gap Analysis

The *earning gap*, also called the *income gap*, is a simple summary measure of the NII sensitivity to a 1% parallel shock in interest rates. The Earning Gap is calculated in the *Earning Gap Analysis*, which has some parallels to the Repricing Gap Analysis discussed in Sect. 2.1.3. As in the Repricing Gap Analysis, the first step is to group assets and liabilities (as well as interest rate sensitive off-balance sheet items) into a table with different buckets according to their first repricing date. The difference, however, is that we limit our analysis to positions that reprice within the first few years. As mentioned above, the *time horizon* for NII forecasts is typically only one to three years. To calculate the first year's earning gap, the aggregated positions for the model bank used in Sect. 2.1.3 are reported in Table 2.9.

Table 2.9 Earning gap schedule

Time to repricing (in months)	<1	1–3	3–6	6–12
$\sum$ Assets	0	0	300	150
$\sum$ Liabilities	0	150	200	0
Net repricing gaps	**0**	**-150**	**100**	**150**

The next step is to calculate the mean of the repricing times of all repricing buckets. They represent the average time to repricing of a position recorded in that repricing bucket.[16] It also calculates the time from the repricing midpoint to the end of the first year; this is the amount of time that an interest rate change will have an impact during the first year. The later the repricing, the fewer months there are for a change in interest rates to affect the NII. Early repricings, on the other hand, have many more months during which the change affects the NII. See Table 2.10.

Table 2.10 Earning gap impact

Time to repricing (in months)	<1	1–3	3–6	6–12
Net repricing gaps	0	-150	100	150
Midpoints	**0.5**	**2**	**4.5**	**9**
1st year impact	**11.5**	**10**	**7.5**	**3**

Finally, for each repricing bucket, *periodic earning gaps* are calculated for a 1% change in interest rates. They are defined as the net repricing gap × 1% × first year impact (as a percentage of a full 12-month period). For example, the periodic earning gap for the 1 - 3-month repricing bucket is -150 × 1% × 10 / 12 = 1.25. This can be interpreted as a loss of 1.25 in NII for positions in the 1- to 3-month repricing bucket. A negative periodic earning gap in this particular bucket implies that there are more liabilities than assets, which means that an increase in interest rates will cause interest expense to rise more than interest income. The sum of the periodic earning gaps of all repricing buckets up to one year is the *total earning gap* for the entire first year. See Table 2.11.

The calculated earning gap of -0.25 implies a decrease in NII of -0.25 in the first year for every 1% parallel increase in interest rates. Thus, if interest rates were to rise immediately by 400 bp, the bank should expect a decline in NII of 1.

Table 2.11 Total earning gap

Time to repricing (in months)	<1	1–3	3–6	6–12
Net repricing gaps	0	-150	100	150
Midpoints	0.5	2	4.5	9
1st year impact	11.5	10	7.5	3
Periodic earning gap	**0**	**-1.25**	**0.625**	**0.375**
Total earning gap		**-0.25**		

2.2.4 NII Simulation

In this section, we provide a simulation of how NII is projected into the future based on a baseline scenario and how NII sensitivity is estimated for a -100 bp interest rate shock scenario. After calculating the NII sensitivity, we apply a hedging transaction and calculate its contribution to reducing NII volatility.

2.2.4.1 Model Bank

For the NII simulation we set up an archetypal bank balance sheet that reflects customer loans and mortgages, investments in fixed income securities, funding through customer deposit and savings accounts, and interbank funding. The model bank's balance sheet is the same as that used in the repricing gap analysis (Sect. 2.1.3) reported in Table 2.2. For ease of reference, the data are restated in Table 2.12, supplemented by the current coupon levels of the positions (from their last interest rate reset).

The product specifications are also the same as those used in the repricing gap analysis (Sect. 2.1.3) and reported in Table 2.3. For ease of reference, the data are restated in Table 2.13, supplemented by the commercial margins of the products (i. e., their product-specific spread over and above the risk-free market rates).

Finally, the current interest rate environment (risk-free interest rates observed in the market) is shown in Table 2.14.

Table 2.12 Model bank balance sheet with current coupon rates

Assets			Liabilities		
	Balance	Coupon		Balance	Coupon
Bonds	50	4%	Term deposits	150	3%
Loans	300	5.5%	Savings accounts	200	1.25%
Mortgages	150	5%	Interbank deposits	100	4%
			Equity capital	50	
Total assets	**500**	**5.2%**	**Total liabilities**	**500**	**2.2%**

Table 2.13 Reset periods and margins for different products

Product	Maturity (months)	Reset period (months)	Margin (bps)
Bonds	60	60	0
Loans	6	6	150
Mortgages	60	12	100
Term deposits	3	3	-50
Savings accounts	36	6	-250
Interbank deposits	24	24	0

Table 2.14 Current interest rate environment

Tenor	Interest rate (%)
1 Month	3.61
3 Months	3.80
6 Months	3.95
1 Year	4.08
2 Years	4.16
5 Years	4.17
7 Years	4.20
10 Years	4.27

The NII simulation is performed in the *baseline scenario* under the following three key assumptions:

- Unchanged balance sheet (static view, as described in Sect. 2.2.1.1).
- Unchanged yield curve (as described in Sect. 2.2.1.2).
- Unchanged commercial margins (also referred to as product margins).

2.2.4.2 Monthly Baseline NII

The next step is to calculate the monthly NII for the baseline. Although volumes do not change from month to month (because we assume an unchanged balance sheet), the coupon of a balance sheet product may have reset to a new level. At the time of a reset, this new level would be the prevailing interest rate plus the product-specific spread, called the commercial margin. Since we are assuming that the prevailing interest rate environment in the future will be the same as the current (spot) rates (because of our assumption of an unchanged yield curve), and since we are assuming that commercial margins will remain unchanged, all we need to do is check whether a rate reset has occurred in a given month and, if so, replace the previous product

Table 2.15 Monthly baseline NII in periods 1 through 3

Assets	*Balance*	*Coupon*	*Monthly Income*
Bonds	50	4%	0.167
Loans	300	5.5%	1.375
Mortgages	150	5%	0.625
Total Income			**2.167**
Liabilities	*Balance*	*Coupon*	*Monthly Expense*
Term deposits	150	3%	0.375
Savings accounts	200	1.25%	0.208
Interbank deposits	100	4%	0.333
Total Expenses			**0.917**
Monthly NII			**1.250**

coupon with the new coupon calculated as the maturity specific interest rate plus the commercial margin.

Starting with the first month, we see that none of the products have a reset before one month (see Table 2.13). Therefore, the NII for the first month can be calculated using the initial product coupons (shown in Table 2.12). The same is true for the second period, which is between one and two months from now, and for the third period, which is between two and three months from now. None of the products reprice within the first three months, so the projected monthly NII is identical for the first three months. See Table 2.15.

In period 4 (starting three months from now and ending four months from now), *term deposits* are set to reprice (see Table 2.13). We can no longer use the 3% coupon rate assumed up to this point, but must calculate the new coupon rate expected in the future. To do this, we use the product's maturity (shown in Table 2.13), which is 3 months, and look up the expected interest rate for the equivalent tenor (reported in Table 2.14), which is 3.8%. Finally, we need to apply the commercial margin (shown in Table 2.13), which is -50 bp. Term deposits pay 50 bp less than the observable 3-month risk-free market rate: 3.8% - 0.5% = 3.3%. This is the new coupon rate for term deposits in period 4. Since term deposits do not reset for another three months (and even when they do, the reset is at the same rate), we can use this rate for periods 5 and 6 as well. Table 2.13 tells us that there are no other resets for other product classes in periods 4 through 6, so the coupons on all other products remain unchanged. Table 2.16 shows the projected monthly NII for periods 4 through 6. Note that the projected monthly interest rate

Table 2.16 Monthly baseline NII in periods 4 through 6

Assets	*Balance*	*Coupon*	*Monthly Income*
Bonds	50	4%	0.167
Loans	300	5.5%	1.375
Mortgages	150	5%	0.625
Total Income			**2.167**
Liabilities	*Balance*	*Coupon*	*Monthly Expense*
Term deposits	150	3.3%	0.413
Savings accounts	200	1.25%	0.208
Interbank deposits	100	4%	0.333
Total Expenses			**0.954**
Monthly NII			**1.213**

expense of term deposits has increased from 0.375 to 0.413, causing the projected monthly NII to decrease from 1.250 to 1.213.

After six months, there is a repricing of both customer *loans* and customer *savings* (see Table 2.13). The ongoing repricing of customer term deposits can be ignored, as any future interest rate reset will reprice to the same 3.3% already assumed from period 4 onwards. Other products are not repriced until period 12. Thus, we can calculate the monthly NII for periods 7 through 12 assuming the same coupon rates. To determine the new coupon rates for *loans* and for *savings*, we follow the same procedure as for term deposits: Identify the appropriate market rate (3.95% in both cases) and apply the margins (150 bp and -250 bp, respectively), resulting in a coupon rate of 5.45% and 1.45%, respectively. See Table 2.17.

In period 13, mortgages will have repriced to 5.08%, with no further repricings expected up to and including period 24. Thus, the projected monthly NII for periods 13 through 24 is as follows (see Table 2.18).

Finally, the *interbank deposits* are repriced after 24 months, resulting in a coupon adjustment to 4.16%. This allows us to calculate the projected monthly NII for periods 25 through 36, as shown in Table 2.19. Note that bonds do not reprice during the first 36 months and do not cause a change in projected NII for the first 60 months.

2.2.4.3 Total Baseline NII

Having calculated the projected monthly NII for the baseline scenario (unchanged interest rates), we can now proceed to aggregate the 36 monthly

Table 2.17 Monthly baseline NII in periods 7 through 12

Assets	*Balance*	*Coupon*	*Monthly Income*
Bonds	50	4%	0.167
Loans	300	5.45%	1.363
Mortgages	150	5%	0.625
Total Income			**2.154**
Liabilities	*Balance*	*Coupon*	*Monthly Expense*
Term deposits	150	3.3%	0.413
Savings accounts	200	1.45%	0.242
Interbank deposits	100	4%	0.333
Total Expenses			**0.988**
Monthly NII			**1.167**

Table 2.18 Monthly baseline NII in periods 13 through 24

Assets	*Balance*	*Coupon*	*Monthly Income*
Bonds	50	4%	0.167
Loans	300	5.45%	1.363
Mortgages	150	5.08%	0.635
Total Income			**2.164**
Liabilities	*Balance*	*Coupon*	*Monthly Expense*
Term deposits	150	3.3%	0.413
Savings accounts	200	1.45%	0.242
Interbank deposits	100	4%	0.333
Total Expenses			**0.988**
Monthly NII			**1.177**

periods into a 3-year total NII. Table 2.20 summarizes the projected monthly NII (Tables 2.15, 2.16, 2.17, 2.18 and 2.19), multiplies the monthly NII by the period lengths (within which the monthly NII remain constant), and calculates the projected 3-year total NII for the baseline.

The monthly evolution of the projected baseline NII is shown in Fig. 2.5.

Table 2.19 Monthly baseline NII in periods 25 through 36

Assets	*Balance*	*Coupon*	*Monthly Income*
Bonds	50	4%	0.167
Loans	300	5.45%	1.363
Mortgages	150	5.08%	0.635
Total Income			**2.164**
Liabilities	*Balance*	*Coupon*	*Monthly Expense*
Term deposits	150	3.3%	0.413
Savings accounts	200	1.45%	0.242
Interbank deposits	100	4.16%	0.347
Total Expenses			**1.001**
Monthly NII			**1.163**

Table 2.20 Total baseline NII

Monthly periods	Monthly NII	Period length	Period NII
1–3	1.250	3	3.750
4–6	1.213	3	3.639
7–12	1.167	6	7.002
13–24	1.177	12	14.124
25–36	1.163	12	13.956
Total 3-year NII		**36**	**42.471**

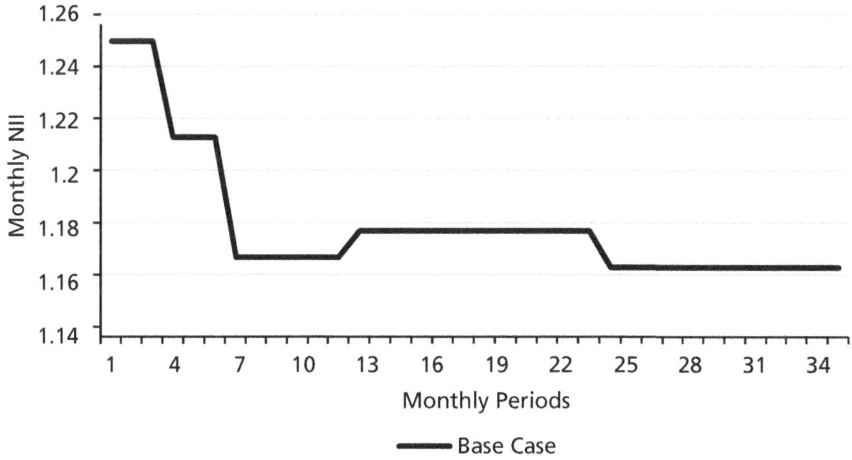

Fig. 2.5 Monthly baseline NII evolution

2.2.4.4 Monthly Shock Scenario NII

Having established a baseline scenario, we can now move on to stress the projected NII by applying an *interest rate shock*. The *shock scenario* applied in this example is an *immediate* and *parallel* 100 bp *downward shift* from current yields.[17]

The initial balance sheet (as shown in Table 2.12) and the product reset periods and commercial margins (as reported in Table 2.13) remain the same. However, the interest rate environment (initially reported in Table 2.14) must be shifted 100 bp lower and is reported in Table 2.21.

The calculation of the monthly NII projections for the -100 bp shock scenario follows the same procedure as before, except that the underlying interest rate at the time of a reset is the shifted yield curve. The resulting monthly NII projections for the shock scenario are shown in Tables 2.22, 2.23, 2.24, 2.25 and 2.26.

2.2.4.5 Total Shock Scenario NII

Having calculated the projected monthly NII for the shock scenario (1% decline in interest rates), we can now proceed to aggregate the 36 monthly periods into a 3-year total NII. Table 2.27 summarizes the projected monthly NIIs (Tables 2.22, 2.23, 2.24, 2.25 and 2.26), multiplies the monthly NIIs by the period lengths (within which the monthly NIIs remain constant), and calculates the projected 3-year total NII projection for the shock scenario.

The monthly evolution of the projected monthly shock scenario and baseline NIIs is shown in Fig. 2.6.

A visual inspection of Fig. 2.6 suggests that the model bank faces significant NII downside risk for a 100 bp move lower in interest rates in the period

Table 2.21 Shifted interest rate environment

Tenor	Interest rate (%)
1 Month	2.61
3 Months	2.80
6 Months	2.95
1 Year	3.08
2 Years	3.16
5 Years	3.17
7 Years	3.20
10 Years	3.27

Table 2.22 Monthly shock scenario NII in periods 1 through 3

Assets	*Balance*	*Coupon*	*Monthly Income*
Bonds	50	4%	0.167
Loans	300	5.5%	1.375
Mortgages	150	5%	0.625
Total Income			**2.167**
Liabilities	*Balance*	*Coupon*	*Monthly Expense*
Term deposits	150	3%	0.375
Savings accounts	200	1.25%	0.208
Interbank deposits	100	4%	0.333
Total Expenses			**0.917**
Monthly NII			**1.250**

Table 2.23 Monthly shock scenario NII in periods 4 through 6

Assets	*Balance*	*Coupon*	*Monthly Income*
Bonds	50	4%	0.167
Loans	300	5.5%	1.375
Mortgages	150	5%	0.625
Total Income			**2.167**
Liabilities	*Balance*	*Coupon*	*Monthly Expense*
Term deposits	150	2.3%	0.288
Savings accounts	200	1.25%	0.208
Interbank deposits	100	4%	0.333
Total Expenses			**0.829**
Monthly NII			**1.338**

from one year to two years from now. Up to one year from now, however, the NII is expected to benefit from a rise in interest rates.

What our NII projections suggest makes intuitive sense: *Term deposits* benefit very *quickly* from a decline in interest rates because they reset after only three months, resulting in significant interest savings on the cost side. *Mortgages*, on the other hand, do not reset for another year, so the decline in interest income comes *later*.

In addition to the unfavorable monthly NIIs in the shock scenario between year 1 and year 2, the shock scenario NIIs are also *more volatile* than the

Table 2.24 Monthly shock scenario NII in periods 7 through 12

Assets	*Balance*	*Coupon*	*Monthly Income*
Bonds	50	4%	0.167
Loans	300	4.45%	1.113
Mortgages	150	5%	0.625
Total Income			**1.904**
Liabilities	*Balance*	*Coupon*	*Monthly Expense*
Term deposits	150	2.3%	0.288
Savings accounts	200	0.45%	0.075
Interbank deposits	100	4%	0.333
Total Expenses			**0.696**
Monthly NII			**1.208**

Table 2.25 Monthly shock scenario NII in periods 13 through 24

Assets	*Balance*	*Coupon*	*Monthly Income*
Bonds	50	4%	0.167
Loans	300	4.45%	1.113
Mortgages	150	4.08%	0.510
Total Income			**1.789**
Liabilities	*Balance*	*Coupon*	*Monthly Expense*
Term deposits	150	2.3%	0.288
Savings accounts	200	0.45%	0.075
Interbank deposits	100	4%	0.333
Total Expenses			**0.696**
Monthly NII			**1.093**

baseline NIIs. Banks typically try to avoid *NII volatility* in order to stabilize earnings over time.

2.2.4.6 Hedging NII

To stabilize the NII in the shock scenario, the model bank looks for an appropriate *hedging transaction*. One way to take advantage of a decline in interest rates is to enter into a fixed-for-floating interest rate swap, where one *receives a fixed rate* and *pays a floating rate*, both on a given notional amount.

Table 2.26 Monthly shock scenario NII in periods 25 through 36

Assets	*Balance*	*Coupon*	*Monthly Income*
Bonds	50	4%	0.167
Loans	300	4.45%	1.113
Mortgages	150	4.08%	0.510
Total Income			**1.789**
Liabilities	*Balance*	*Coupon*	*Monthly Expense*
Term deposits	150	2.3%	0.288
Savings accounts	200	0.45%	0.075
Interbank deposits	100	3.16%	0.263
Total Expenses			**0.626**
Monthly NII			**1.163**

Table 2.27 Total shock scenario NII

Monthly periods	Monthly NII	Period length	Period NII
1–3	1.250	3	3.750
4–6	1.338	3	4.014
7–12	1.208	6	7.248
13–24	1.093	12	13.116
25–36	1.163	12	13.956
Total 3-year NII		**36**	**42.084**

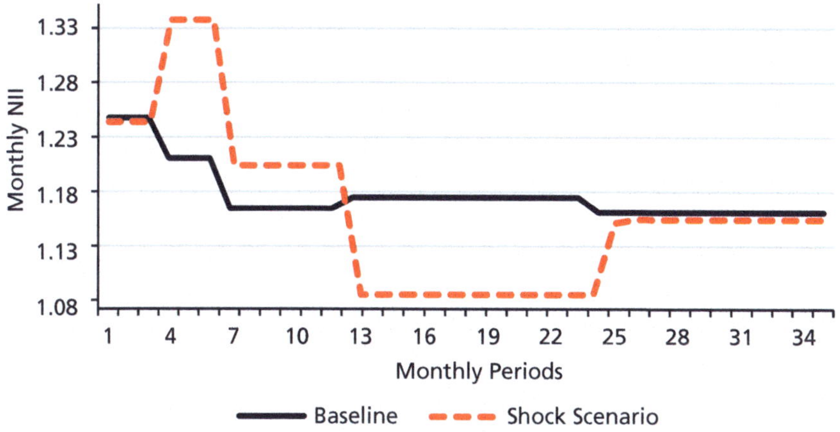

Fig. 2.6 Monthly baseline and shock scenario NII evolution (I)

As an illustration, assume that the bank enters into a 3-year EUR 100 (notional) *receiver swap*[18] where the fixed leg of the swap pays 4.16% and the floating leg is linked to floating interest rate that is initially set at 3.95% and reprices every six months thereafter.

To include the receiver swap in the NII analysis, the two legs of the swap are treated as assets and liabilities. The fixed leg of the swap, which creates a positive cash flow for the bank, is recorded as an asset (equivalent to a bond that also pays a fixed coupon), while the floating leg of the swap is recorded as a liability because the bank must make recurring interest payments (similar to floating interest payments on short-term customer deposits).

The calculation of the monthly NII projections for the -100 bp shock scenario hedged by the interest rate swap follows the same procedure as before and is reported in Tables 2.28, 2.29, 2.30, 2.31 and 2.32.

Table 2.28 Monthly hedged shock scenario NII in periods 1 through 3

Assets	*Balance*	*Coupon*	*Monthly Income*
Bonds	50	4%	0.167
Loans	300	5.5%	1.375
Mortgages	150	5%	0.625
Swap Receive	100	4.16%	0.347
Total Income			**2.513**
Liabilities	*Balance*	*Coupon*	*Monthly Expense*
Term deposits	150	3%	0.375
Savings accounts	200	1.25%	0.208
Interbank deposits	100	4%	0.333
Swap Pay	100	3.95	0.329
Total Expenses			**1.246**
Monthly NII			**1.268**

Table 2.29 Monthly hedged shock scenario NII in periods 4 through 6

Assets	*Balance*	*Coupon*	*Monthly Income*
Bonds	50	4%	0.167
Loans	300	5.5%	1.375
Mortgages	150	5%	0.625
Swap Receive	100	4.16%	0.347
Total Income			**2.513**
Liabilities	*Balance*	*Coupon*	*Monthly Expense*
Term deposits	150	2.3%	0.288
Savings accounts	200	1.25%	0.208
Interbank deposits	100	4%	0.333
Swap Pay	100	3.95	0.329
Total Expenses			**1.158**
Monthly NII			**1.355**

Table 2.30 Monthly hedged shock scenario NII in periods 7 through 12

Assets	*Balance*	*Coupon*	*Monthly Income*
Bonds	50	4%	0.167
Loans	300	4.45%	1.113
Mortgages	150	5%	0.625
Swap Receive	100	4.16%	0.347
Total Income			**2.251**
Liabilities	*Balance*	*Coupon*	*Monthly Expense*
Term deposits	150	2.3%	0.288
Savings accounts	200	0.45%	0.075
Interbank deposits	100	4%	0.333
Swap Pay	100	2.95%	0.246
Total Expenses			**0.942**
Monthly NII			**1.309**

2.2.4.7 Total Hedged Shock Scenario NII

We can now proceed to aggregate the 36 monthly periods into a 3-year total NII. Table 2.33 summarizes the projected monthly NIIs (Tables 2.28, 2.29, 2.30, 2.31, and 2.32), multiplies the monthly NIIs by the period lengths (within which the monthly NIIs remain constant), and calculates the projected 3-year total NII projection for the hedged shock scenario.

Table 2.31 Monthly hedged shock scenario NII in periods 13 through 24

Assets	*Balance*	*Coupon*	*Monthly Income*
Bonds	50	4%	0.167
Loans	300	4.45%	1.113
Mortgages	150	4.08%	0.510
Swap Receive	100	4.16%	0.347
Total Income			**2.136**
Liabilities	*Balance*	*Coupon*	*Monthly Expense*
Term deposits	150	2.3%	0.288
Savings accounts	200	0.45%	0.075
Interbank deposits	100	4%	0.333
Swap Pay	100	2.95	0.246
Total Expenses			**0.942**
Monthly NII			**1.194**

Table 2.32 Monthly hedged shock scenario NII in periods 25 through 36

Assets	*Balance*	*Coupon*	*Monthly Income*
Bonds	50	4%	0.167
Loans	300	4.45%	1.113
Mortgages	150	4.08%	0.510
Swap Receive	100	4.16%	0.347
Total Income			**2.136**
Liabilities	*Balance*	*Coupon*	*Monthly Expense*
Term deposits	150	2.3%	0.288
Savings accounts	200	0.45%	0.075
Interbank deposits	100	3.16%	0.263
Swap Pay	100	2.95%	0.246
Total Expenses			**0.872**
Monthly NII			**1.264**

The monthly evolution of the hedged and unhedged shock scenario, together with the baseline NIIs, is shown in Fig. 2.7.

The hedge helped to stabilize the NII in the event of a -100 bp interest rate shock. In particular, the NII downside in the 13–24-month period was reduced.

Table 2.33 Total hedged shock scenario NII

Monthly periods	Monthly NII	Period length	Period NII
1–3	1.268	3	3.804
4–6	1.355	3	4.065
7–12	1.309	6	7.854
13–24	1.194	12	14.328
25–36	1.264	12	15.168
Total 3-year NII		**36**	**45.219**

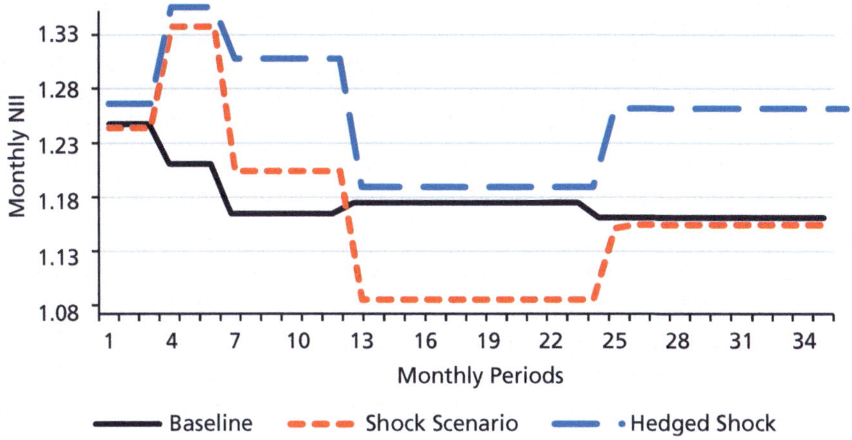

Fig. 2.7 Monthly baseline and shock scenario NII evolution (II)

2.2.4.8 Caveats

There are three aspects of the NII projections presented above that warrant further discussion.

First, the picture painted by Fig. 2.7 seems *too good to be true*: the expected NII for the hedged balance sheet is not only better than that in the unhedged shock scenario, but also better than that in the baseline scenario. If the receiver swap seems to miraculously improve NII in *every period*, why not *just* enter into a receiver swap (instead of doing any customer business at all), or at least *increase* the "hedge"? Something seems wrong!

To understand why the receiver swap has such a positive impact on NII, we need to go back to the assumptions we used for the NII projections in this example. We have chosen to *hold the current interest rate constant*, i. e. there is no expected increase in short-term interest rates. This is a rather specific assumption that makes *any* asset paying a long-term fixed interest rate and funded with short-term rates look attractive in an upward sloping yield curve environment. For example, a 5-year or 10-year bond financed by successive short-term repo transactions would also have extremely positive NII projections if short-term rates are not allowed to rise. If we assume that interest rates will rise in line with what forward rates imply, the short-term benefit of receiving a higher fixed rate and paying a currently lower floating rate would disappear over time, and at some point in the future, short-term rates would even *exceed* the fixed rate. You can think of the fixed rate as an kind of *average* of the expected floating rates over the life of the transaction. Common sense tells us that if this weren't the case, there would be few, if any, market participants willing to be the counterparty to a receiver swap.

This again illustrates the importance of making *alternative* assumptions about future interest rates, and not limiting the NII simulation analysis to one set of assumptions. For example, in 2019 and 2020, the fixed rate on a 10-year receiver swap was -0.25% or lower, and some market participants still felt compelled to enter into receiver swaps because the floating rate (6-month EURIBOR) was *even lower* at around -0.5%. If one assumes that one will continue to pay -0.5% (the equivalent of receiving +0.5%), then receiving -0.25% (the equivalent of paying +0.25%) for 10 years sounds attractive (generating a 25 bp positive NII p. a.). However, shortly thereafter, the 6-month EURIBOR rose above 4% in 2023 (which is not only higher than the -0.5% during the previous EURIBOR settings, but also higher than what forward rates would have implied in 2019 or 2020), changing the actual *realized* NII from +25 bp to -425 bp p. a.

The second caveat relates to the economic value perspective, which we have ignored in the NII analysis. As discussed in Sect. 2.2.5, the economic value perspective (based on EVE) and the earnings perspective (based on NII) often show a *contradictory reaction* to changes in interest rates. The impact of the 3-year receiver swap as a "hedge" on the economic value perspective risk is shown in the tables below. In Sect. 2.1.3, we have already calculated the repricing gap risk to be 1.74 (see Table 2.34). Adding the receiver swap to the economic value risk analysis increases the repricing gap to 3.63 (see Table 2.35).

Given that the bank's capital is 50, the risk after including the receiver swap corresponds to a 7.26% (up from 3.48% without the swap) decline in capital for a 100 bp upward shock in interest rates.

Since the *supervisory outlier test*, or Basel interest rate shock, is defined for a 200 bp change in interest rates, the bank's Basel II-Ratio (relative risk of a ±200 bp interest rate shock) would be twice as high, or 14.52% (up from 6.96% without the swap).

Table 2.34 Repricing gap analysis without receiver swap

				Assets				
time to repricing (in months)	<1	1-3	3-6	6-12	12-24	24-36	36-48	48-60
Bonds								50
Loans			300					
Mortgages				150				
Σ Assets	**0**	**0**	**300**	**150**	**0**	**0**	**0**	**50**
				Liabilities				
time to repricing (in months)	<1	1-3	3-6	6-12	12-24	24-36	36-48	48-60
Term deposits		150						
Savings accounts			200					
Interbank deposits					100			
Equity								
Σ Liabilities	**0**	**150**	**200**	**0**	**100**	**0**	**0**	**0**
Net repricing gaps	**0**	**-150**	**100**	**150**	**-100**	**0**	**0**	**50**
Mod. Duration (%)	0.04	0.16	0.36	0.72	1.39	2.25	3.07	3.86
Weighted gaps	0	-0.24	0.36	1.08	-1.39	0	0	1.93
Total repricing gap				**1.74**				

Thus, the receiver swap “hedge” helped to stabilize and improve the NII, but at the same time it increased the EVE risk.

Third, our cash flow projections ignore the intratemporal investment of NII. If the projected monthly NII (as shown in Table 2.20) were to be invested in, say, short-term interbank deposit accounts before being paid out at the end of the year as part of an annual dividend payment, these short-term investments would also be subject to interest rate risk. For simplicity, the analysis presented in this section implicitly assumes that all NII earned is immediately distributed to shareholders.

Fourth, the estimate of future NII based on the assumption of a constant balance sheet, unchanged interest rates, and constant margins ultimately results in a constant NII after the repricing of the product with the longest reset period has occurred. According to the reset schedule shown in Table 2.13, this is the case after 60 months. From that point on, the NII does not change any more. This is another reason, why NII analyses are typically only performed only a few years into the future.

Table 2.35 Repricing gap analysis with receiver swap

				Assets				
time to repricing (in months)	<1	1-3	3-6	6-12	12-24	24-36	36-48	48-60
Bonds								50
Loans			300					
Mortgages				150				
Swap Receive						100		
$\sum$ *Assets*	**0**	**0**	**300**	**150**	**0**	**100**	**0**	**50**
				Liabilities				
time to repricing (in months)	<1	1-3	3-6	6-12	12-24	24-36	36-48	48-60
Term deposits		150						
Savings accounts			200					
Interbank deposits					100			
Swap Pay			100					
Equity								
$\sum$ *Liabilities*	**0**	**150**	**300**	**0**	**100**	**0**	**0**	**0**
Net repricing gaps	**0**	**-150**	**0**	**150**	**-100**	**100**	**0**	**50**
Mod. Duration (%)	0.04	0.16	0.36	0.72	1.39	2.25	3.07	3.86
Weighted gaps	0	-0.24	0	1.08	-1.39	2.25	0	1.93
Total repricing gap					**3.63**			

2.2.5 Economic Value vs. Earnings Measures: A Critique

Both, economic value measures and earnings measures are appropriate measures for quantifying interest rate risk. Changes in interest rates affect both, EVE and NII. However, EVE and NII often *react in opposite ways* to changes in interest rates. For example, an increase in the general level of interest rates may be a positive for NII if floating-rate assets (e. g., loans with periodically resetting interest rates) generate more interest income, while the same interest rate increase causes the net present value of fixed-rate assets to decline.

The difficulty of immunizing a bank against interest rate risk from both an EVE and NII perspective is illustrated by the following example. Suppose a bank has EUR 10 mm of equity, EUR 90 mm of funding on the liabilities side of its balance sheet in the form of 3-year fixed-rate customer deposits, and assets consisting entirely of a EUR 100 mm 10-year fixed-rate bond (see the left panel of Fig. 2.8). The NII is constant for the next three years and can be calculated as EUR 100 mm × 5% - EUR 90 mm × 3% = EUR 2.3 mm p. a. Thus, there is no NII risk at all for the next three years. From an EVE perspective, however, the situation is different. Assuming a modified duration of 8 for the 10-year fixed-rate bond and a modified duration of 2.8 for the 3-year fixed-rate deposit, the duration gap is

$$\left(\frac{\text{EUR}\,100\,\text{mm} \times 8}{\text{EUR}\,100\,\text{mm}}\right) - \left(\frac{\text{EUR}\,90\,\text{mm} \times 2.8}{\text{EUR}\,100\,\text{mm}}\right) = 5.48$$

With a duration gap of 5.48, a 1% increase in interest rates results in a loss of 5.48% on EUR 100 mm, or EUR 5.48 mm. This is 54.8% of the EUR 10 mm of equity, so that the Economic Value of Equity (EVE) risk is 54.8%.

Applying the supervisory outlier test, or Basel interest rate shock, defined as a 200 bp change in interest rates, the bank's Basel II-Ratio would be double that, or about 110%. This is significantly higher than the regulatory limit of 15% and bakes the bank an *outlier bank.*

Suppose the bank restores its asset side of the balance sheet by selling the EUR 100 mm position in 10-year fixed-rate bonds and by establishing two EUR 50 mm positions, one as a 6-year fixed-rate bond and the other as an overnight loan currently yielding 1% (see the right panel of Fig. 2.8). From an EVE perspective, the bank is now in good shape. Assuming a modified duration of 5 for the 6-year fixed-rate bond, a modified duration of 0 for the overnight loan, and a modified duration of 2.8 for the 3-year fixed-rate deposit, the duration gap is

$$\left(\frac{\text{EUR}\,50\,\text{mm} \times 5}{\text{EUR}\,100\,\text{mm}} + \frac{\text{EUR}\,50\,\text{mm} \times 0}{\text{EUR}\,100\,\text{mm}}\right) - \left(\frac{\text{EUR}\,90\,\text{mm} \times 2.8}{\text{EUR}\,100\,\text{mm}}\right) \approx 0$$

With a duration gap of 0, a change in interest rates causes no loss and the economic value of equity (EVE) risk is zero. However, from an NII perspective, the bank is no longer safe. In the NII baseline scenario, the bank earns EUR 0.3 mm p. a. for the next three years, calculated as EUR 50 mm × 5% + EUR 50 mm × 1% - EUR 90 mm × 3%. With a -100 bp decline in interest rates, the overnight loan would only pay 0% and the resulting NII of this shock scenario is minus (!) EUR 0.2 mm for the next three years, calculated as EUR 50 mm × 5% + EUR 50 mm × 0% - EUR 90 mm × 3%.

This example highlights the fact that neither of the two interest rate risk measures, EVE and NII, is suitable for quantifying interest rate risk on its own. In addition, liquidity risk is not reflected in either measure. In fact, EBA requires banks not to rely on a single measure of risk, but instead to use a *range* of quantitative tools and models appropriate to their specific risk exposures.[19]

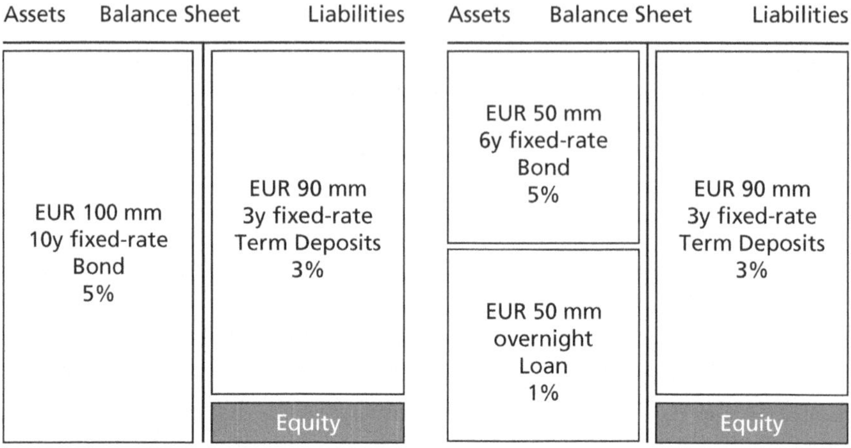

Fig. 2.8 NII vs. EVE risk immunization

2.2.6 Change in Market Value Outside of the NII Horizon

A fundamental problem with NII calculations is that they only measure the impact of interest rate changes within the NII horizon. One way of addressing this shortcoming is to calculate the impact of interest rate changes on the *market value* (MV) of instruments beyond the NII horizon. To avoid double counting, cash flows within the NII horizon are excluded from the calculation of market value changes (Δ MV).

This inclusion of MV changes blurs the definition of NII, as it relies on the same process used in economic value (EV) calculations (e.g., EVE) and creates an overlap between NII and EV measures. Therefore, Δ MV should be considered mainly for the purpose of *monitoring* the earnings risk that is not captured within the NII horizon.

Banks using IFRS standards can extract market value changes of positions held at fair value with relative ease, while smaller institutions reporting under local GAAP face some difficulties (and may have few positions with P&L impact in different interest rate environments anyway).

In 2022, the EBA has included in its IRRBB guidelines a requirement to *monitor* the market value changes of instruments held at fair value due to interest rate changes.[20] This was implemented by Commission Delegated Regulation (EU) 2024/857 and entered into force on May 14, 2024.[21] Details of the supervisory reporting requirements relating to market value changes are provided in Sects. 5.2.1 and 5.5.1.

2.3 Funds Transfer Pricing (FTP)

Funds Transfer Pricing is an *internal* process that aims to assign a funding rate to each asset-side position and an earning rate to each liability-side position within the banking book.

For example, a bank that provides a 5-year mortgage loan to a customer wants to know, how much it would cost to refinance the position. Obviously, it would be wrong to assume that funding is free because the bank has excess liquidity on its balance sheet that could be used. This would be a violation of the economic principle of *opportunity cost*, which states that one should include in the cost calculation the potential foregone profit from a missed opportunity that could otherwise be taken. For example, if excess liquidity is used to finance the mortgage loan, it can no longer be used to repay bank liabilities (e. g., an interbank loan), and the interest rate savings from doing so are foregone. It would also be inappropriate to use *a single* rate, such as the bank's weighted average cost of capital (WACC), as the funding and as the earnings rate for all assets and liabilities, respectively. Longer-term assets require longer-term funding, which is typically more expensive than shorter-term funding.

Once an interest rate is determined that appropriately reflects the funding of each position, an internal allocation of a position's interest income can be made. The *customer area* of a bank should receive the portion of the earned income that results from its ability to secure a better-than-market *customer rate*, but without having to worry about funding, while the unit responsible for funding, the *treasury department*, is allocated the portion of the earned income that results from the need to borrow or to invest the appropriate funds at prevailing market rates, but without having to worry about the specific customer rate of each transaction.

2.3.1 Net Interest Margin

The difference between the interest income (II) and interest expense (IE) is called the Net Interest Margin, or NIM. NIM can be calculated on a position basis or aggregated over a group of assets all the way up to the bank-wide level. Figure 2.9 shows an example of a bank that funds itself with 1-year customer deposits at 1% and uses all the funds to make a 1-year customer loan at 3%. Based on this example, the net interest margin is 2%.

As asset and liability positions are perfectly matched in terms of both size and maturity, the bank is not exposed to any interest rate risk. The net interest

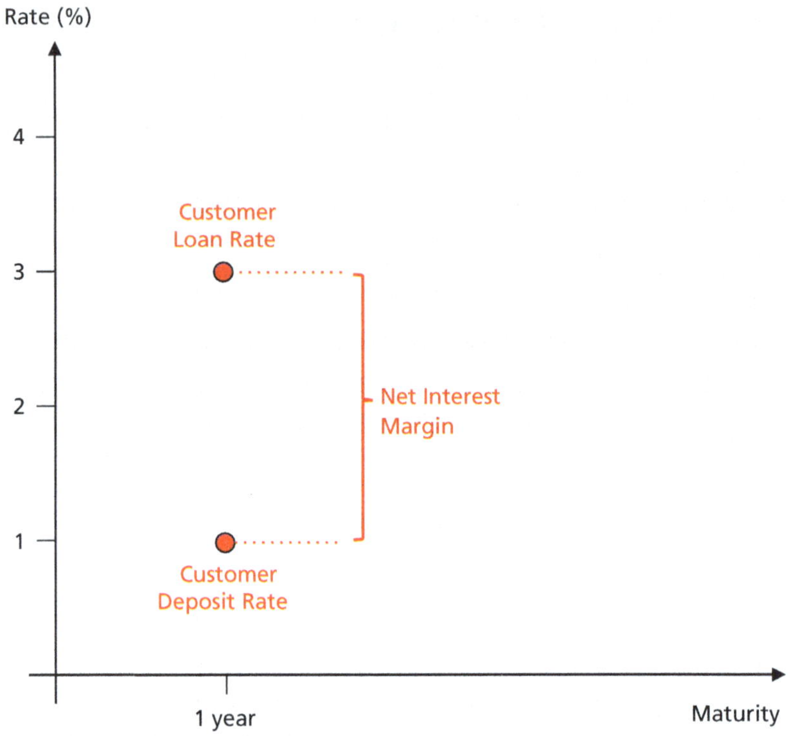

Fig. 2.9 NIM without duration mismatch

margin is maintained for one year and there is no interest rate risk to net interest income (NII).

While this example seems to eliminate the need for a funds transfer pricing process, there is still a question that cannot be answered by a simple NIM calculation. Knowing that the bank is earning a net interest margin of 2%, but that two different departments are responsible for this (namely the customer deposit department, which acquired the funds, and the customer loan department, which made a matching loan), how should the NIM be allocated between them? To answer this question, the total margin contribution must be divided into two individual margin contributions for the customer deposit and for the customer loan departments, respectively.) This requires an FTP system.

2.3.2 Cost of Funds

A problem arises when asset and liability positions don't match, either in size or in term of maturity. In an example shown in Fig. 2.10, a bank makes a 1-year loan to a customer, but has no matching funding from customer business. What is the margin contribution of the loan? The margin contribution of the loan depends on the interest rate level at which the bank can fund itself in the market. This funding is done by a central funding center, typically a bank's treasury department. The rate that the treasury department deems appropriate for raising funds on the capital market (using bank-specific funding channels) is the *cost of funds*. The difference between the customer lending rate and the cost of funds is the margin contribution assigned to the lending area.

The cost of funding depends on the term. A 2-year loan is typically more expensive than a 1-year loan. Therefore, the cost of funds for a 2-year customer loan is higher than the cost of funds for a 1-year customer loan. The margin contribution of a 2-year customer loan is the difference between the 2-year customer loan rate and the 2-year cost of funds rate. See Fig. 2.11.,

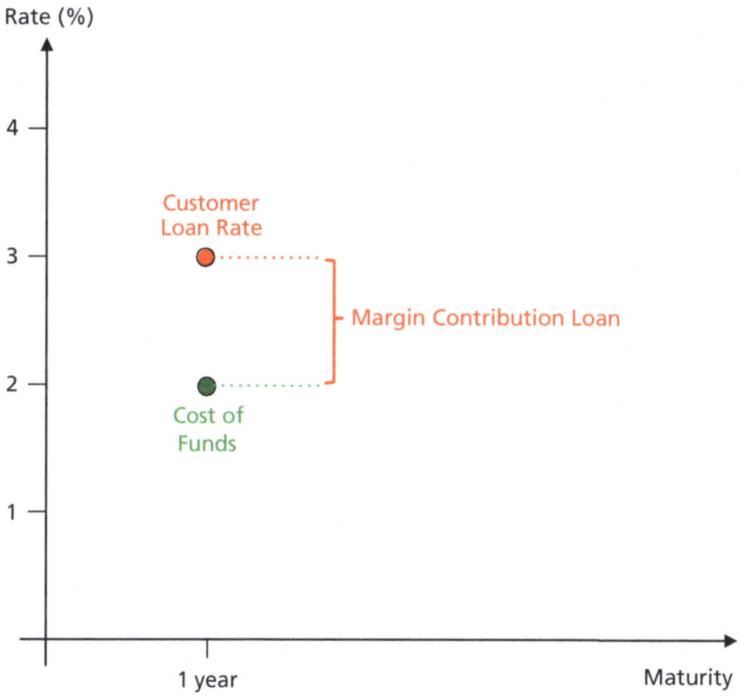

Fig. 2.10 Cost of funds (I)

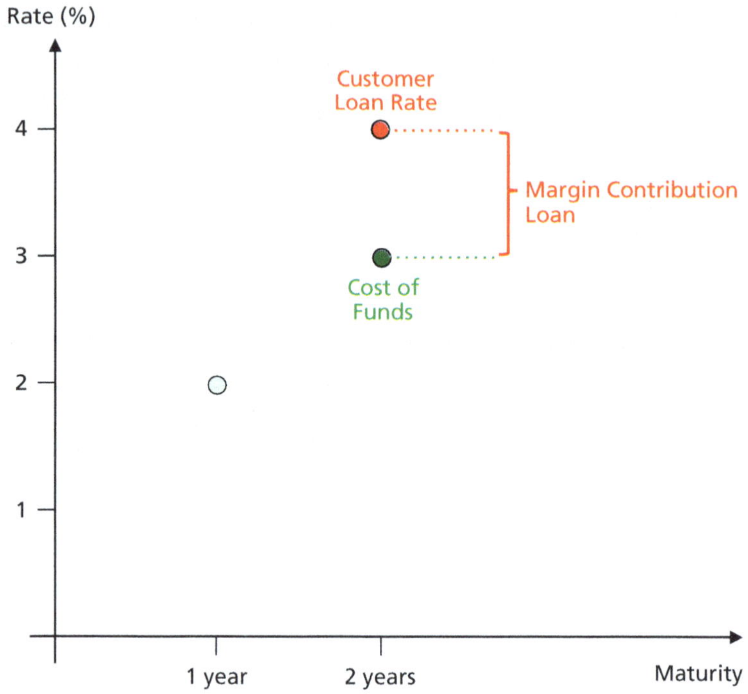

Fig. 2.11 Cost of funds (II)

2.3.3 Transfer Price Curve

Combining all points of cost of funds rates for different maturities gives the transfer price curve. It is also known as the Cost of Funds Curve or the Funds Transfer Price Curve.

In the *matched maturity method* of FTP implementation, each originated asset or liability position is assigned an FTP rate from the transfer price curve that matches the maturity of the position. FTP helps allocate a bank's net interest margin (NIM) among different business units based on the types, characteristics, and riskiness of the asset and liability positions they originate.

Figure 2.12 illustrates the following situation: A bank's deposit department accepts a one-year deposit from a customer at a low interest rate of 1%, while its lending department makes a two-year loan to another customer at 4%. Thus, the net interest margin (for the first year) is 3% p. a. However, a 1-year deposit cannot be directly compared to a 2-year loan; instead, the 1-year deposit rate is compared to an internal 1-year transfer price rate of 2%. The difference, 1%, is the margin contribution of the deposit area. The 2-year loan rate is compared to the corresponding transfer price rate, which is 3%,

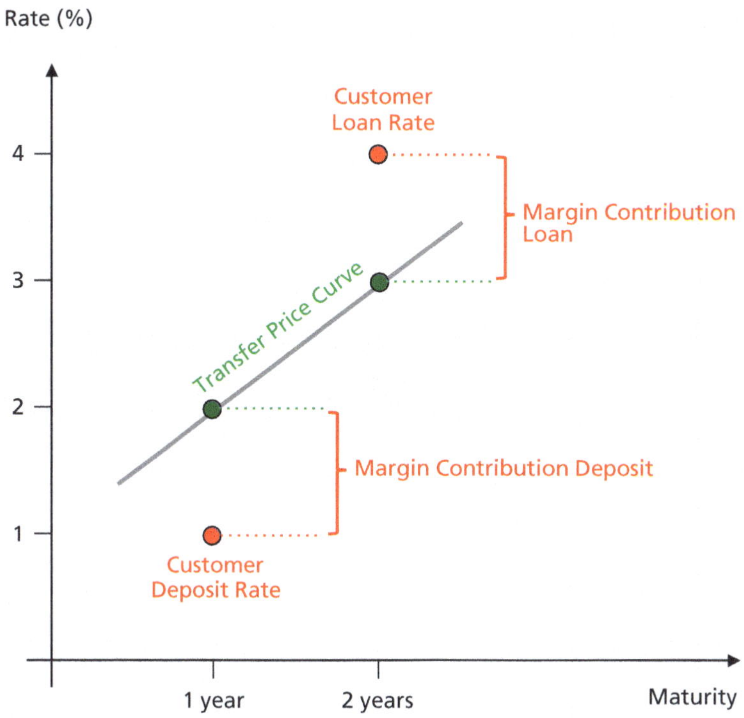

Fig. 2.12 Transfer price curve

and the resulting margin contribution of the lending department is 1%. The difference between a 1- and a 2-year rate on the FTP curve, called structural contribution, is discussed in the next section.

2.3.4 Structural Contribution

The *structural contribution* is the compensation to the treasury department for taking on two different risks, liquidity risk and interest rate risk.

In the example discussed earlier, a bank has funded a 2-year loan with a 1-year deposit. At the end of the 1-year term, the customer deposit area needs to *roll* its position because the funds generated by the deposit are still tied up for another year in what was originally a 2-year loan. If the deposits cannot be rolled, the bank faces a liquidity shortage. Thus, by entering into maturity mismatched asset and liability positions, the bank creates *refinancing risk*, which is a form of *liquidity risk*. In addition, since the interest rate on the liability is only fixed for the one-year term of the deposit, if the interest rate rises in the second year, the deposits will be rolled into a higher interest rate, resulting in an erosion of the net interest margin. Therefore, the mismatched asset and liability positions also create *interest rate risk*. See Fig. 2.13.

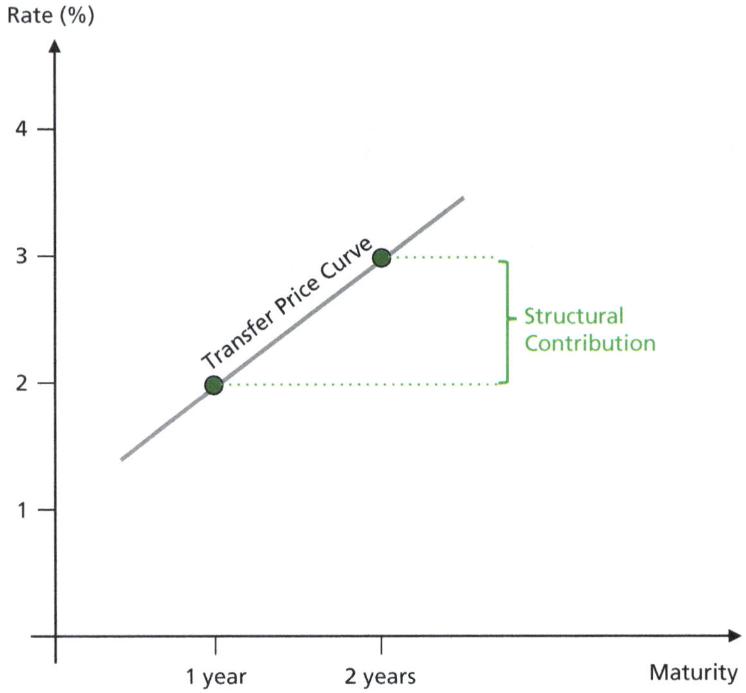

Fig. 2.13 Structural contribution

2.3.5 Interest Rate vs. Liquidity Risk

Since the FTP curve compensates the treasury department for both, *interest rate* and *liquidity risk*, it is useful to *separate* this combined risk into its *two components*. This is done by constructing a *pure interest rate risk curve* and then adding a *funding spread* to it. See Fig. 2.14.

Several approaches have been proposed to construct a term structure of risk-free interest rates (also called a risk-free yield curve).[22] Each approach has its advantages and disadvantages:

- For countries where the government has the power to print money, a risk-free yield curve can be constructed from government bonds. This is commonly done in the U.S., where a U.S. Treasury yield curve can be constructed from the prices of newly issued (and therefore very liquid) U.S.

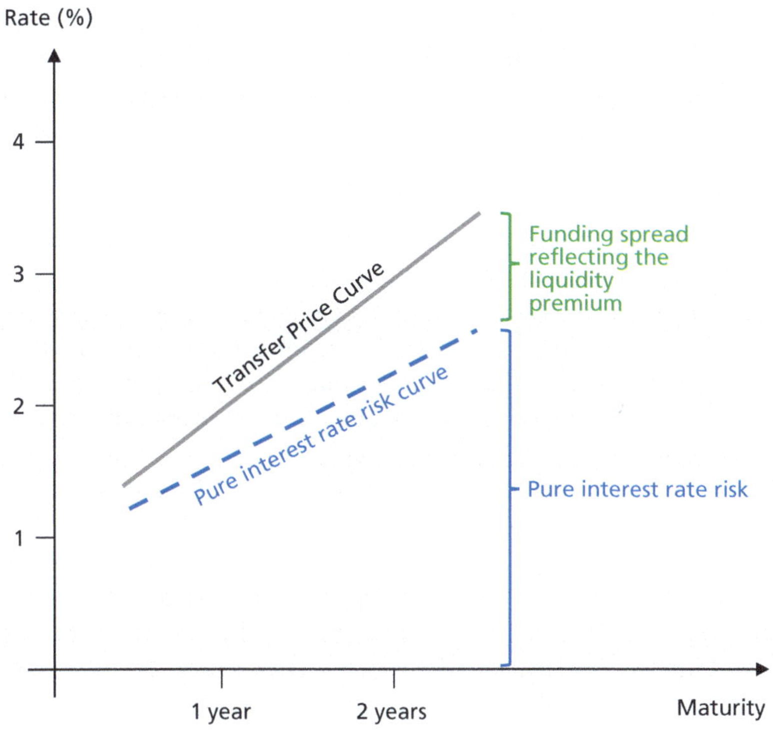

Fig. 2.14 Pure interest rate risk curve

Treasury securities of various maturities.[23] In Europe, however, no single country has the power to print the legal tender (euro), and thus European sovereign debt includes a default risk premium that varies from country to country.

- In Europe, it is possible to construct an *almost* risk-free yield curve from eurozone central government bonds that have the best credit risk rating from the rating agencies, i. e. "AAA-rated" government bonds.[24] The downside is that there are very few (only five as of 2024) AAA-rated European governments.[25]
- A third approach is to use the euro short-term interest rate (€STR) and €STR-based derivatives (such as the Eurex-traded three-month €STR future contract or €STR overnight index swaps).[26] The €STR is the eurozone's version of so-called risk-free rates (RFRs), which are designed to represent observable funding rates in the market.[27] A potential disadvantage is that €STR-based yields do not (yet) have a (forward-looking) term structure. Instead, they are accrued over time and are calculated in arrears.

- A fourth approach would be to construct a risk-free curve from repo rates.[28] Since repo rates are based on collateralized lending and borrowing, and counterparty credit risk[29] can be even further reduced through triparty repo and central counterparty (CCP)-cleared repo, the resulting yield curve can be considered virtually risk-free. The downside of this approach is that the repo market is short-term in nature and typically only liquid out to one or two years. In addition, the repo market can become illiquid at times (e. g. during the banking crisis of 2007 / 2008).
- A fifth method is to use the EURIBOR-based interest rate swap curve[30] as a proxy for the risk-free yield curve. The main advantage of using the swap curve as a benchmark is that it extends out to 30 years and is quite liquid. Because interest rate swaps do not involve an exchange of the notional amounts and are typically collateralized, swap transactions are virtually risk-free. However, the rate that is exchanged in a EURIBOR interest rate swap is based on unsecured borrowing and lending between banks, and, therefore the swap rate reflects the counterparty credit risk between banks. In fact, EURIBOR may eventually be replaced by €STR (the current fallback rate should EURIBOR cease to exist in the future) due to manipulation of interest rate benchmarks, which occurred between 2005 and 2011 with the London Interbank Offered Rate[31] (LIBOR).

Funding spreads over and above the risk-free interest rate are asset specific. For example, a liquid, high-quality security that can be used as a collateral can be funded in the repo market.[32] A mortgage loan can also be funded at attractive levels if the mortgage can be used as a collateral in a mortgage-backed security (MBS) issue. An illiquid, lower-quality asset, on the other hand, is unlikely to be able to be used as a collateral and will have to be funded on an unsecured basis (which is more expensive). In theory, there could be a separate FTP curve for each balance sheet item. Since it is not practical to have many separate funding curves, it is more appropriate to use *a single FTP-curve* that reflects an *average funding spread* and then to adjust the spread on a case-by-case basis as necessary. Calculating a bank's average liquidity premium can be done by *calibrating* the FTP curve to the bank's prevailing funding and investment opportunities. For example, if the bank currently issues 2-year fixed rate notes at 3% and 2-year floating rate notes at 2.2%, then the funding spread for a 2-year term would be 80 bp over the interest rate risk-free curve.

The Separation of FTP into two risk sub-components has the advantage of allowing the pricing of products where the *contractual reset reference interest*

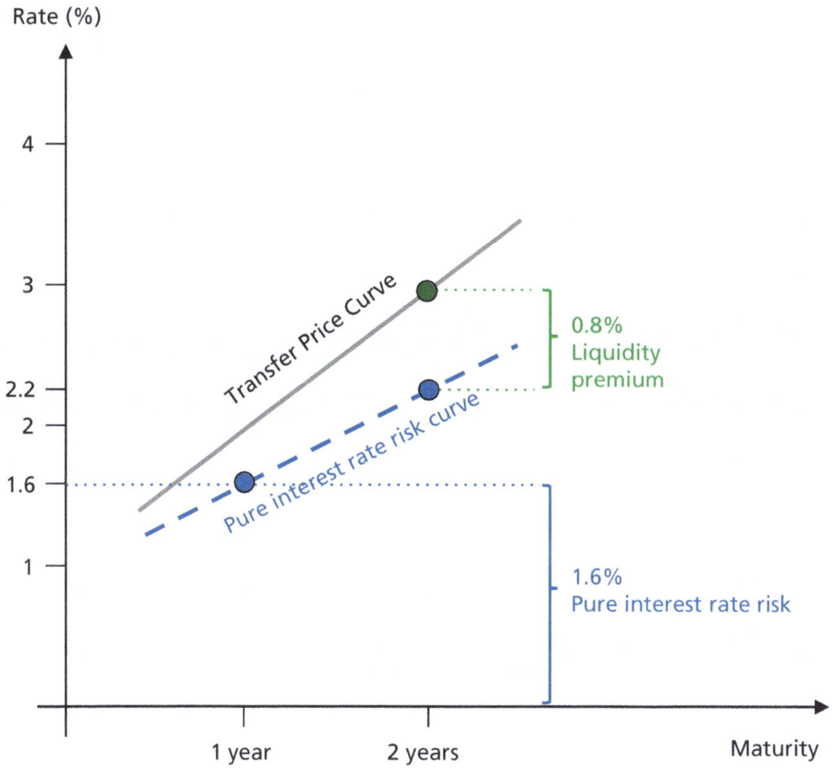

Fig. 2.15 Pure interest rate risk vs. liquidity premium

rate index has a different maturity than the *contractual maturity of the instrument*. For example, a 2-year customer loan with an initial 1-year rate fix that resets after 1 year would have an FTP rate calculated as 1.6% interest rate risk +80 bp liquidity premium = 2.4%. See Fig. 2.15.

2.3.6 Multi-currency FTP Curve

If assets or liabilities are denominated in a currency other than the base currency of the FTP curve, either a new FTP curve needs to be constructed or the existing FTP curve needs to be adjusted to reflect the different currency.

If the bank has subsidiaries in different currency zones, the local ALM desks may be able to create currency-specific FTP curves, based on market activity (funding, deposits etc.) in those regions. In this case, the local ALM desk may also make funding and investment decisions in the local currency.

If the alternative currency position is managed by a centralized ALM desk, it may not be practical to create multiple FTP curves for multiple currencies,

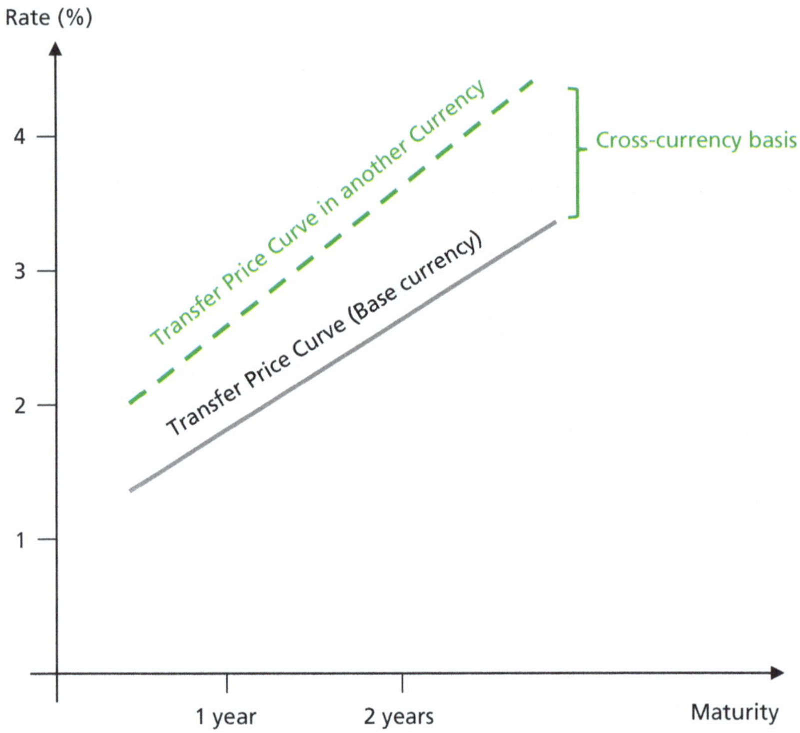

Fig. 2.16 Transfer price curve in another currency

but rather to price the non-base currency position on the base currency FTP curve after applying a cross-currency adjustment to the funding spread. For all major currencies, this cross-currency adjustment can be observed in the cross-currency swap market.[33] See Fig. 2.16.

2.3.7 Steering the Bank's Customer Business

So far, we have discussed two purposes of FTP:

- Internal allocation of the net interest margin to different business units.
- Centralization of interest rate and liquidity risk in the treasury department at an appropriate transfer price based on the riskiness of the positions.

There is a *third* possible function of FTP: it can be used to *steer* the bank's customer business and as a tool to influence the evolution of the balance sheet structure. For example, a bank facing a balance sheet mismatch resulting from an overhang of customer liabilities (customer deposits) and a lack of customer assets (customer loans) could address the situation by shifting the FTP curve downward. This will reduce the margin contribution allocated to the customer deposit department, while increasing the margin contribution to the loan department. This is likely to act as an *incentive* for the loan department to make more loans to customers, while *discouraging* deposit business. See Fig. 2.17.

The steering function of FTP is highly *political*. FTP is essentially the single source of truth for assessing the perceived value added by different business lines. Small changes in FTP can paint significantly different pictures of which business line contributed to a bank's overall NII. Schäfer et al. (2017, 584) put it this way:

> Reflecting [Boston Consulting Group's] client work from the early 2000s onwards, we were surprised to see how frequently the impact of the FTP scheme was underestimated. Based on years of experience and habit, managers tend to focus on a bank's (or, for that matter, business unit's) net interest

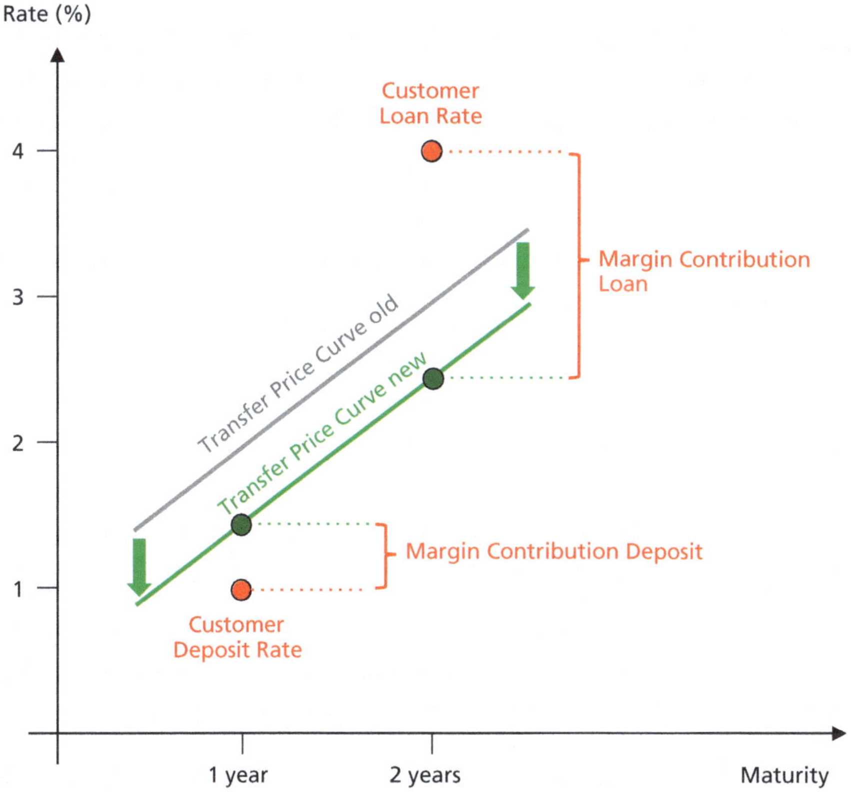

Fig. 2.17 Steering the bank's customer business

income as an aggregated metric to measure the top line of an interest-generating business. In reality, the disaggregation into interest income and interest expense shows that a significant portion of the net interest income is usually primarily driven not by client margins but by internal models that value the cost of funding provided from or to the bank's treasury department. Any change in such models – such as adjusting the behavioural maturity assumption for a corporate sight deposit portfolio, or a different interest rate applied to calculate capital benefit – will distort the net interest income significantly without the slightest change to the bank's actual business relationships to the outside world.

Not surprisingly, the business units are very well aware of how even small changes in FTP can make them look good or bad. Business unit resistance to unrealistic FTP assumptions limits the bank's ability to use (or abuse) the FTP framework for steering (and other) purposes.

2.3.8 Regulatory Requirements

In response to the financial market crisis of 2007 / 2008, a number of regulatory requirements have been adopted that have an impact on the funding costs of both on- and off-balance sheet positions of banks. Each requirement, when triggered by a position to be priced on the FTP curve, results in some cost (at the margin) to the bank. For example, if the duration of funding needs to be extended, cheaper short-term debt needs to be replaced by more expensive longer-term debt (assuming an upward-sloping yield curve); if margin needs to be posted for a derivative transaction, the interest earned on the margin account may be less than the bank's overall cost of capital. The main regulatory cost drivers are listed below.[34]

2.3.8.1 Liquidity Coverage Ratio

The liquidity coverage ratio (LCR) requires banks to hold sufficient high quality liquid assets (HQLA) to withstand a 30-day stressed funding scenario.[35] "To the extent that [a position to be priced on the funds transfer curve] requires additional funding beyond the normal strategy, this additional cost of HQLA should probably be transfer priced. If this is not the case, then new business will tend to deteriorate the bank's LCR as the incremental cost of additional HQLA will not be priced."[36]

Some FTP systems already address the cost of doing business from a *regulatory constraint perspective* by allocating LCR costs to both liabilities and assets, thereby incentivizing assets that generate an LCR inflow and reduce the size of the required liquid asset portfolio holdings.

2.3.8.2 Net Stable Funding Ratio

The Net stable funding ratio (NSFR) requires banks to maintain a stable funding profile in relation to the composition of their assets and off-balance sheet activities.[37] This may result in additional costs and will need to be reflected in funds transfer pricing. Some positions (e. g., derivatives positions) do not require regular funding (they are considered self-funded positions), but lead to a deterioration of a bank's NSFR. This may force the bank to raise additional (and more expensive) long-term funding. To reflect the additional cost of remediating the NSFR, positions that impact the NSFR should be penalized on the funds transfer pricing curve.

2.3.8.3 Clearing Mandate

Clearing is a post-trade process in which a central counterparty (CCP) directly or indirectly interposes itself between the counterparties to a trade to assume their rights and obligations. Standardized over-the-counter (OTC) derivatives are required to be centrally cleared,[38] which in turn results in additional funding costs due to the margin requirements set by the CCPs.[39]

2.3.8.4 Margin Requirements

Regulatory margin requirements for non-centrally cleared derivatives aim to reduce systemic risk associated with non-standardized derivatives by reducing contagion and spillover risks and promoting central clearing.[40] Like the margin requirements set by the CCPs, regulatory margin requirements for non-centrally cleared transactions impose additional costs.

2.3.9 Relation to Funding Value Adjustment

The bank's internal funds transfer pricing process is somewhat related to a similar area within derivatives pricing called funding value adjustment (FVA). Since most derivatives transactions require the posting of collateral (in the form of initial and variation margin), the funding of the collateral plays an

Table 2.36 Funding amounts: customer banking business vs. derivatives

	Funding amount	Concept used
Customer loan	Notional amount	FTP
Plain interest-rate swap	Collateral amount	FVA
Cross-currency swap	Notional and collateral amount	

important role. To reflect the impact of funding, the valuation of a derivative is adjusted for the cost of funding.

Most derivative transactions do not require an exchange of notional amounts between counterparties.[41] Thus, most derivatives are *self-funded* positions with funding built in (except for margin funding). A bank's customer business, on the other hand, is not self-funded. In fact, the primary purpose of a bank is to provide funding. Thus, while funding is a primary concern for banks, it is a secondary concern for most derivatives, since it affects only a small fraction of the notional amount of a transaction. See Table 2.36.

Although funding issues are a secondary concern for derivatives, the competitive nature of the derivatives business has forced industry and academia to invest a great deal of energy in developing concepts and techniques. FTP, on the other hand, is merely an *internal* process that cannot be arbitraged by aggressive market participants (such as hedge funds) and therefore can live with a certain lack of accuracy. For this reason, it is reasonable to assume that FVA techniques are more advanced than typical FTP models.

While the funding of a bank's customer business is handled by the treasury department, the funding of the derivatives business conducted by a dealer desk is handled by the derivatives funding desk. This derivatives funding desk is part of a broader risk management area called the X-Value Adjustment, or XVA, desk. The XVA desk calculates and charges not only a funding fee (the Funding Value Adjustment, FVA), but also a fee for credit protection (the Credit Value Adjustment, CVA), for liquidity-related costs (the Liquidity Value Adjustment, LVA), and a fee for the use of economic capital (the Capital Value Adjustment, KVA). In an FTP framework, credit value considerations do not play a role because the treasury department typically does not absorb the counterparty credit risk that remains with the customer business areas, while liquidity and economic capital costs have been slow to be recognized as components of the FTP rate.

There is a large body of literature on XVA, FVA, CVA, LVA and KVA from which a further development of the FTP framework stands to benefit.[42]

2.3.10 Further Developments

In addition to the aspects already mentioned above (regulatory compliance charges in Sect. 2.3.8 and funding value adjustments in Sect. 2.3.9), there are several other potential improvements to the standard FTP framework.

One possible extension relates to climate risk. This is discussed further in Sect. 6.4. Three other refinements relate to contingent liquidity, optionality, and counterparty credit and operational risk:

2.3.10.1 Contingency Liquidity

Contingency liquidity consists of cash, cash equivalents, and unencumbered high quality liquid assets held for liquidity risk management and for regulatory purposes (as discussed in Sects. 2.3.8.1 and 2.3.8.2).[43]

Contingency liquidity costs are added to the FTP rate, similar to the LVA discussed in Sect. 2.3.9.

An example of a bank customer transaction that gives rise to contingency liquidity costs is a committed line of credit to a customer.

2.3.10.2 Optionality

The FTP rate should be adjusted for optionality. Depending on whether a position creates a short or a long optionality, the adjustment to the FTP curve is a mark-up or a discount. The bank is "short" optionality when the *customer* who has the right to change the cash flow of a transaction (e. g., the customer having the right to prepay a loan) and "long" optionality when the *bank* that has a choice (e. g., after issuing a callable bond). One can imagine the treasury department having to buy options in the market to offset short optionality, and being able to sell options in the market when the bank is long optionality. Unfortunately, some of the optionality comes from so-called embedded options that are difficult to quantify (and will be discussed in more detail in Sect. 2.4.3) and / or are based on behavioral assumptions (to be discussed in Sect. 3.3), so that their value cannot be calculated with standard option pricing models and / or cannot be hedged with standard options traded in the financial market.

2.3.10.3 Counterparty Credit and Operational Risk

In general, only risks that are to be transferred to the treasury department for management should be priced in the FTP framework. Counterparty credit risk and operational risk are typically not considered such a risks because the client-facing customer area is much better equipped to identify, quantify and manage these risks. Moreover, if the customer area were to be no longer impacted by adverse credit events and operational risks, there is a potential for misallocation of the bank's funds due to adverse selection[44] and the potential for negligent risk monitoring after the customer transaction due to moral hazard.[45]

On the other hand, the treasury department may offer to hedge the counterparty credit risk, e. g. by entering into a credit default swaps (CDS), in which case the CDS premium could be used as an add-on to the FTP curve.[46]

2.3.11 Conclusion

As we have shown, the FTP is a tool for *measuring risk-adjusted performance and profitability*. By allocating net interest margin on a risk-adjusted basis, the FTP promotes sound origination and pricing practices and aligns business unit activities with the bank's overall risk appetite.

Misallocating funding costs to business unit activities can incentivize a business unit to take *excessive risk* to improve its own performance metrics, while such activities may not be aligned with a bank's policies and risk limits. A properly implemented FTP system helps *align business unit risk-taking activities* with the bank's overall strategy, business plan, and risk tolerance.

FTP is also a tool for *centralizing the management of various risks*, particularly interest rate and liquidity risk. FTP provides a method to aggregate these risks in a *centralized unit* within the bank and provides a broader view of all exposures and their inherent risks for *better hedging and mitigation planning*.

Farahvash (2020, 934–936) identifies ten characteristics of a good FTP system, of which the following are particularly noteworthy:

- Alignment of the complexity and scope of a bank's FTP system with the balance sheet size, complexity of its activities and products, and its risk appetite.
- Assignment of an FTP rate to a position that is consistent with its economics and its inherent risk.
- Choice of an appropriate level of granularity for the FTP system.
- Implementation of an appropriate governance structure.

- Commitment of appropriate resources (human capital, IT etc.).
- Aiming for consistency across business units and product types.
- Ongoing analysis, questioning of assumptions and proper documentation.

2.4 Non-maturity Products

One of the most difficult tasks in measuring interest rate risk is how to model positions where the *behavioral maturity* differs from the *contractual maturity* or where there is no stated contractual maturity. These positions are classified as *non-maturity products*,[47] although the term can be somewhat misleading. A non-maturity product (NMP) will *eventually* mature; it is just that the *expected* maturity date is either not contractually agreed at inception or the bank customer has the option (i. e., the right, but not the obligation) to change its cash flows. In Sect. 1.2.2.3, we emphasized that ALM must consider both "automatic" and "behavioral" interest rate options for all instruments with explicit or embedded options.

2.4.1 Examples of Non-maturity Products

On the asset side of the balance sheet, NMP may include *mortgages* and mortgage-related securities that may be subject to prepayment risk. Depending on contractual terms and local consumer rights, borrowers often have the ability to prepay portions of their mortgages with little or no penalty, creating uncertainty about the timing of the mortgage-related cash flows.

On the liabilities side, NMP may include non-maturity deposits (NMDs) such as *sight deposits* and *savings deposits* that can be withdrawn at the discretion of the depositor, often without penalty.

2.4.2 Liquidity and Interest Rate Profile

The liquidity profile defines the *expected lifetime* of the product and how the volume changes over time. The interest rate profile defines the *rate reset frequency* and the *reset reference rate*, also called the indicator rate. Typically, the reset reference rate has the same maturity as the contractual maturity of the instrument. In this case, the *liquidity profile* and the *interest rate profile* are identical. See Fig. 2.18.

If there is a difference between the time to reset of the reference rate and the contractual maturity of the instrument, the liquidity and interest rate

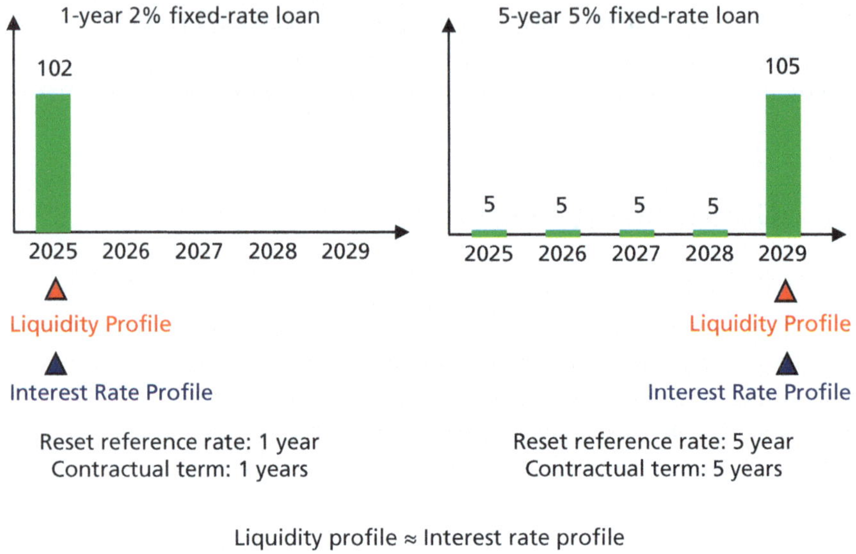

Fig. 2.18 Typical liquidity and interest rate profile

profiles are no longer identical. For example, a floating rate instrument will have a value of par at the next reset date (ignoring changes in credit risk and other factors); therefore, the interest rate risk is only up until the next reset date. Liquidity, however, is tied up until the final maturity of the instrument. Figure 2.19 illustrates this using the example of a 5-year floating rate loan based on 12-month EURIBOR. If the first floating rate reset (of the 12-month EURIBOR rate) just occurred at 2%, the interest rate profile of the bond is *one year* (because the interest rate is now fixed for one year). However, the contractual maturity of the loan for which the bank needs to provide liquidity is *five years*. Therefore, the liquidity profile is five years.

Some customer products, such as sight deposits, have *no contractual agreement* on either the *maturity* or *the reset reference rate*. The lack of contractual features regarding the maturity of a product prevents ex ante knowledge of the precise liquidity profile. Regarding the reset reference rate, these products typically have a so-called *administered rate*, where the bank has the right to change the interest rate paid to the depositor at its discretion (in some cases with an agreed notice period). This prevents an ex ante knowledge of the precise interest rate profile. In Sect. 2.5 we will discuss the fact that administered rates are only loosely related to market rates.

Several conceptual frameworks have been developed to estimate the interest rate and the liquidity profile of non-maturity products. These include:

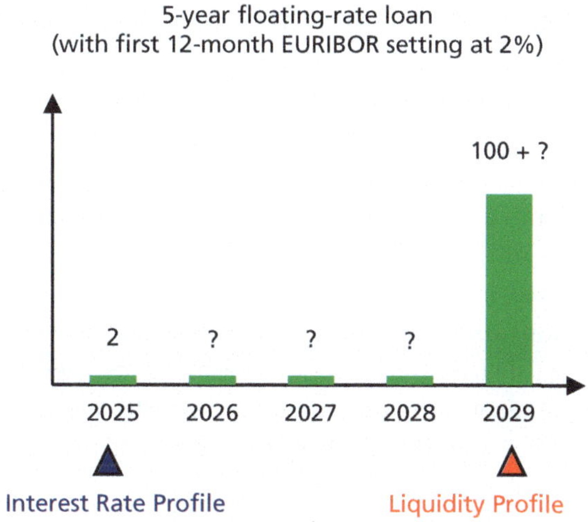

Fig. 2.19 Atypical liquidity and interest rate profile

- Option-adjusted spread (OAS) models, in which the value of the embedded options of the non-maturity products is estimated using standard option pricing theory.
- Replicating models, discussed in Sect. 2.5, in which the non-maturity products are replicated by a portfolio consisting of mainly liquid and tradable financial instruments, where the evolution of the volume and interest rates of the replicating portfolio is a realistic approximation of the expected behavior of the non-maturity product.
- Lifecycle models, based on historical customer observations (e. g., customer type, account opening date, initial interest rate) to explain their influence on the expected maturity, volume and interest rate of the non-maturity products.
- Autoregressive integrated moving averages (ARIMA) models, based on historical observations of volumes and interest rates.

2.4.3 Embedded Options

ALM needs to consider both, "automatic" and "behavioral" interest rate options. Automatic options execute rule-based, such as interest rate caps and floors and swaptions. *Embedded options*, also known as *behavioral* or *nested* options, give the customer the right to make individual decisions about cash flows.

Examples of behavioral options include the right of a bank customer to close a product-specific bank account or to terminate the relationship with a bank altogether. They also include options to change the volume of certain loans or deposits, e. g., by withdrawing deposits from sight deposit accounts (the so-called *deposit redemption option*), paying off mortgage loans earlier than originally planned (referred to as prepayment[48] option), or taking out an overdraft. Even filing for *bankruptcy* can be considered as a behavioral option and is referred to as a default option.[49]

Behavioral options may also exist for products that have a stated contractual maturity (e. g., floating-rate loans, consumer mortgages).

Because behavioral options potentially reduce the expected (contractual) maturity, they have a significant impact on economic value of equity and earnings measures (EVE and NII).

Figure 2.20 illustrates how the behavioral option to prepay a loan changes its expected cash flows.

To predict the future cash flow profile of a customer transaction, it is necessary to *model* the customer's behavior. In the example shown in Fig. 2.20, a simple, if not *the* simplest, assumption is that a constant percentage p of all customers will prepay their loan (based on empirical observation). In modeling a loan of EUR 100, one would represent it as a combination of a loan of $p \times$ EUR 100 with maturity to the prepayment (call) date and a loan of $(1 - p) \times$ EUR 100 with maturity to the final maturity date. A more realistic model would make the prepayment percentage, p, a function of the interest rate environment at the prepayment date. In this more complex model, the stream of payments from the loan is no longer invariant to changes in the level of interest rates.

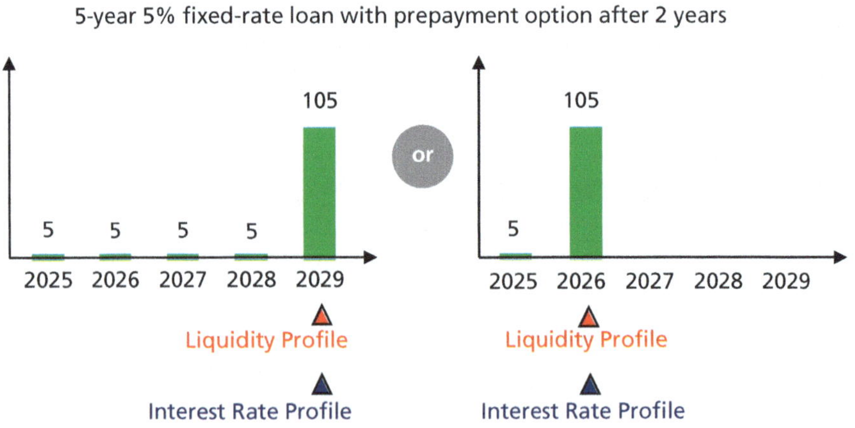

Fig. 2.20 Change in cash flows due to prepayment option

The fundamental problem with modeling is that a model is only be as good as its assumptions. Wrong model assumptions can lead to a severe distortion of reality. The impact of so-called *model risk* can be enormous. Banks should use robust models based on a sufficiently long observation period and regularly review and update the models as necessary. This is recognized in the EBA guidelines, which even limit the range of certain assumptions in order to avoid nonsensical model conclusions:

> [T]he assumed behavioural repricing date for retail deposits and wholesale deposits from non-financial customers and operational deposits (...), without any specific repricing dates (non-maturity deposits), should be constrained to a maximum weighted average repricing date of 5 years.[50]

It is worth noting that a bank also has a number of options that work in its favor. Examples include the right to change the interest rate for bank products with an administered rate or, in certain cases, the right to terminate an account.

Standard option pricing theory assumes that *rule-based*, or *automatic*, options are exercised in a rational manner. For example, the holder of a standard financial option would never execute an out-of-the-money call option because, in doing so, the price paid for the underlying instrument would be higher than the prevailing market price. *Behavioral* options, on the other hand, may not be executed optimally, partially, in part because of demographic factors (such as death, divorce, or job change). For example, a mortgage loan may be prepaid even though the contractual interest rate is well below the prevailing market rate because the borrower's divorce necessitates the sale of the home. In this case, the bank benefits from the exercise of the behavioral option, even though the bank is short the option.

2.5 Replicating Model

A *replicating model* aims to replicate non-maturity products by means of a portfolio consisting mainly of liquid and tradable financial instruments, where the volume and interest rate development of the replicating portfolio is a realistic approximation of the expected behavior of the non-maturity product. The model is sometimes referred to as a vintage run-off model.

2.5.1 Intuition

In Sect. 2.4, we defined non-maturity products as positions where the *behavioral maturity* differs from the *contractual maturity* or where there is no stated contractual maturity. In order to conduct meaningful risk management for non-maturity product, an assumption must be made about *run-off*. The run-off measures the decay of deposits in existing accounts over time.

Figure 2.21 illustrates the modeled run-off of a bank's EUR 50 mm sight deposit position. We assume that there is no replacement business and that the position will run off (due to withdrawals) about EUR 10 mm within the next month (e.g. from customers who have parked their money for the short term) and the remaining EUR 40 mm will be withdrawn in equal tranches over the next 5 years.

Thus, a previously homogeneous EUR 50 mm sight deposit book (in our example) is modeled as a portfolio of six individual deposit positions with different expected maturities.

The modeled portfolio can already be used to calculate the *average expected duration* of the sight deposit book. It is the sum of the modified durations

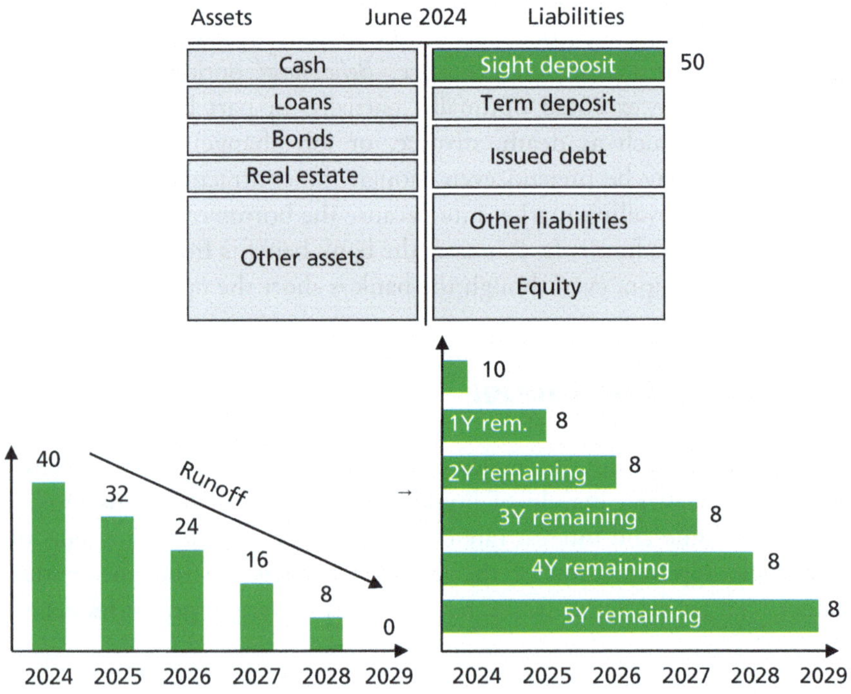

Fig. 2.21 Modeled run-off of sight deposits

(*modD*) of the six components, weighted by their national amounts:

$$modD = \sum_{n=1}^{6} modD \,\text{of component}\, n \times \text{weight of component}\, n$$

If we assume the modified duration of a 1-month deposit to be 0.03, that of a 1-year deposit to be 0.9, that of a 2-year deposit to be 1.8, that of a 3-year deposit to be 2.7, that of a 4-year deposit to be 3.6, and that of a 5-year deposit to be 4.5, the resulting modified duration of the sight deposit book would be:

$$modD = 0.03\frac{10}{50} + 0.9\frac{8}{50} + 1.8\frac{8}{50} + 2.7\frac{8}{50} + 3.6\frac{8}{50} + 4.5\frac{8}{50} = 2.166$$

In addition, the modeled portfolio can be used to calculate the *average expected maturity* of the sight deposit book. While the average expected duration reflects the risk arising from the interest rate profile, the average expected maturity measures the risk from a liquidity perspective. It is the sum of the maturities of the six components, weighted by their national amounts:

$$\sum_{n=1}^{6} maturity \,\text{of component}\, n \times \text{weight of component}\, n$$

$$= 0.083\frac{10}{50} + 1\frac{8}{50} + 2\frac{8}{50} + 3\frac{8}{50} + 4\frac{8}{50} + 5\frac{8}{50} = 2.417 \text{ [years]}$$

2.5.2 Rolling Portfolio

Continuing with the assumption that 80% of the sight deposits remain with the bank for up to 5 years (while the remaining 20% are withdrawn and replaced on a monthly basis), we can establish a *timeline for the cash flows* (in a *steady state* loan book). The EUR 8 mm we expect to be withdrawn in one year may be a deposit made four years ago. The EUR 8 mm outflow in two years could be a deposit made three years ago. This continues up to today's EUR 8 mm deposit, which is expected to remain in the bank for another five years. See Fig. 2.22.

Viewing the deposit book as a *portfolio of deposits* made over time is more realistic than viewing it as a sum of homogeneous customer deposits. This is particularly true for a bank that has built up a loan book over a longer period of time (as opposed to a bank that has recently entered the market).

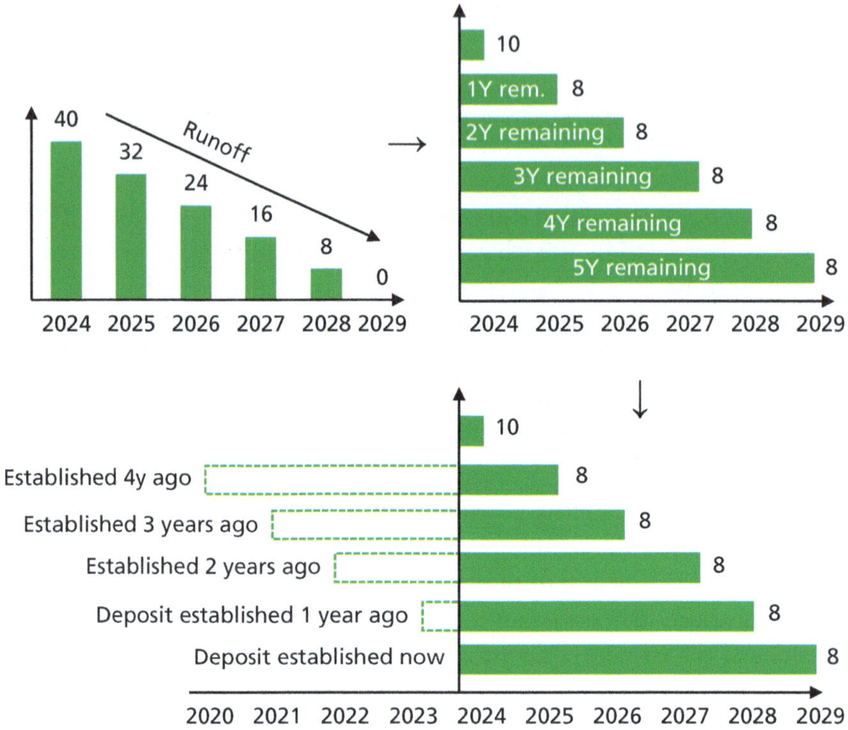

Fig. 2.22 Rolling portfolio construction

If the deposit book is modeled as a *rolling* portfolio in which decaying deposits due to withdrawals are fully replaced by new customer deposits, the bank's overall (sight) deposit position does not change over time.

Having established a (hypothetical) timeline for cash flows, we can derive opportunity interest rates at which the customer funds could have been invested in the market. This assumes that the bank's ALM / treasury department is mandated to receive the customer funds passed through from the customer lending area and to manage them at prevailing market rates. Whether or not the ALM / treasury department actually invests customer funds in the market (or passes the funds on to the customer lending area) is irrelevant. The relevant question is: what would be the opportunity interest rate that the bank could have earned in the market? This rate is nothing other than the FTP rate we discussed in Sect. 2.3.

Since (hypothetical) investments of customer business occur at different points in time, the average opportunity interest rate is a mix of historical rates, the so-called *moving average* (MA) of interest rates. See Fig. 2.23.

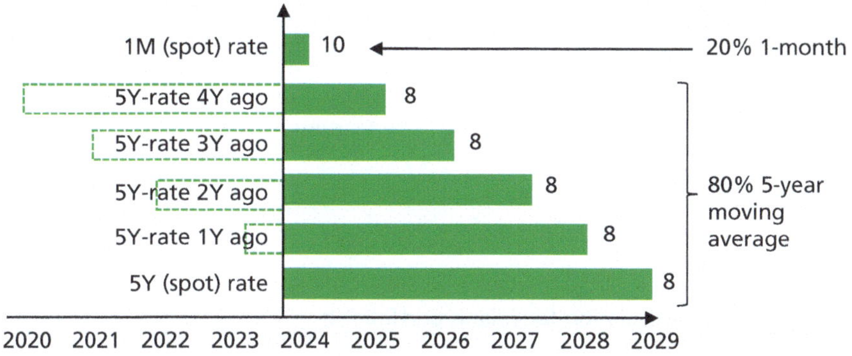

Fig. 2.23 Moving average interest rate of rolling portfolio (I)

The rolling portfolio construction is now used to calculate the *average return* from investing customer funds at historical rates. For example, using the EUR swap rate as the bank's opportunity investment rate, four years ago, EUR 8 mm in sight deposits would have been invested for 5 years at the then prevailing (swap) rate of -0.3%. However, the most recent tranche of EUR 8 mm yields 3% (i. e., the current 5-year swap rate).[51] On average, the investment of EUR 50 mm sight deposits yields 0.8%. See Fig. 2.24.

If we assume that the treasury department passes this 0.8% on to the customer lending department as a *funds transfer pricing rate*, then the margin contribution of the customer department overseeing the sight deposit business is 0.8% minus what is currently being paid to bank customers for sight deposits.

The customer rate for sight deposits is typically set in the marketplace as a result of competitive interaction among many banks. Let's say our bank is forced to pay 1% on sight deposits because that is the current customer

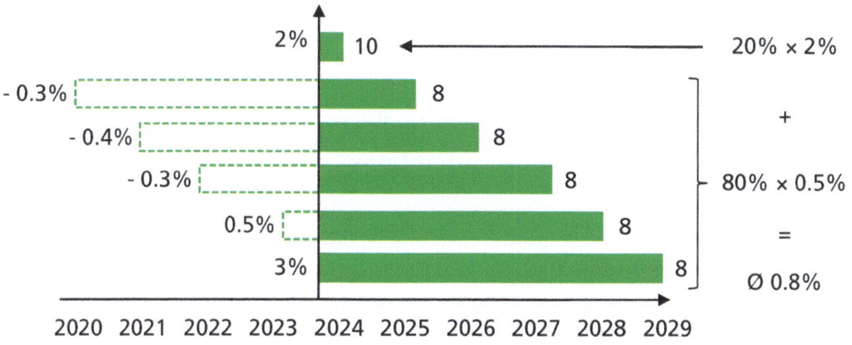

Fig. 2.24 Moving average interest rate of rolling portfolio (II)

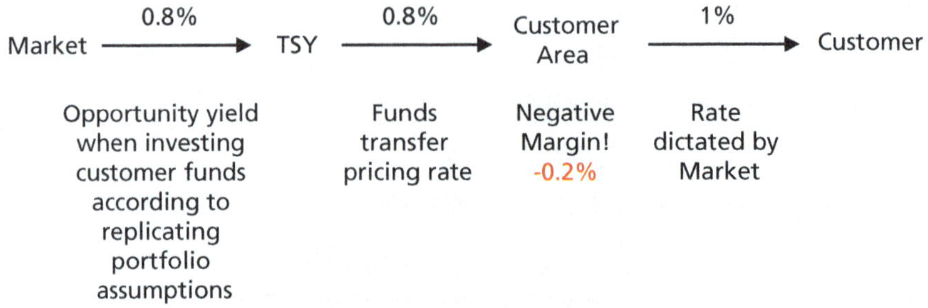

Fig. 2.25 Margin calculation for rolling portfolio (I)

rate. In this case, the customer margin earned on sight deposits is -0.2%. See Fig. 2.25.

2.5.3 Replication Over Time

The rolling portfolio approach helps formulate a *replication strategy* over time. Since the portfolio of funding instruments *recycles* itself through the process of replacing customer withdrawals with new customer deposits, a replication of this rolling portfolio must also address the reinvestment of the replacement business.

Using the example shown in Fig. 2.23, if we now move forward one year in our analysis, we see that what was a 5-year customer deposit 4 years ago is now a 5-year customer deposit 5 years ago. Therefore, we assume that this deposit has been withdrawn and the former 5-year investment has matured. Since we assume that the customer withdrawal is replaced by a new deposit, the total volume does not change. However, this new deposit is assumed to remain with the bank for another 5 years, so the replicating hedge would be a 5-year instrument. See Fig. 2.26.

The moving average interest rate will capture this replication over time effect by throwing out the historical interest rates and replacing them with current rates.

Figure 2.27 illustrates the effect of replication over time on the customer margin. We make the following assumptions:

- One year has passed.
- The 5-year investment made 5 years ago has matured.
- The 1-month (Euribor) rate has increased from 2% to 2.5%.
- The new prevailing 5-year rate is 3.5% (0.5% higher than a year ago).

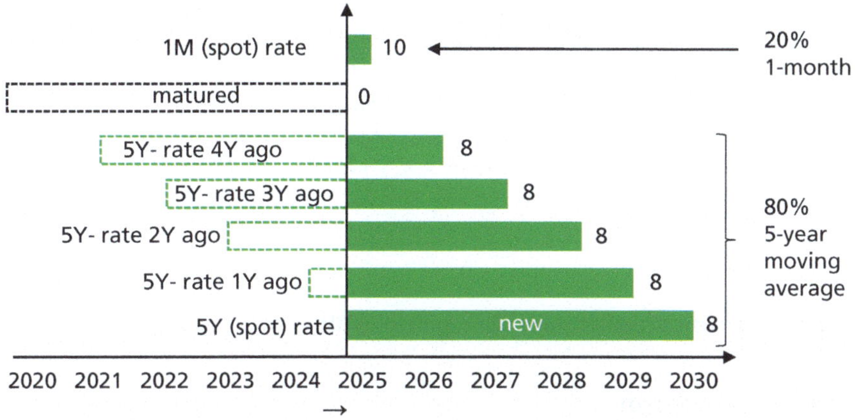

Fig. 2.26 Moving average interest rate of rolling portfolio (III)

- Customers are still getting paid 1% on sight deposits (perhaps because banks are reluctant to pass higher interest rates on to their customers).

The 5-year moving average has increased from 0.5% to 1.26% (due to the fact that EUR 8 mm of new customer deposits can be invested in a higher yielding interest rate environment). The total opportunity interest rate increased from 0.8% to 1.5%.

The customer area is now credited with 1.5% through the funds transfer pricing system, while (still) paying only 1% to the customers. The margin of the customer area improves to +0.5%. See Fig. 2.28.

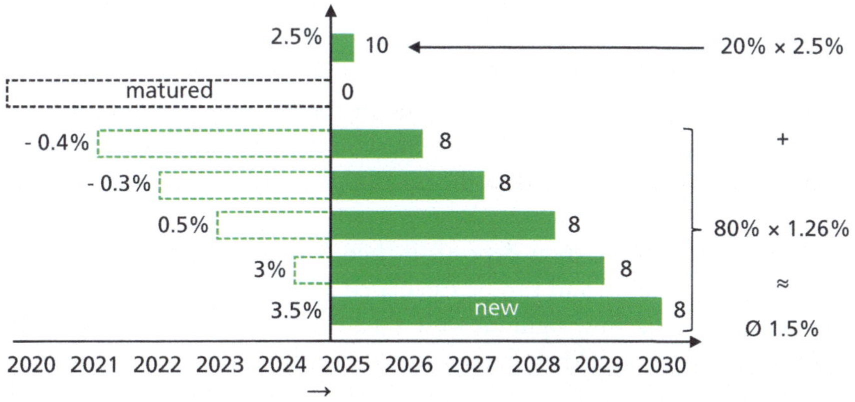

Fig. 2.27 Moving average interest rate of rolling portfolio (IV)

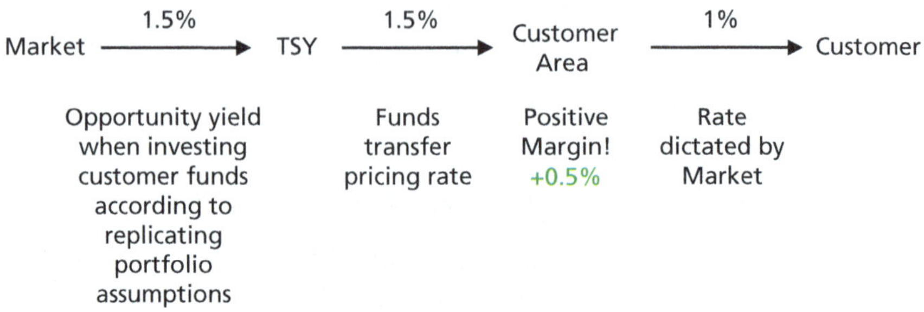

Fig. 2.28 Margin calculation for rolling portfolio (II)

2.5.4 Calibration

The idea of *calibrating* the replicating portfolio with a wide range of key rates (not just the 1-month and the 5-year rates as in our previous example) is to identify a portfolio of fixed-income assets with different maturities in which to invest the available volume of deposits, optimized for which a *specific objective criterion* subject to *specific constraints.*

- The *objective criterion* used for optimization is bank-specific and depends on a bank's business and risk management strategy.
  - One objective may be to generate the *most stable margin* above the deposit rate over a given sample period, i. e., to identify the portfolio that minimizes the standard deviation of the margin.
  - Another objective may be to *maximize the expected margin* earned above the deposit rate.
  - Yet another objective may be to maximize the *risk-adjusted margin,* as measured by the *Sharpe ratio* of the margin, i. e. the ratio of the average expected margin to the standard deviation of the margin.
- *Constraints* include that that the portfolio best replicates the dynamics of outstanding deposit balances over some historical sample period, but also restrictions imposed by regulators, supervisors, and bank management on which products may be used in the portfolio and to what extent.[52]

The duration of the savings deposits is then determined as the duration of the replicating portfolio and can be calculated analytically.

In our case, modeling sight deposit rates with a 5-year key rate (here: the 5-year swap rate) yields a *lower volatility* of the expected margin, while modeling with a 10-year key rate (here: the 10-year swap rate) yields a *higher expected margin.* Thus, there is a *trade-off* between using these two key rates in order to optimize both high expected returns and low volatility of returns. When looking for the *highest Sharpe ratio of the margin*, calculated as the expected margin per unit of risk, or $\mathbb{E}(M)$ / σ (M), the 10-year key rate looks more attractive at 1.804 (83 bp / 46 bp) than the 5-year key rate at 1.026 (39 bp / 38 bp). See Fig. 2.29.

Replicating models typically use a *combination* of two to four different key rates to produce a positive and stable expected customer margin. For example, a combination of *two* key rates may result in better risk / return characteristics than either rate alone. The best rolling portfolio will have the highest *risk-adjusted margin*, i. e., the *highest Sharpe ratio of margin*, with a reasonable number of key rates. See Fig. 2.30.

The interest rate difference between the best-fitting rolling portfolio and the customer rate would then be the bank's expected margin (assuming ALM succeeds in funding the customer business according to the rolling portfolio).

While the expected margin would be attributed to the customer business area, any deviation from this margin would be attributed to the ALM desk.

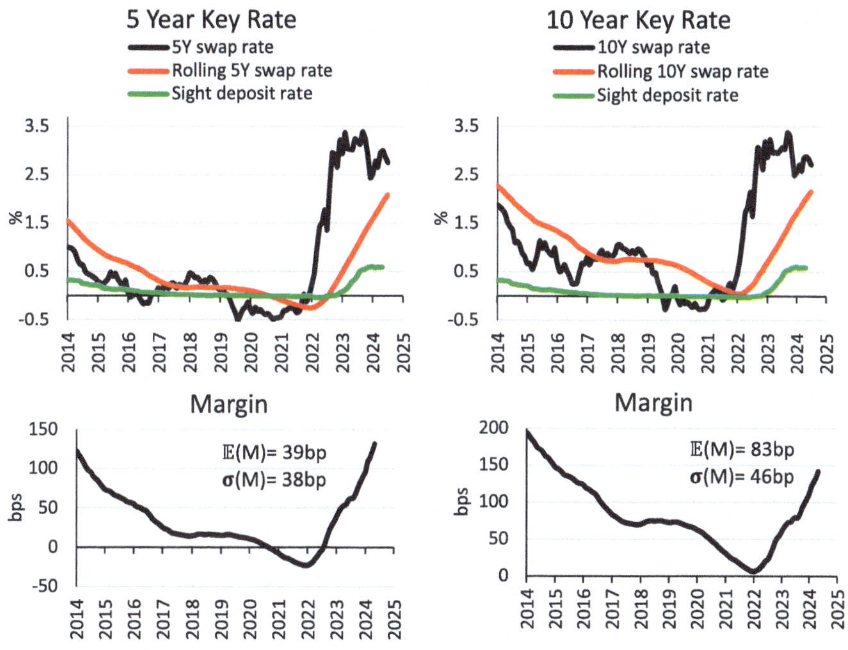

Fig. 2.29 Calibration of rolling portfolio (I)

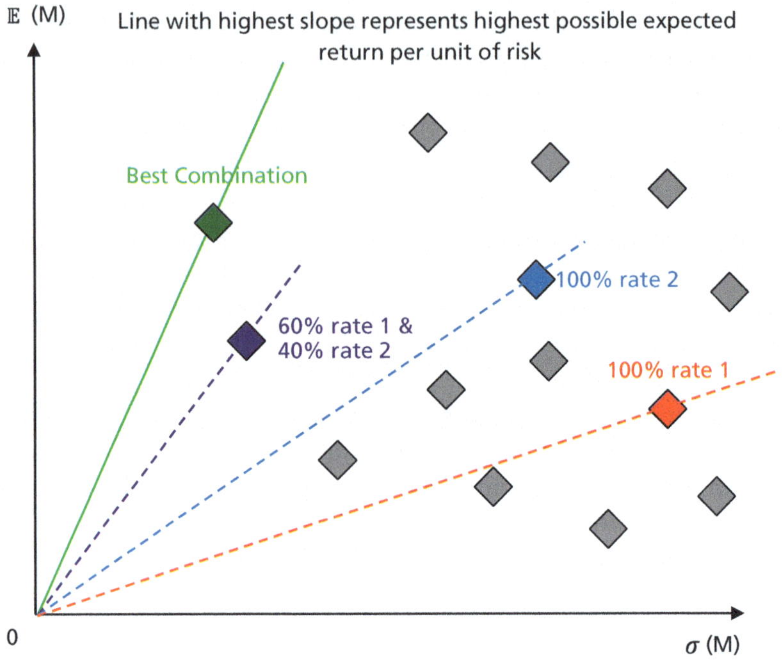

Fig. 2.30 Calibration of rolling portfolio (II)

2.5.5 Volume Changes

The representation of the bank's customer business with a portfolio that remains unchanged once established takes the *run-off view* of the balance sheet, where maturing products are not replaced by new positions.

Replication models with a rolling portfolio (of constant size) based solely on rolling moving averages take a *static view* of the balance sheet, where maturing positions are replaced by comparable positions of the same size at maturity dates.

Replicating the bank's customer business with a constantly adjusting rolling portfolio takes a *dynamic view* of the balance sheet, taking into account the impact of projected changes in the balance sheet. See Fig. 2.31.

There is a link between the maintenance of the rolling portfolio and the planned new customer business: if new customer business does not compensate for natural run-off, ALM will have to "peel off" some of the rolling portfolio over time; if new customer business exceeds the run-off, the replicating portfolio will have to be increased.

How realistic is it to take a static view of the balance sheet where new business is relatively constant (and then to replicate the bank's customer business

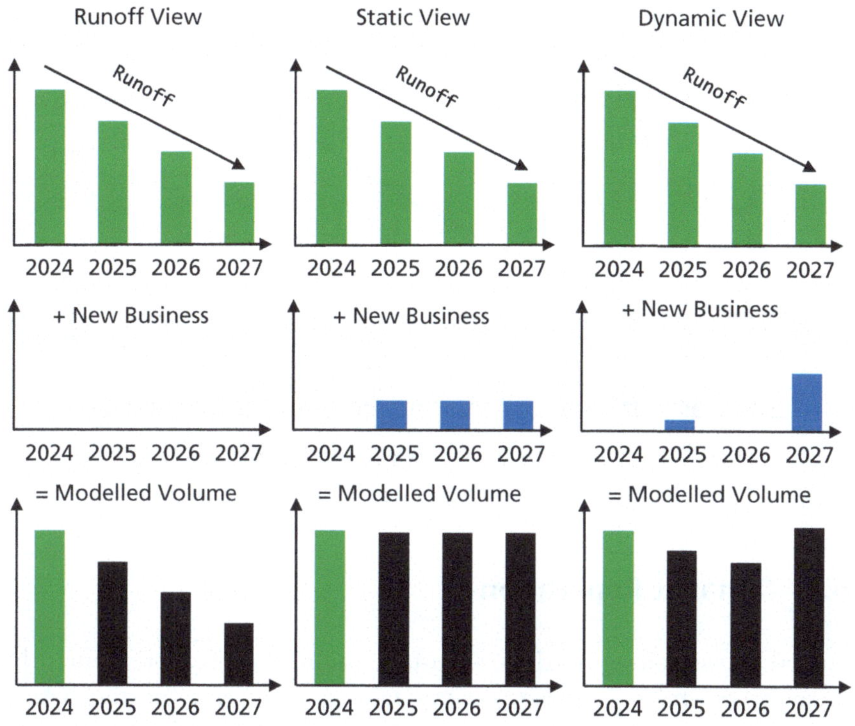

Fig. 2.31 Volume changes

with a rolling portfolio of constant size)? Fig. 2.32 shows the new business volume of sight-deposits from private households at German banks, along with the associated product interest rate over the period from 2003 to 2024.[53] During the period of falling interest rates (2009–2022), the new business in sight deposits was not constant at all, but rather grew rapidly. When interest rates rise, the volume of sight deposits is also not constant. It is also noteworthy that deposit rates never went negative. This illustrates the widely observed practice that negative interest rates are often not immediately passed on by banks to consumers.

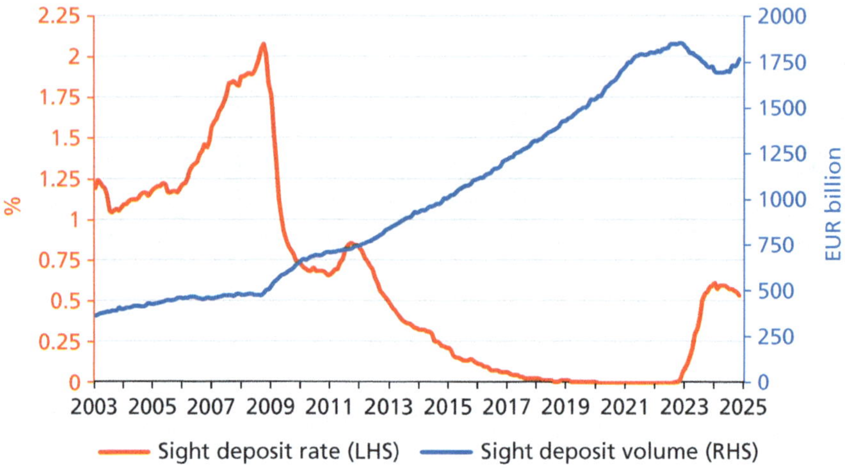

Fig. 2.32 Volume vs. rates

2.5.6 Dynamic Replication

As noted above, rolling portfolio (constant volume) replication models that rely solely on *rolling moving averages* take a *static view* of the balance sheet, where maturing positions are replaced at maturity dates by comparable positions of equivalent size. Only if the central premise of a constant volume holds, will the constant moving average method provide an adequate valuation.

If, on the other hand, there are changes in the volume, additions or deductions must be made to the replicating portfolio.

If the effects of volume changes are not taken into account, this will lead to an incorrect assessment of the opportunity interest rate and incorrect margins. It also distorts the assessment of sales success or the profitability of a product. A commonly used model to account for volume changes is based on *dynamic replication.*

To illustrate the concept of dynamic replication, we consider an increase in sight deposits from 50 to 100 (see Fig. 2.33).

The core idea of dynamic replication is to integrate volume changes through a separate portfolio that is priced at current market interest rates.

Since the treasury department can't go back in time to create hedge positions at historical rates, volume changes must be hedged at *current rates.* See Fig. 2.34.

If interest rates rise over time and the volume also increases, the additional hedge will be established at higher interest rates (compared to the historically low interest rates previously locked in). This is illustrated in Fig. 2.35: While

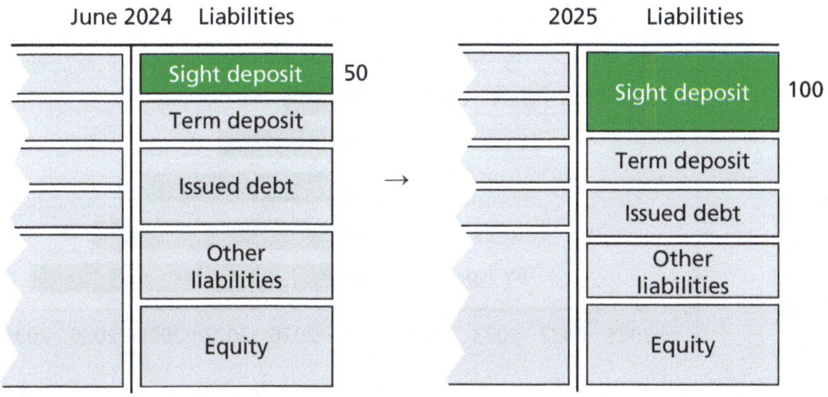

Fig. 2.33 Increase in sight deposits (I)

EUR 8 mm invested *4 years ago* for 5 years will only generate an annual interest income of -0.4% for the remaining year, a 1-year investment established *now* will generate an interest income of 2.7%. Thus, the additional sight deposit business has an increased margin of 2% (instead of 0.5%), assuming an (unchanged) customer interest rate of 1%.

While it makes sense to incentivize the deposit franchise by passing on higher interest rates through an increased FTP rate, it is difficult to distinguish between replacement business (necessary to maintain a stable volume) and incremental business beyond that.

If volume were to decline at a time of rising interest rates, this would result in losses to the dynamic replication portfolio, as previously established hedges would have to be unwound at a mark-to-market loss.

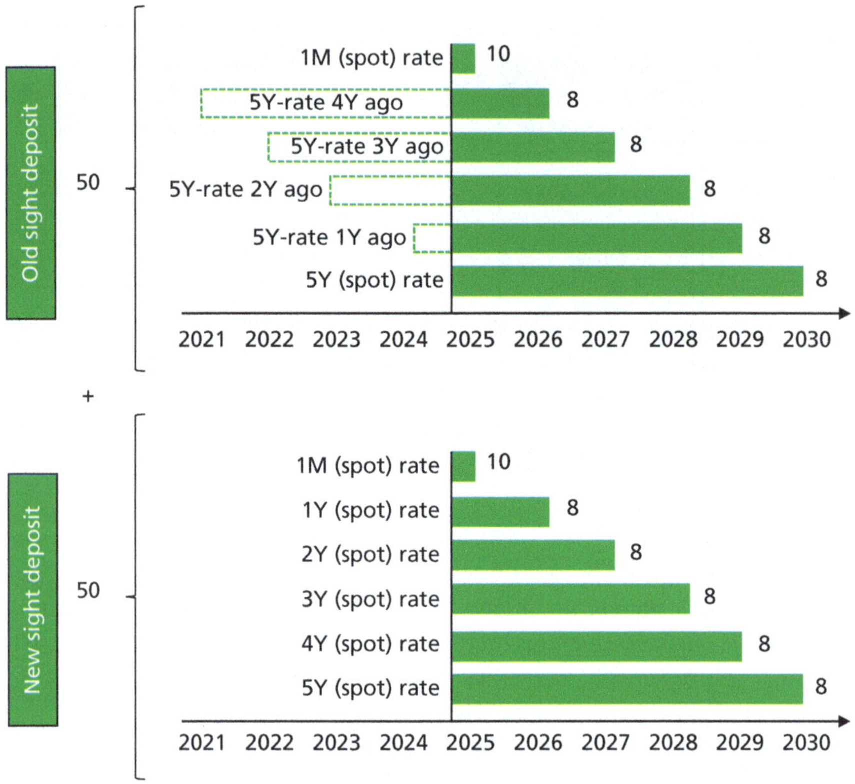

Fig. 2.34 Increase in sight deposits (II)

2.5.7 Further Developments

Since what is widely considered to be the first formal presentation of the replication model by Jarrow and Van Deventer (1998), a number of variations and extensions have been developed to improve goodness of fit, stability, and transparency. Some of these are mentioned here.

One method, described by Maes and Timmermans (2005), is based on classifying deposits into different categories, such as *core*, *volatile*, and *remaining*, with a specific duration modeled for each of these categories.[54] The core consists of rigid deposits, which are assumed to have little or no sensitivity to interest rates and are modeled to decline gradually over time; deposits assigned to the volatile category are assumed to be withdrawn by depositors over a short horizon and their contractual maturities are used; only for the remaining part of deposits is a replication model used.

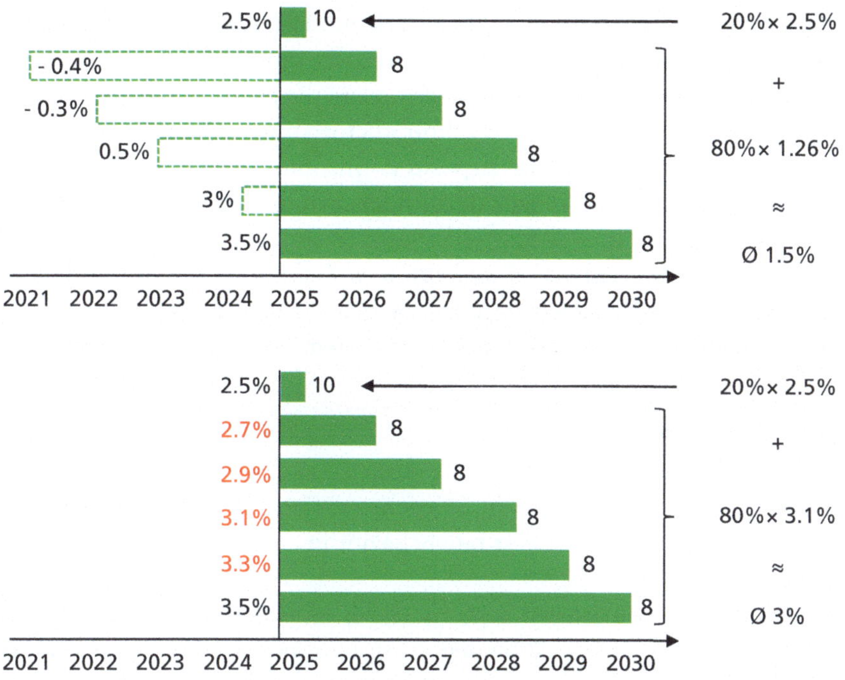

Fig. 2.35 Increase in sight deposits (III)

Elkenbracht and Nauta (2006) propose two value-based variants of the replication model, in which the margin (rather than the value) on non-maturity deposits (NMDs) is stabilized for either the original (and amortizing) volume or the future volume, given an expected evolution of the future volume.

As an extension to better capture the impact of interest rate uncertainty on customer deposit balances and interest rates, *Monte Carlo simulation models* can be used to generate a large number of possible market interest rate paths. The net present value (NPV) of all simulated future economic rents is calculated; the process is then repeated with shocked interest rates. Finally, the difference in NPVs caused by the interest rate shocks relative to the size of the interest rate shocks is used to estimate the duration of deposits.

At the heart of the so-called *monetary economics models* are the assumed purposes of customers for holding a fraction of their total financial assets in a deposit account. These include *transactional*, *precautionary* and *speculative* purposes. In different market scenarios, the amount of assets allocated to non-maturity deposits varies.

Stochastic models aim to describe the stochastic evolution of interest rates, deposit rates, and deposit volumes through stochastic processes and stochastic programming in discrete time. Unlike static models, stochastic models adapt dynamically to changing market conditions over time.[55]

Linear and nonlinear behavioral models relate the evolution of deposit rates and volumes to various factors based on microeconomic liquidity preference theory. These factors could be depositors' income, the growth rate of the economy, or even depositors' lack of confidence in the bank's creditworthiness and the accountability.

In the *statistical individual account model*, information on individual deposit accounts is collected over several years and the sensitivity of each customer to changes in deposit rates is estimated.

2.5.8 Criticism

The replication model is not without its critics. There is some evidence that it is a poor fit for modeling interest rate behavior in current interest rate market conditions.

Modeling of non-maturity deposits (NMDs) is complicated by the fact that the interest rates received by depositors tend not to move in close correlation with changes in the general level of market interest rates. The rates set by the bank, known as administered rates, are only *loosely related* to market rates. Empirical studies suggest that the pass-through of changes in market rates to sight deposit rates is partial: only 9% of changes in market rates are passed on to deposit rates in the short run, and only 29% in the long run.[56] Because banks only *sluggishly* adjust deposit rates, deposit rates are *sticky*. This is illustrated in Fig. 2.36, which compares the average customer deposit rate of European banks with the 3-month and 5-year risk-free market rate (represented by the yields on triple-A-rated euro area government bonds).[57]

One explanation for the difference between market rates and overnight deposit rates is provided by Jarrow and Van Deventer (1998): Using the market segmentation argument that only banks, not individual investors, can issue overnight deposits, it is suggested that overnight deposits are equivalent to a special exotic interest rate swaps whose principal depends on the past history of market rates.

The imperfect correlation between deposit rates and market rates is partly due to the fact that deposit rates are to some extent *policy* rates. Banks do administer the interest rates on accounts with the specific *intention* of managing the volume of deposits retained.

The sensitivity of a bank's deposit rate to changes in short-term market interest rates also appears to have increased over the past decade. Acharya et al. (2023) note that since "interest rates on close substitutes [for bank

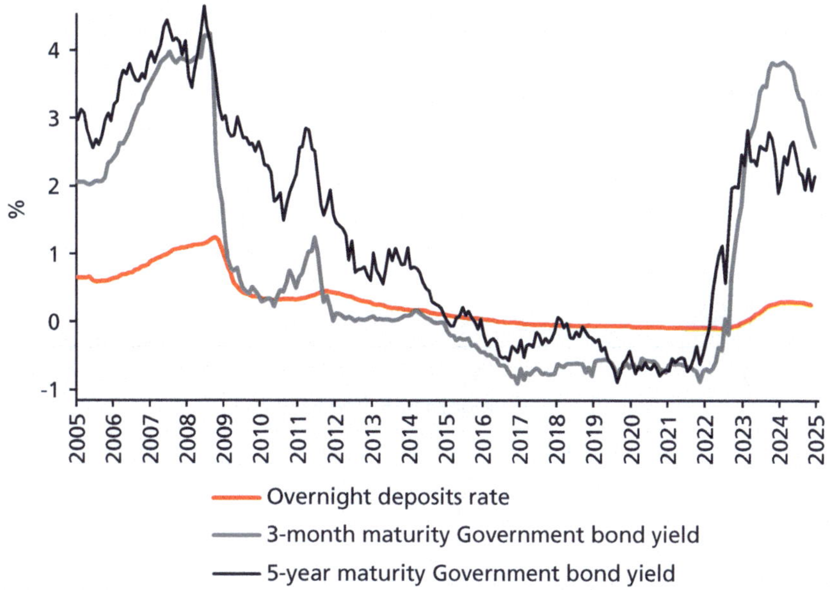

Fig. 2.36 Sticky deposit rates

deposits] (like money market funds) rose substantially, as they did during 2022, the pressure on banks to compete for funds, i. e., the so-called 'deposit beta,' rose in ways that they had not experienced since at least 2008."[58] *Deposit beta* is a measure that expresses the change in the deposit rate relative to the change in appropriate risk-free rate observable in the market. Thus,

$$\text{deposit beta} = \frac{\text{change in deposit rates}}{\text{change in market rate}}.$$

In Fig. 2.37, we regress the average customer deposit rate of European banks against the three-month risk-free market rate (represented by the yield on triple-A rated euro area government bonds) for three different time frames and estimate that the deposit beta declines from about 21% between 2014 and 2017 (when interest rates were falling) to less than 3% in 2017 to 2021 (when interest rates were negative) and back to more than 20% since 2023 (when interest rates rose again).

Unstable deposit betas complicate the use of the replication model because the parameterization of the replicating portfolio depends on how sticky deposit rates are. Not only do deposit betas vary widely over time, but they also vary across banks, possibly reflecting bank-specific deposit rate-setting behavior and customer-specific withdrawal behavior.[59]

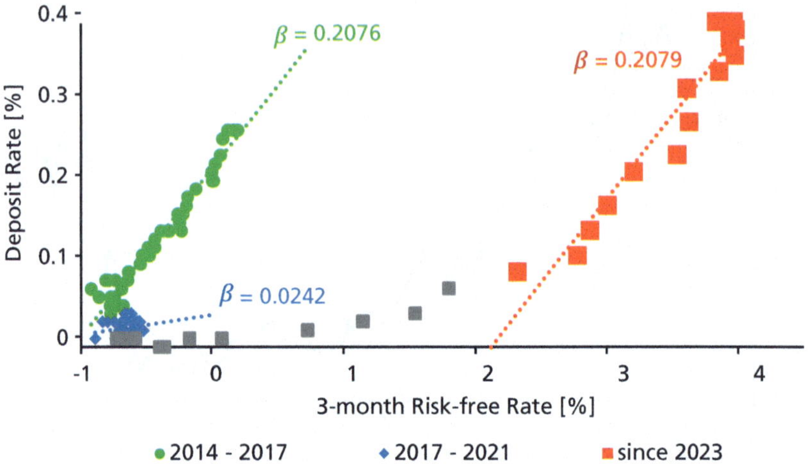

Fig. 2.37 Deposit beta estimates for different time frames

In addition, the relatively long estimated durations of the rolling portfolio are mainly rooted in the low interest rate environment of recent years. Deposit volumes have changed little, as there have been no opportunity cost incentives for bank customers to withdraw deposits. At the same time, deposit rates are stuck at 0%. As market interest rates rise further, durations should shorten as deposits become *less sticky* and volumes decline again. This effect is more pronounced for banks where customers are more sensitive to opportunity costs. The choice of simulation horizon is perhaps the most important driver of the duration estimates.[60]

Notes

1. EBA (2022a, 14).
2. As specified in Article 3(3) of Commission Delegated Regulation (EU) 2024/856: "All CET1 instruments and other perpetual own funds without any call dates shall be excluded from the [EVE] calculations"; OJ L, 2024/856, 24.4.2024, ELI: http://data.europa.eu/eli/reg_del/2024/856/oj. Nevertheless, a bank could choose to include equity in an alternative version of the economic value calculation, but it cannot be EVE. An alternative measure might suggest that the bank is able to invest more and/or longer in fixed-income assets, especially if there are no other long-term items on the liabilities side that could serve as a natural hedge. Nevertheless, banks must remain below the regulatory

limit for EVE, which does not include equity, so an alternative model that includes equity would only help to improve the calculations for *internal* limits.

3. See BCBS (1997, 29–32).
4. This is somewhat of a simplification, assuming that spreads / margins are unchanged, there is no optionality / convexity, or any other product-specific changes.
5. The inverse relationship between the direction of an interest rate change and the expected change in the value of EVE (Δ EVE $\approx -$ Gap $\times$ *ModD* $\times$ Δ *i*) can be explained by the *inverse* relationship between price and yield ($\Delta P \approx - P \times ModD \times \Delta i$), where *ModD* denotes the modified duration and Δi denotes the change in interest rates. It is worth noting that in some gap analysis frameworks, the gap is defined as liabilities minus assets, in which case the relationship between Δ EVE and Δi is no longer inverse.
6. See BCBS (1997, 31–32).
7. EBA (2022a, 14).
8. A bank that pays 3% interest on deposits, earns 6% on loans, and at 3 in the afternoon, everyone goes to the golf course.
9. This can be illustrated by an example simulation. Using the example from the previous section, a bank with EUR 100 mm in 6% loans, funded by EUR 100 mm in 3% deposits, has a current NII of EUR 3 mm. There is a significant difference between assuming an unchanged balance sheet or a reduced balance sheet for the forecasted NII. For example, if we assume a future balance sheet of EUR 80 mm, the forecasted NII falls to EUR 2.4 mm, a reduction of EUR 0.6 mm. If we now calculate the NII sensitivity for a 50 bp increase in the funding rate, the change from the forecast is EUR 0.5 mm for a balance sheet of EUR 100 mm and EUR 0.4 mm for a balance sheet of EUR 80 mm. Thus, in this example, the deviation of the NII sensitivity is only EUR 0.1 mm, or one-sixth of the deviation of the NII itself.
10. Farahvash (2020, 614). From a supervisory reporting perspective, banks shall consider in their NII calculations interest income and interest expenses over a one-year period; Article 4(2) of Commission Delegated Regulation (EU) 2024/856; OJ L, 2024/856, 24.4.2024, ELI: http://data.europa.eu/eli/reg_del/2024/856/oj.
11. ALM hedges are typically put in place to protect against a specific mismatch. It is not clear whether the same hedge would be needed in the future, given a new interest rate environment. Therefore, it is

not advisable to roll over these hedges. Instead, NII analysis (forecasting, simulation, etc.) will identify new potential risks that may require hedging activities different from those implemented in the past.

12. Article 4(4) of Commission Delegated Regulation (EU) 2024/856; OJ L, 2024/856, 24.4.2024, ELI: http://data.europa.eu/eli/reg_del/2024/856/oj.
13. The Pure Expectations Hypothesis (PEH) states that, in equilibrium, the expected returns from different investment strategies with the same horizon should be the same. For a more detailed discussion, see, e. g., Hull (2021, 117).
14. See, e. g., Fama (1990).
15. Article 1(1) of Commission Delegated Regulation (EU) 2024/856; OJ L, 2024/856, 24.4.2024, ELI: http://data.europa.eu/eli/reg_del/2024/856/oj.
16. Of course, the analysis would be even more accurate if the specific repricing date were taken into account for each individual transaction. Given sufficient computing power, this is possible.
17. Other interest rate shocks could have been chosen, such as an *increase* in interest rates, a *non-parallel* yield curve shift, or a *gradual* change in interest rates, to name a few.
18. Interest rate swaps are designated according to the direction of the cash flow on the fixed leg (i.e., the cash flow stream tied to the fixed interest rate). From the perspective of the swap counterparty that *receives* the fixed rate, the swap is called a *receiver swap*; from the perspective of the swap counterparty that *pays* the fixed rate, the swap is called a *payer swap*.
19. EBA (2022a, 34).
20. Article 20 of EBA (2022b).
21. OJ L, 2024/857, 24.4.2024, ELI: http://data.europa.eu/eli/reg_del/2024/857/oj.
22. Kenyon and Stamm (2012, 70–71).
23. The process involves a process of bootstrapping a yield curve that perfectly fits the price / yield quotes of instruments traded in the market, as well as some interpolation techniques to calculate odd maturities. On Bloomberg, the I25-curve provides a yield curve, which is based on the yield-to-maturity of actively traded coupon-paying U.S. Treasury bonds. The so-called spot par curve can then be used to derive continuously compounded zero rates that are useful for discounting purposes.

24. This curve is calculated and published daily by the European Central Bank. See https://www.ecb.europa.eu/stats/financial_markets_and_interest_rates/euro_area_yield_curves/html/index.en.html.
25. Germany, Luxembourg, Denmark, Norway and Netherlands. See https://countryeconomy.com/ratings.
26. The €STR is calculated and published daily by the European Central Bank. See https://www.ecb.europa.eu/stats/financial_markets_and_interest_rates/euro_short-term_rate/html/index.en.html. The €STR reflects the wholesale cost of unsecured overnight credit in euro for euro area banks. It is based on actual transactions in euro conducted and is calculated using overnight unsecured fixed-rate deposit transactions over EUR 1 million as a volume-weighted trimmed average of the relevant transactions, with the highest and lowest 25% in terms of volume removed before calculating the average. See Amorese et al. (2022).
27. RFRs in other currencies are: Secured Overnight Financing Rate (SOFR) for USD; Tokyo Overnight Average Rate (TONAR) for JPY; Sterling Overnight Index Average (SONIA) for GBP; Swiss Average Rate Overnight (SARON) for CHF.
28. Repo stands for "repurchase agreement," which is a contract to sell a financial market instrument at a specified price to a counterparty with the obligation to repurchase the instrument at a future date at a pre-agreed price. The annualized interest rate implied by the price at which the security is sold and repurchased is the repo rate. A transaction in which a market participant sells a security and implicitly borrows money is called a *repo*, while the opposite transaction (buying a security and implicitly lending out money) is called a *reverse repo*. While most repo transactions take place overnight (called an *overnight* or O / N repo), they can extend over several days, weeks, or months (called a *term repo*). See Tata (2020, 102–103).
29. Counterparty credit risk is the risk that one party to a transaction will fail to make contractual payments to the other party. It is also called *credit risk* or *default risk*.
30. EURIBOR stands for Euro IBOR, or Euro Interbank Offered Rate, which is the average euro-denominated interest rate at which banks in the eurozone lend or borrow excess reserves from one other. See https://www.euribor-rates.eu/en/.
31. For a timeline of the LIBOR fixing scandal see https://www.bbc.co.uk/news/business-18671255.

32. The question of which interest rate should be used as the risk-free rate is addressed in Sect. 2.3.5. Since cash collateral typically accrues at the overnight rate of interest and repo collateral (which is also very liquid but not as liquid as cash) accrues at the repo rate, the spread (difference) between the term repo and the overnight index swap (OIS) rate could be used to reflect this funding spread.
33. In a cross-currency swap, the parties exchange currency notional amounts at the spot exchange rate. Throughout the life of the swap transaction, they exchange coupon payments for two currencies. At maturity, the notional amounts of both currencies are swapped back. Cross-currency swaps effectively reflect the interest rate differential between two currencies, as implied by the market.
34. Gregory (2020, 395).
35. See BCBS (2019a).
36. Gregory (2020, 406).
37. See BCBS (2019b).
38. Regulation (EU) 2019/834 of the European Parliament and of the Council of 20 May 2019, OJ L 141, 28/05/2019, p. 42–63. ELI: http://data.europa.eu/eli/reg/2019/834/oj.
39. Margin requirements consist of initial margin (posted at the outset) and variation margin (to cover price fluctuations in the funded position). See Gregory (2020, 81).
40. See BCBS (2020).
41. A notable exception from this is the cross-currency swap, where the notional amounts of the two "legs" of the trade (pay and receive) are swapped at the start of the trade and then reversed at the end.
42. E. g., Green (2016), Henrard (2014), Kenyon and Stamm (2012), Lu (2015), Ruiz (2015).
43. Farahvash (2020, 933).
44. Adverse selection is a form of market failure due to asymmetric information. For example, in the case of a customer loan, the customer line of business may know more about a potential borrower's poor credit than the treasury department, but may still extend the loan because the credit risk is transferred to the treasury department through an FTP system that includes compensation for credit risk.
45. Moral hazard occurs when a market participant is not (fully) affected by its behavior because it affects a third party, and therefore makes less effort to mitigate risk. For example, in the case of a customer loan, the

front office may create unnecessary operational risk because the operational risk is transferred to treasury via an FTP system that includes an operational risk offset.

46. This is only possible if the counterparty whose loan needs to be hedged trades as a "name" in the credit derivatives market. If this is not the case, the credit spread component of the FTP rate must be determined by assuming a *probability of default* (PD), the *exposure at default* (EAD) and the *loss given default* (LGD). The expected loss (EL) is the product of these expected values, i. e. PD × EAD × LGD.
47. Often also referred to as "non-maturing products."
48. A prepayment is the settlement or the partial repayment of a debt before its maturity date.
49. For default options in the context of mortgage termination, see Deng et al. (2000).
50. EBA (2022a, 39).
51. In practice, instead of creating tranches of *annual* investments, rolling replicating portfolios are used on a *monthly* basis.
52. E. g., short selling is typically not allowed.
53. Source: Deutsche Bundesbank. Series keys BBK01.SUD101 and BBK01.SUD201.
54. According to Maes and Timmermans (2005, 146), "the replicated deposits are only a portion of total deposits, since banks, in practice, classify total deposits into interest-rate insensitive core deposits, volatile deposits, and remaining balances. Only the latter will get replicated, whereas core deposits are assumed to be invested at a discretionary long horizon and volatile deposits at the interest rate risk free short horizon."
55. See, for example, Nyström (2008) or Frauendorfer and Schürle (2003).
56. Hoffmann et al. (2023, 3).
57. Source: ECB Data Portal. Series keys MIR.M.U2.B.L21.A.R.A. 2250. EUR.N, YC.B.U2.EUR.4F.G_N_A.SV_C_YM.SR_3M and YC.B.U2.EUR. 4F.G_N_A.SV_C_YM.SR_5Y.
58. Acharya et al. (2023, 22).
59. Maes and Timmermans (2005, 144).
60. Hoffmann et al. (2023, 21–22).

References

Acharya, Viral V., Mathew P. Richardson, Kermit L. Schoenholtz, and Bruce Tuckman (eds.). 2023. SVB and Beyond: The Banking Stress of 2023. NYU Stern White Paper. https://www.stern.nyu.edu/experience-stern/about/departments-centers-initiatives/centers-of-research/volatility-and-risk-institute/research/svb-and-beyond-banking-stress-2023. Accessed on January 18, 2025.

Amorese, Ludovica, Javier Huerga, and Ronald Rühmkorf. 2022. The Euro Short-Term Rate (€STR): The New Role of Central Bank Statistics in Financial Markets—A Financial Benchmark Fully Based on Statistical Microdata. 11th Biennial IFC Conference on "Post-pandemic Landscape for Central Bank Statistics" BIS Basel, 25–26 August 2022. https://www.bis.org/ifc/publ/ifcb58_21.pdf. Accessed on January 18, 2025.

BCBS. 1997. Principles for the Management of Interest Rate Risk. Basel Committee on Banking Supervision, September 1997. https://www.bis.org/publ/bcbs29a.pdf. Accessed on January 18, 2025.

BCBS. 2019a. LCR: Liquidity Coverage Ratio, First Version in the Format of the Consolidated Framework, Version Effective as of December 15, 2019. Basel Committee on Banking Supervision. https://www.bis.org/basel_framework/standard/LCR.htm. Accessed on January 18, 2025.

BCBS. 2019b. NSF: Net Stable Funding Ratio, First Version in the Format of the Consolidated Framework, Version Effective as of 15 Dec 2019. Basel Committee on Banking Supervision. https://www.bis.org/basel_framework/standard/NSF.htm. Accessed on January 18, 2025.

BCBS. 2020. MGN: Margin Requirements, First Version in the Format of the Consolidated Framework, Version Effective as of April 3, 2020. Basel Committee on Banking Supervision. https://www.bis.org/basel_framework/standard/MGN.htm. Accessed on January 18, 2025.

CRD IV. 2013. Directive 2013/36/EU of the European Parliament and of the Council of 26 June 2013 ("Capital Requirements Directive IV"). OJ L 176, 27.6.2013, pp. 338–436. ELI: http://data.europa.eu/eli/dir/2013/36/oj.

Deng, Yongheng, John M. Quigley, and Robert Van Order. 2000. Mortgage Terminations, Heterogeneity and the Exercise of Mortgage Options. *Econometrica*, Vol. 68, No. 2, 275–307.

EBA. 2022a. Guidelines on the Management of Interest Rate Risk and Credit Spread Risk Arising From Non-trading Book Activities, Final Report, EBA/GL/2022/14 From October 20, 2022, Mandated by Article 84 (6) of Directive 2013/36/EU (Capital Requirements Directive, CRD), European Banking Authority. https://www.eba.europa.eu/sites/default/files/document_library/Publications/Guidelines/2022/EBA-GL-2022-14%20GL%20on%20IRRBB%20and%20CSRBB/1041754/Guidelines%20on%20IRRBB%20and%20CSRBB.pdf. Accessed on January 18, 2025.

EBA. 2022b. Draft Regulatory Technical Standards Specifying Standardised and Simplified Standardised Methodologies to Evaluate the Risks Arising From Potential Changes in Interest Rates That Affect Both the Economic Value of Equity and the Net Interest Income of an Institution's Non-trading Book

Activities in Accordance With 84(5) of Directive 2013/36/EU, Final Report, EBA/RTS/2022/09 From 20 October 2022, European Banking Authority. https://www.eba.europa.eu/sites/default/files/document_library/Publications/Draft%20Technical%20Standards/2022/EBA-RTS-2022-09%20RTS%20on%20SA/1041755/Final%20draft%20RTS%20on%20SA.pdf. Accessed on January 18, 2025.

Elkenbracht, Marije, and Bert-Jan Nauta. 2006. Managing Interest Rate Risk for Non-maturing Deposits. *Risk*, Vol. 19, No. 11, 82–87.

Fama, Eugene F. 1990. Term-Structure Forecasts of Interest Rates, Inflation and Real Returns. *Journal of Monetary Economics*, Vol. 25, No. 1, January 1990, 59–76.

Farahvash, Pooya. 2020. *Asset-Liability and Liquidity Management*. Newark, NJ: Wiley.

Frauendorfer, Karl, and Michael Schürle. 2003. Management of Non-maturing Deposits by Multistage Stochastic Programming. *European Journal of Operational Research*, Vol. 151, No. 3, 602–616.

Green, Andrew. 2016. *XVA: Credit, Funding and Capital Valuation Adjustments*. Chichester, UK: John Wiley & Sons.

Gregory, Jon. 2020. *The XVA Challenge: Counterparty Risk, Funding, Collateral, Capital and Initial Margin*. Chichester, UK: John Wiley & Sons.

Henrard, Marc. 2014. *Interest Rate Modelling in the Multi-Curve Framework: Foundations, Evolution and Implementation*. Cham, CH: Palgrave Macmillan.

Hoffmann, Peter, Sebastian Frontczak, and Federico Pierobon. 2023. Modelling the Duration of Retail Bank Deposits, Draft Paper Prepared for Submission to the 2023 EBA Policy Research Workshop. https://www.eba.europa.eu/sites/default/files/document_library/Calendar/Conference-Workshop/2023/12th%20Annual%20Research%20Workshop%20-%20Interest%20rate%20and%20Liquidity%20Risk%20Management,%20Regulation%20and%20the%20Macro-economic%20environment/pepers%20and%20presentations/1063514/Federico%20Pierobon.pdf. Accessed on January 18, 2025.

Hull, John C. 2021. *Options, Futures, and Other Derivatives*. Boston, MA: Pearson Prentice Hall.

Jarrow, Robert A., and Donald R. Van Deventer. 1998. The Arbitrage-Free Valuation and Hedging of Demand Deposits and Credit Card Loans. *Journal of Banking & Finance*, Vol. 22, No. 3, 249–272.

Kenyon, Chris, and Roland Stamm. 2012. *Discounting, LIBOR, CVA and Funding: Interest Rate and Credit Pricing*. Cham, CH: Palgrave Macmillan.

Lu, Dongsheng. 2015. *The XVA of Financial Derivatives: CVA, DVA and FVA Explained*. Cham, CH: Palgrave Macmillan.

Maes, Konstantijn, and Thierry Timmermans. 2005. Measuring the Interest Rate Risk of Belgian Regulated Savings Deposits. *Financial Stability Review*, Vol. 3, No. 1, 137–151.

Nyström, Kaj. 2008. On Deposit Volumes and the Valuation of Non-maturing Liabilities. *Journal of Economic Dynamics and Control*, Vol. 32, No. 3, 709–756.

Ruiz, Ignacio. 2015. *XVA Desks—A New Era for Risk Management*. Cham, CH: Palgrave Macmillan.

Schäfer, Robert, Pascal Vogt, and Peter Neu. 2017. Funds Transfer Pricing in the New Normal. In: Bohn, Andreas, and Marije Elkenbracht-Huizing (eds.): *The Handbook of ALM in Banking*, Second Edition, Risk Books, 583–604.

Tata, Fidelio. 2020. *Corporate and Investment Banking: Preparing for a Career in Sales, Trading, and Research.* Cham, CH: Palgrave Macmillan.

3

Bank ALM in Practice

There is no *one-size-fits-all*-ALM. The *heterogeneity* of European banks requires a tailored approach to the use of risk management techniques.

In this chapter, we look at how banks in Europe differ in terms of balance sheet evolution, regional differences, varying business models, and whether ALM is treated as a profit center or a cost center. We then discuss the implications for selecting an appropriate ALM framework. Another practical aspect we will cover is the process of planning NII. A hot topic that has recently made its way into ALM is behavioral economics, which we will also outline. We then look at making ALM into a strategic factor that a bank can use to differentiate itself and increase its competitiveness. Finally, we turn our attention to the roller coaster ride that interest rates have taken over the past decade. We highlight the impact on ALM by first analyzing the negative interest rate environment of the eight years starting in 2014, and then the period of dramatic interest rate changes starting in 2022.

The original version of the chapter has been revised. A correction to this chapter can be found at https://doi.org/10.1007/978-3-031-80205-8_7

F. Tata, *Bank Asset-Liability Management*, https://doi.org/10.1007/978-3-031-80205-8_3

3.1 Bank-Specific ALM

No two banks are alike. From the smallest local savings bank to the pan-European investment bank, from the long-established institution to the neobank, institutions differ in size, scope, geographic footprint, strategy, structure, governance, technological sophistication and, perhaps most importantly, customer base.

Just as we would not expect a doctor to prescribe the same medicine for all patients, the ALM tools and techniques we have covered so far need to be applied on a case-by-case basis and possibly modified to suit the idiosyncrasies of a particular bank. We will do this by covering various dimensions of how banks differ from one another, illustrating the differences by presenting the size, structure and nature of stylized balance sheets, and discussing the implications for ALM and interest rate risk management.

3.1.1 Composition of Banks' Balance Sheets Over Time

The composition of assets and liabilities on current balance sheets has changed significantly since the turn of the century. Figure 3.1 illustrates this development for monetary financial institutions[1] (MFIs) in Germany between EoY 1999 and EoY 2021.[2]

At first glance, several observations can be made:

- The secular decline in interest rates between 1999 and 2021 has led to a significant increase in customer sight deposits (from 7.9% to 29.3%). More than half of this 21.4% increase was driven by customers moving out of term deposits (from 17.3% to 9.3%) and savings accounts (from 10.8% to 5.8%), as term deposits and savings accounts did not offer sufficient compensation over and above that of sight deposits.
- Consumer loans did not absorb the increase in funding from customer business (from 36% to 44.4%); on the contrary: Consumer loans fell from 57.7% to 48.3%. This may be because banks were reluctant to increase their consumer loan book due to economic uncertainty.
- Banks responded to this shift in retail customer business by making the following ALM-adjustments to their funding and investment profiles:
  - A large part of the inflow of overnight retail deposits was parked with the central bank as excess reserves, leading to an increase in the overall cash position of banks' balance sheets from 1% to 11.4%.

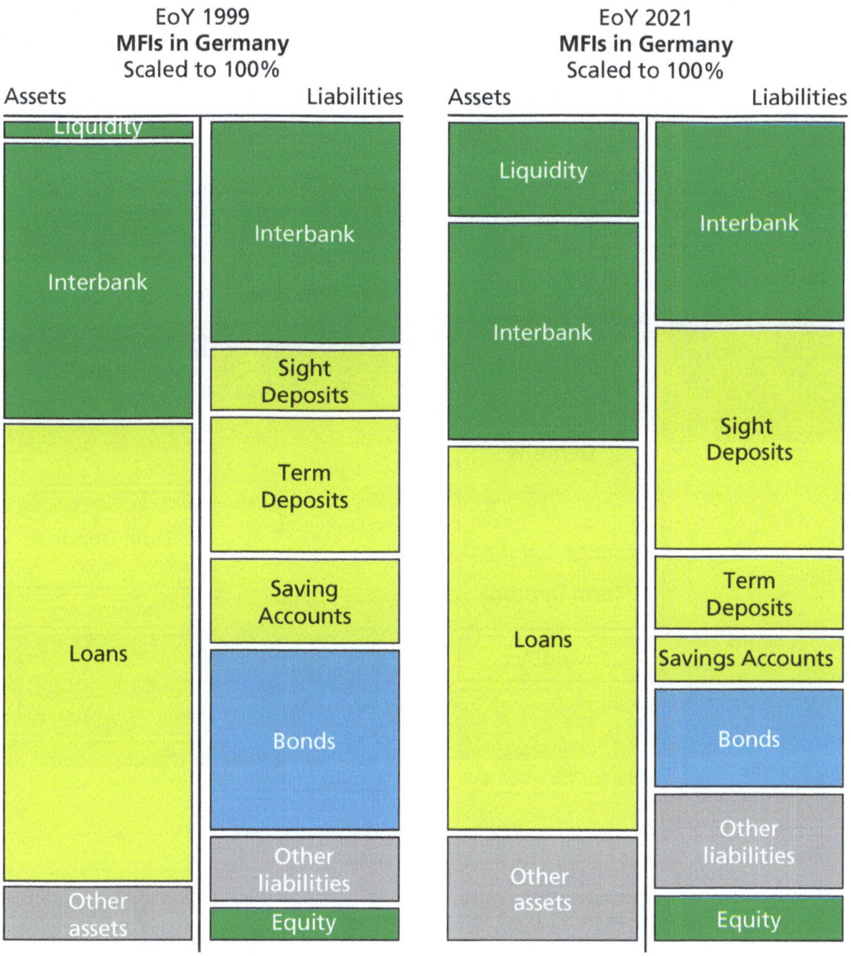

Fig. 3.1 Balance sheet evolution 1999–2021

- Another part of the inflow of sight deposits was invested in other assets (up from 6.8% to 13.3%), including liquid traded securities such as government bonds.
- Finally, the inflow of short-term customer deposits replaced some of the banks' funding through bond / note issuance (which declined from 23.2% to 12.5%).

Figure 3.2 shows how quickly balance sheets adjust to rising interest rates over the next two years (between EoY 2021 and EoY 2023).

In just two years, the rise in interest rates caused banks to reduce their excess reserves at the central bank, bringing their liquidity back to 1% (roughly the level prior to the low interest rate environment). Customer

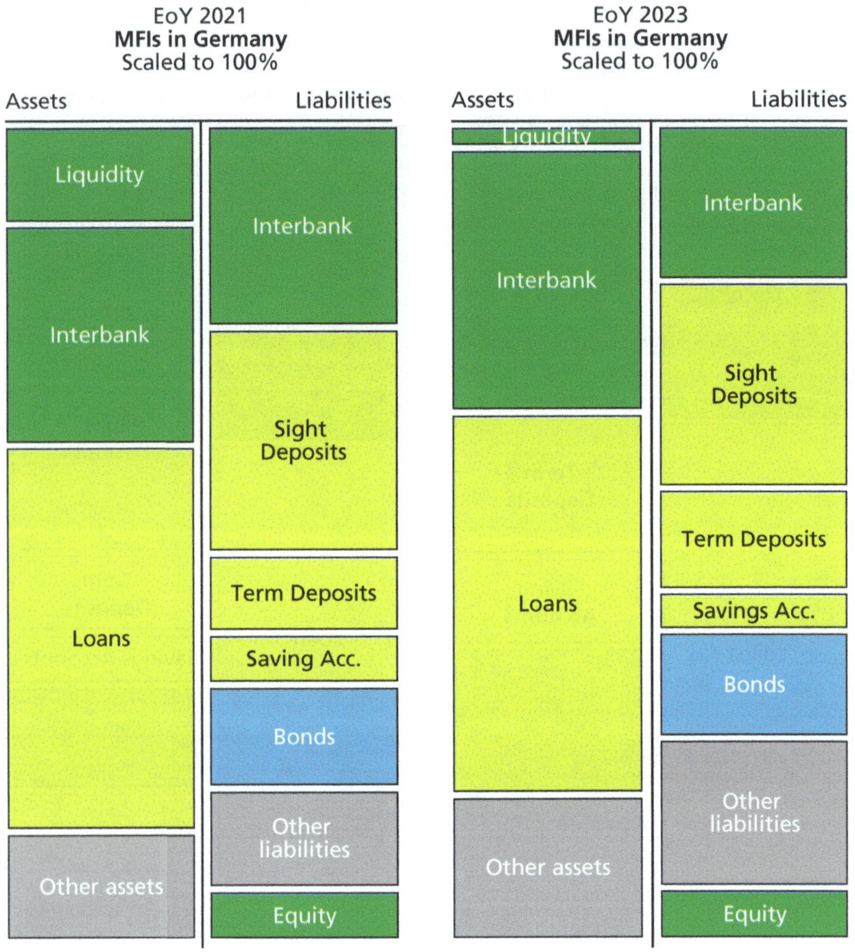

Fig. 3.2 Balance sheet evolution 2021–2023

sight deposits declined from 29.3% to 26.1%, while customer time deposits increased. The largest increase was in customer time deposits under one year, which rose from 2.6% to 5.9%.

The pronounces whipsaw in the balance sheet structure of banks in response to changes in interest rates illustrates the importance of modeling volumes (especially retail volumes) with realistic ALM assumptions.

3.1.2 Regional Differences

European banking is subject to a large heterogeneity of customer preferences across countries. This is particularly striking in the case of mortgage loans. Fixed-rate mortgages dominate in Belgium, France, Germany and the Netherlands, while adjustable-rate mortgages (ARMs) are more common in Austria, Greece, Italy, Portugal and Spain.[3]

Attempts have been made to explain regional differences by factors such as different degrees of concentration in the banking system,[4] institutional diversity (public, state, cooperative, mutual and private banks),[5] divergences in the quality of banks' assets,[6] or the level of economic and financial literacy.[7]

A recent study highlights regional differences that underscore the need for rather different ALM strategies in different local markets, pointing out that "in France, the overall low sensitivity of parts of the deposit base to interest rate changes is matched by the offer to retail clients of long-dated fixed rate residential mortgages, whereas such products exhibit a much shorter duration where depositors are way more reactive to interest rate changes, e. g. in Germany or Finland, ceteris paribus".[8]

Although some of these regional differences appear to be disappearing as a result of a more pan-European young customer base, banks' balance sheets are still plagued by what used to be country-specific customer business.

3.1.3 Balance Sheets for Different Business Models

The role of ALM also depends to a large extent on the bank's business model. An international investment bank has a different need to balance its customer business than a regional savings bank.

For example, banks with a high degree of retail deposit-generating infrastructure (i. e., networks of branches and offices) cannot fully control the amount of retail deposits they receive through that infrastructure; turning down deposits is simply not an option. Other banks that are less dependent on retail deposits and more reliant on the interbank market and other forms of funding have more discretion over their funding sources.

This is illustrated in Fig. 3.3 by comparing the balance sheet of Deutsche Bank (a former global investment bank, albeit now with a somewhat reduced level of ambition) with that of Landesbank Berlin (LBB); balance sheet items are scaled / normalized for comparability.

Generalizing this observation, the following differences can be observed:

- Investment banks tend to have larger trading books
- Savings banks are more dependent on funding through sight deposits
- Savings banks are more involved in the mortgage business

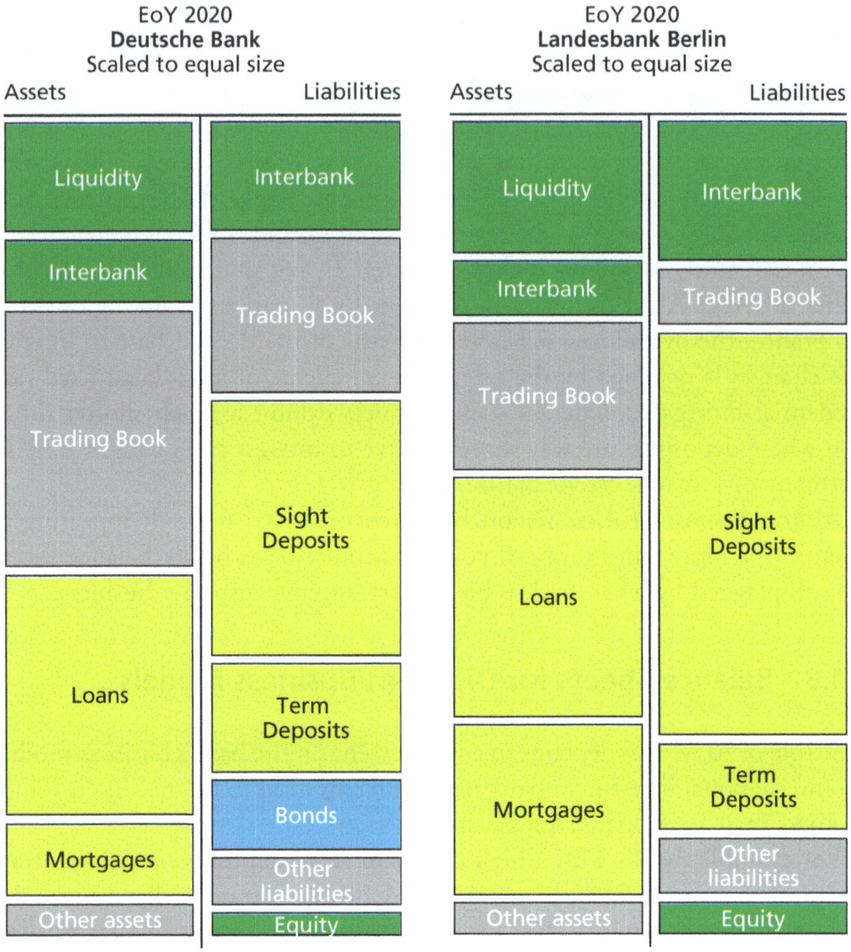

Fig. 3.3 Balance sheet comparison: Deutsche Bank vs. LBB

ALM must adapt to the specific needs of a bank's business model. For example, the strong sight deposit business of savings banks creates potential problems in the event of negative interest rates.

3.1.4 ALM as a Profit or a Cost Center

Funds Transfer Pricing (FTP) allows the ALM department to become a *profit center*.

When ALM is organized as a profit center, financial risks are transferred to the interest rate risk profit center (within ALM). ALM then decides whether and how to hedge the assumed risk through open market transactions. The profit generated within ALM is then periodically redistributed to the customer business units.

When structured as a profit center, ALM could be further subdivided into individual profit centers that reflect separate areas of risk. Examples include:

- Interest rate risk profit center
- Liquidity risk profit center
- Foreign exchange risk profit center
- Inflation risk profit center
- Volatility risk profit center
- Model risk profit center

Alternatively, ALM can be run as a *cost center*. In this case, ALM aggregates the costs of all necessary interest rate risk management activities without the objective of generating a profit through market positioning and timing. These costs must be passed on to the customer business units' overhead.

3.1.5 Implications for ALM

There is *no one-size-fits-all* ALM. ALM must be tailored to the specific needs of the bank. The requirements for ALM change over time, as the market environment, behavioral aspects of the customer base, best practices in theory and modeling, access to and liquidity in the financial markets, and regulatory requirements change. Examples of questions to ask when designing a tailored ALM include

- How has my balance sheet structure evolved over time?
- What is my geographic footprint?
- What is my target business model?
- Who are my key customers?
- What products can I use to hedge within ALM? Do they include derivatives?
- What is my level of sophistication in modeling and risk management?
- What are my execution capabilities?
- Do I want to run ALM as a profit center?

The extent and rigor with which ALM tools and concepts should be applied in a *bank-specific* situation also depends on the *size* and *sophistication* of the institution; sometimes it is better to keep them simple, but have good intuition about the process, than to create a *false sense of accuracy* by using overly complicated models.

3.2 NII Planning

Because NII is an important, if not *the* most important, measure of a bank's success from an earnings perspective, NII is not only calculated backward for reporting purposes, but also projected into the future. The process of planning NII goes beyond setting reasonable expectations for future NII; the whole exercise has a significant *political* dimension. Business units are typically reluctant to plan for a decline in NII, even if this is objectively the most likely scenario, because of the strategic implications, such as reduced allocation of resources (including personnel), diminished decision-making power within the organization, and, in the extreme, the discontinuation of the entire business unit. At the same time, there is some reluctance to plan for a very large increase in NII because it would set the bar very high, increasing the likelihood of disappointment and decreasing the likelihood of exceeding the plan (which could be the basis for promotions and bonuses).

These behavioral biases in the *psychology of planning* make it even more important to strive for as much objectivity as possible, to test any assumptions made, and to keep the process as data-driven as possible.

3.2.1 Planning Horizons

When projecting NII into the future, various planning horizons are typically used. While bank-specific terminology may vary, a common notation is to *forecast* NII in the *current* calendar or fiscal year, *budget* for the *next* calendar or fiscal year, and *plan* for calendar or fiscal years *thereafter* for a horizon of up to 3–5 years.

The forecast is a combination of known results (from past months) and a prediction for future months. The quality of the current year's forecast typically improves as the calendar or fiscal year progresses. A forecast is often done three to four times a year, sometimes more.

The budget and plan, on the other hand, are pure predictions of the future. *Assumptions* about future key factors (volumes, margins, interest rates, etc.) have a significant impact on the results and quality of these predictions.

3.2.2 Scenario Planning

The (annual) NII planning process of a bank includes, as a minimum, the planning of *volumes* and *expected margins* for *each business line*, as well as the expected future *interest rate environment*.

Volumes are reflected by the assumed changes in the balance sheet structure. The level of new customer business must be planned. New customer business counteracts the natural attrition (run-off) of existing business.

Volumes and margins depend on the interest rate environment. Therefore, several alternative interest rate environments must be modeled and a consistent view of volumes and margins must be established for each.

One of the scenarios can be referred to as the *baseline scenario*, which is the most widely expected interest rate environment. This is often the current interest rate environment (i. e., current *spot* rates) or the one reflected in current *forward* rates.

Alternative scenarios provide an idea of the potential distribution of NII (under uncertainty). See Fig. 3.4.

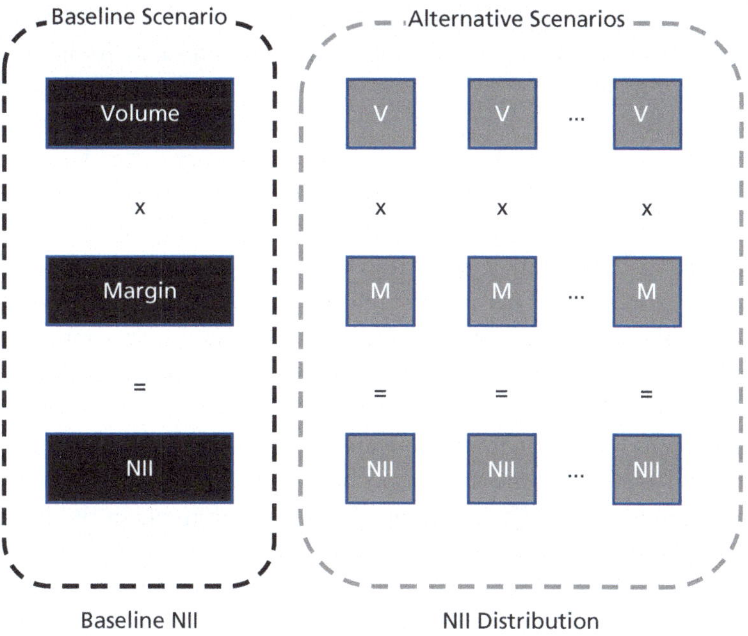

Fig. 3.4 Baseline vs. alternative NII scenarios

3.2.3 Volume Planning

The volume of each business line needs to be planned separately because the run-offs are different (e. g., some business lines give customers prepayment options, while others don't).

The *run-off* needs to be estimated and is a function of the assumed interest rate environment and the assumed behavior of the bank's customers. Then, *new* business must be planned (which is also a function of the assumed interest rate environment). As discussed in Sect. 2.5.5 on volume changes in the context of the replicating model, different assumptions can be made about new business. See also Fig. 2.31.

After adding new customer business to the (shrinking) legacy customer business, an estimate of future volume is obtained.

3.2.4 Margin Planning

The *net interest margin* of each business needs to be planned separately because margins evolve differently (e. g., due to the competitive environment in different business areas). Estimating a potential *margin compression*, which could be affected by the assumed interest rate environment itself, is part of the planning process.

Adjusting the *current margin* for the expected *margin compression* (or potential margin expansion) results in the *planned margin*. See Fig. 3.5.

Some empirical evidence suggests that net interest margins are to some extent directional with respect to the general level of interest rates. For example, using data from a quantitative survey of German banks, Busch et al.(2021) estimate that net interest margins decline by 5 bp for every additional year following a 100 bp downward shift in the interest rate level.[9] In another study looking at a broad panel of banks from 32 countries over the period 2008 to 2014, Cruz-García et al. (2019) estimate that interest margins move by about 19 bp for every 100 bp shift in short-term market interest rates. If we have to assume a "margin-beta," then planned margins would need to be adjusted for different interest rate environments in the future.

Margin planning also tends to be a highly political issue within the bank's panning process. Managers tend to shy away from planning for a reduction in margin. Often enough, the current margin is assumed to remain unchanged.

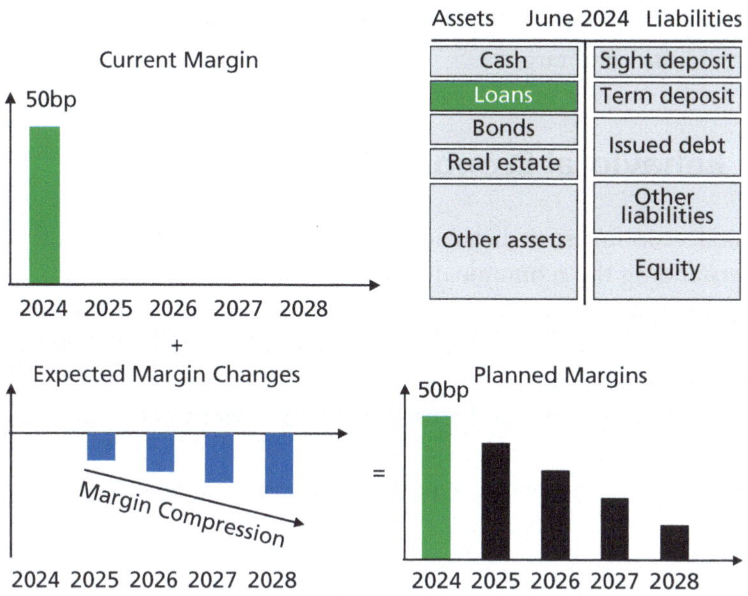

Fig. 3.5 Margin planning

3.2.5 Comprehensive ALM Plan

ALM closes the gap between assets and liabilities. To do this, it requires a closer look at the plans of other business units, as these affect the volume development of the bank's assets and liabilities.

ALM planning involves forecasting the bank's future interest rate risk. To do this, expected EVE and NII sensitivities should be calculated for the future. This requires ALM to have a *detailed plan* of the different business units that goes beyond a pure volume plan:

- Different customer interest rate behaviors should be taken into account by dividing the planned volume into segments with different assumed interest rate behaviors.
- Expected maturities for new business need to be specified. For example, it makes a big difference whether a business unit plans fixed-rate business with a maturity of 5 years or 20 years.

Forecasts of future liquidity risk (e. g., liquidity coverage ratio, net stable funding ratio) and capital requirements should also be considered as they can have a significant impact on the ALM plan. A comprehensive ALM plan should help meet all regulatory and supervisory requirements as well as internal limits and targets.

3.3 Behavioral Economics

Behavioral economics, or behavioral finance, applies psychological insights to understanding the economic decisions of individuals and institutions.[10] It challenges the idea of rational decision-making typically assumed by standard neoclassical economics and takes a more realistic approach to describing and predicting human behavior.

Behavioral economics can be used to better understand a bank's *customer base* and the *behavior of other banks* alike. The latter is important because banks are typically *price-takers* when it comes to *product rates* (e. g., the interest rate on sight deposits).

3.3.1 Behavioral Assumptions About Bank Customers

In the context of bank customers, behavioral economics addresses the fact that bank customers vary in their personal circumstances and in their ability to manage their financial affairs in their own long-term interest.

To anticipate a bank customer's behavior, especially when it comes to executing behavioral options, it is necessary to understand his or her economic and non-economic motivations and preferences. For example, the decision to move from one city to another (either based on non-economic considerations or, for example, on job-related economic considerations that are unknown to the bank) may force a bank customer to prepay a mortgage loan on the house that needs to be sold.[11]

In the past, only some banks made explicit assumptions about the behavioral aspects of their customers, but in the future this will be a regulatory requirement set by the EBA, for all banks:

> Behavioural assumptions for customer accounts with embedded customer optionality for the purpose of IRRBB:
> In assessing the implications of optionality, institutions should take into account:
> (a) The potential impact on current and future loan prepayment speeds arising from the interest rate scenario, underlying economic environment and contractual features. Institutions should take into account the various dimensions influencing the embedded behavioural options.

(b) The elasticity of adjustment of product rates to changes in market interest rates.[12]

Behavioral modeling is particularly important for balance sheet items with embedded options. Examples of customer transactions that require behavioral modeling include

- Non-maturity deposits (NMDs) with respect to behavioral maturity.
- Loans with prepayment options (such as certain mortgage loans).
- Lending facilities, such as overdrafts, in terms of drawdown and repayment speed.
- Certain term deposits with respect to early withdrawal (even if the customer is subject to a penalty for breaking the contract).

The modeling of key behavioral assumptions must be based on appropriate underlying historical data and on prudent hypotheses. However, *backtesting*[13] is often difficult due to the ever-changing market environment, change in customer sophistication and the development of new banking products. In addition, negative interest rates can lead to atypical behavior; therefore, data from the negative interest rate environment cannot be used for backtesting in a positive interest rate environment and vice versa.

3.3.2 Behavioral Assumptions About Banks

Since banks are typically not monopolists in any of the banking services they offer, their pricing power with respect to so-called product rates is limited. At the extreme, a bank could be a mere price-taker, meaning that whatever the market equilibrium rate for a particular banking product (say, sight deposits) is, it is also be the rate the bank has to offer to its own customer base.[14] Thus, it is not enough to model the behavior of bank customers based on their investment opportunities and preferences, but also to understand the behavior of all other banks behavior based on idiosyncratic factors, such as their funding strategy.

In some cases, the competitive relationship between banks is obvious. There are cases where two competing banks in a small town, perhaps even next door to each other, post their product rates on a notice board next to the front door for all to see. If one of the two banks decided to change a product rate (e. g., increase the demand deposit rate from 1% to 1.5%), it would force the other bank to match that rate or appear less competitive. At the same time, the rate offered by online banks may be of little importance (since small-town bank customers may prefer physical banking and may not pay much attention to what neobanks are doing). In this case, behavioral assumptions must be made about a single, specific bank.

In another case, the competitive relationship is less obvious. A bank with branches in small towns, large cities, and a strong online franchise competes with a large number of banks. Here, behavioral assumptions must be made about many different banks. This is particularly difficult because different banks have different business models and their FTP rates from their respective ALM frameworks are likely to be different. For example, an established bank using a replicating portfolio model approach may pass on only a fraction of a market rate change to its non-maturity deposit customer base because a large portion of the deposits have been originated in the past and are already hedged at historical rates. Alternatively, a start-up online bank with few legacy deposits can afford to pass on most of the interest rate change (because it can also lock in this higher funding rate with investments at current rates).

On an aggregate basis, the extent to with which changes in interest rates are reflected in the rates of non-maturity products is estimated through deposit beta modeling. Deposit betas are a measure of the pass-through of risk-free rates, typically the monetary policy rate, to the deposit market, measured as the portion of a change in the risk-free market rate that is passed through to the deposit rate. As discussed in Sect. 2.5.8 in the context of the replicating model and illustrated in Fig. 2.37, deposit betas are highly unstable. Thus, extracting *implied* patterns of banks behavior from empirical observations of product rates does not work very well. In fact, it may be necessary to model bank behavior explicitly, even if it is cumbersome and based on many assumptions.

3.4 Holistic ALM

Holistic ALM goes beyond the narrow *tactical* ALM functions that include *operational* tasks related to regulatory compliance, P&L, capital, liquidity and risk management (IRRBB, etc.). It takes a broader and more *strategic* approach, incorporating aspects from the bank's ecosystem. Examples include

- Adopting ALM to the ALM used by key competitors to avoid becoming an "outlier".
- Incorporating the interests of stakeholders (beyond equity owners), e. g., customers and employees.

- Consideration of interaction with other business areas of the bank, e. g., fee business generated in the M&A department.
- Consideration of capital market aspects (collateral management, dependence on the derivatives market, etc.).
- Aligning ALM with the bank's global / international strategy.
- Consideration of reputational issues (e. g. use of derivatives).
- Listening to politicians and their constituencies, e. g., regarding the level of risk taking.

See Fig. 3.6.

Investments in holistic ALM can give a bank a *strategic advantage* over its competitors. This includes investments in hardware, software, risk management tools, AI / machine learning capabilities, databases and access to alternative data,[15] human capital and research units.

Examples of how successful banks are embracing new technologies for ALM and other risk areas include

- BlackRock (approximately USD 11+ trillion in assets under management by 2025) established an AI lab in Palo Alto, California in 2018.[16]
- JP Morgan Chase spent USD 17 bn on technology in 2024 (equal to the combined spending of the top eight banks, and that's just on technology!), including on robotics and AI.[17]

Fig. 3.6 Holistic vs. tactical ALM

- Goldman Sachs has employed 10,000 developers in 2020, a quarter of its total workforce.[18]

ALM capabilities can even be made available to customers and other market participants for a fee. JPMorgan's Value-at-Risk (VaR) framework, developed by its risk management department in the 1980s, was later turned into a commercial offering (RiskMetrics) and spun off.

A bank with a sound ALM could even go so far as to lobby lawmakers for stricter risk management regulations, knowing that it would be better prepared to meet them than its competitors.

3.5 Negative Interest Rates

On June 5, 2014, the Governing Council of the ECB lowered the rate on the deposit facility (DF) to -0.10%. The eight years that followed are often referred to as the period of zero interest rate policy (ZIRP) or negative interest rate policy (NIRP). Historically, a basic truism of finance would reject the idea of negative interest rates, similar to that of negative probabilities or negative commodity prices. Previously, modeling assumptions were mostly based on zero-bound interest rates (e. g., assuming that interest rates are log-normally distributed with a zero probability of negative interest rates).

3.5.1 0% Interest Rate Floor

The use of negative interest rates in *institutional* transactions, such as interbank interest rate swaps or repo transactions, is hardly a problem.[19] Conceptually, *nominal* interest rates are the *real* interest rate plus an adjustment for inflation. If inflation is negative, negative nominal interest rates do not necessarily imply a lack of compensation. Banks would normally be able to pass on their costs of holding excess liquidity[20] at the central bank to corporate customers by charging negative interest rates on corporate deposits. Also, negative *indicator* rates (market-based interest rates, such as EURIBOR, used to calculate the customer rate) do not necessarily result in negative cash flows, as cash flows are often based on an indicator rate *plus a spread*. For example, in the case of floating rate corporate loans, even if the indicator rate on which the loan is based becomes negative, the credit spread, and the margin applied to the indicator rate could easily make the customer rate used for cash flow calculations positive.

The situation is different in *retail* banking. Charging retail depositors negative interest rates may be prohibited by consumer protection laws or may be impractical from a customer relationship perspective. If a bank expects to pay retail depositors an interest rate of $r_I \pm x$, based on a floating rate indicator rate r_I and a spread x, the actual deposit rate is not $r_I \pm x$, but the greater of $r_I \pm x$ and zero percent, or max ($r_I \pm x$; 0%). This *floor* at zero percent was hardly relevant when interest rates were high; the situation is different in a negative interest rate environment.

To draw an analogy from the area of automatic interest rate options, where execution is rule-based, such as interest rate caps and floors, a 0% floor is *out of the money*, i. e., has little value, when interest rates are high, but is *at the money*, or even *in the money*, when interest rates are low or negative. The ability of consumers to resist being charged negative interest rates on retail deposits is an example of embedded options or behavioral options. Their value also increases in a low interest rate environment.

There are two types of floors, depending on the features of the contract and how consumer protection laws are implemented: The *coupon floor* and the *indicator floor*. In the case of a *coupon floor*, the customer's interest rate cannot fall below 0%. However, the indicator rate used to calculate the customer interest rate can be negative as long as the spread applied above the indicator rate ensures that the resulting customer rate is not negative. Thus, the customer rate is max ($r_I + x$; 0%). While the customer will never be charged a negative interest rate charge, the customer may not receive the expected margin x. An example of a coupon floor is a retail savings account (where consumer protection laws in some countries prevent retail customers from paying interest on such account types). In the case of an *indicator floor*, the indicator rate used to calculate the customer rate cannot be less than 0%. In this case, the customer rate is calculated as max (r_I; 0%) + x. Here, the margin x is protected even if the indicator rates fall below 0%. An example of an indicator floor is a corporate loan with a corresponding contract feature.

Figure 3.7 illustrates the effect of a decreasing indicator rate on the customer rate for both types of floors.

Whether a 0% floor is good or bad from a bank's perspective depends on whether the floor is applied to an asset or a liability. Coupon floors are bad for liabilities (e. g., customer deposits) because they limits the bank's ability to "charge" negative interest rates on funding transactions. Coupon floors are good for assets (e. g., customer loans) because they prevent the bank from having to pay negative interest rates on investments.

If a bank faces indicator floors on assets and coupon floors on liabilities, a negative interest rate environment is beneficial (all else being equal); if a bank

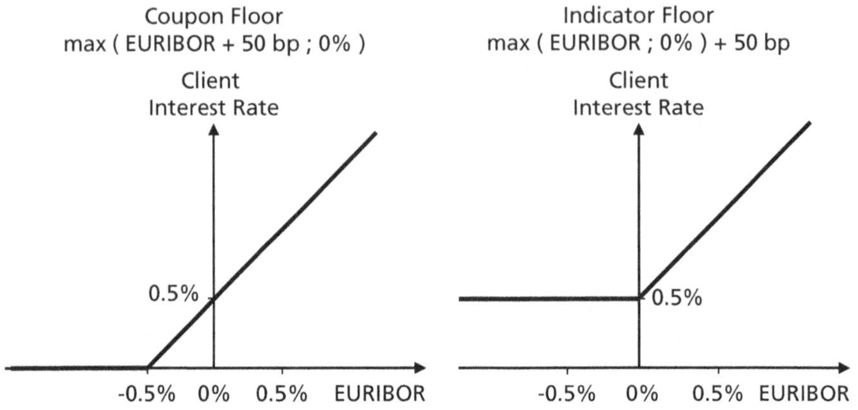

Fig. 3.7 Coupon floor vs. indicator floor

faces coupon floors on assets and indicator floors on liabilities, a negative interest rate environment causes potential losses.[21]

3.5.2 Economic Implications

In a negative interest rate environment, non-negatively remunerated sight deposits become an attractive asset class for bank customers compared to other low-risk alternatives such as short-term fixed income investments.[22] Not surprisingly, banks experienced a significant inflow into sight deposits during the ZIRP / NIRP period (see Fig. 2.32). These deposits became what can be called *rigid deposits*,[23] defined as deposits whose interest rate becomes inelastic when market interest rates fall below zero.

From an economic perspective, ZIRP / NIRP creates frictions in banks' funding mix, as banks' retail deposits do not reprice when policy rates are cut below zero. According to Demiralp et al. (2021), "[r]ate cuts resulting in negative policy rates are unlikely to operate in the same fashion as conventional rate cuts because banks may not be able to charge their retail customers negative rates on their deposits. Banks' inability to adjust a part of their funding costs may be due to the forces of competition – in combination with the high regulatory value of retail deposits due to their stability – as well as the existence of banknotes, which offer an alternative store of value with a yield of zero. Therefore, NIRP should have an impact on banks' profitability as the remuneration of banks' assets declines as a consequence of NIRP while a significant part of their funding costs remains unchanged, leading to declining intermediation margins."

The negative interest rate environment encouraged *some* of the most deposit-dependent banks to shift the composition of their balance sheets toward higher-yielding assets in order to protect or restore profitability,[24] *others* that were highly NII-dependent to compensate for lost deposit margins by increasing lending margins, and *still others* to seek more fee and commission income.[25]

3.5.3 Regulatory Implications

Regulators expect banks to consider negative interest rate scenarios and their impact on retail customer behavior. According to the EBA:

> In low interest rate environments, institutions should also consider negative interest rate scenarios and the possibility of asymmetrical effects of negative interest rates on their interest rate sensitive instruments. (…) In making behavioural assumptions about accounts without specific repricing dates (…), institutions should (…) consider potential constraints on the repricing of retail deposits in low or negative interest rate environments and the effect that such constraints may have on the stability of deposits under different interest rate scenarios.[26]

3.5.4 Challenges

A number of challenges remain with respect to negative interest rates. These include:

- Data availability is still limited due to the relatively short period of negative interest rates. This can lead to calibration issues for ALM models.
- Models are still adapting to the inclusion of negative rates, and no benchmark model has yet taken hold.
- In the transition from EURIBOR to risk-free rates (RFRs), indicators and customer spreads on existing contracts will change. This could impact the resulting floors.
- Legal challenges are still working their way through the legal system, with few high court decisions yet. Legal implications may vary by jurisdiction.[27]
- Changes in consumer behavior are not fully understood.
- Reputational issues are also potentially important. Banks must *balance* legal positions with maintaining good customer relationships. *Social responsibility* may ultimately trump the pursuit of a legal position. Behavioral

aspects (of the bank) need to be considered and interest rate floors may not be "executed" by banks for strategic / reputational reasons.
- The focus on the 0% floor should not distract from the analysis of the risks associated with a sudden rise in interest rates (see Sect. 3.6).

In summary, the 0% interest rate floor on retail deposits caused different problems for different banks and, as a result, banks *reacted differently*. This illustrates how bank-specific an ALM framework must be to deal with shocks such as negative interest rates. The governance of models and model risk remains a key responsibility of banks management.

3.6 Rapid Rise in Interest Rates

The extended period of relatively stable and declining interest rates through 2022 has been ingrained in the thinking of an entire generation of risk managers, leading them to believe that interest rate risk would remain muted.

Acharya et al. (eds.) (2023) explain the impact of risk management complacency on the modeling of *non-maturity deposits* (NMDs) as follows:

> The zero-lower bound period was likely also a factor. During the 2016-2019 interest rate cycle, which was relatively shallow, these uninsured checking and savings deposits appeared 'sticky' and remained in banks despite historically low deposit betas. Banks may have assumed these low betas would persist during the current cycle. This is risky because uninsured deposits can become unstuck and their betas can rise quickly.[28]

Indeed, in 2022 and 2023, bank customers shifted a significant portion of their deposits from sticky sight deposits to other products (term deposits, savings accounts, etc.) in order to earn higher interest rates (see Fig. 3.2). This led to an increase in banks' duration gaps and the materialization of interest rate risk.[29]

It is worth noting that in 2017, the ECB conducted a sensitivity analysis of the banking books of the largest European banks, focusing on interest rate changes.[30] The stress test was designed to provide the ECB with sufficient information to understand the interest rate sensitivity of a bank's banking book assets and liabilities, as well as net interest income, to hypothetical interest rate changes. The results showed that "[b]anks heavily rely on models of customer behavior which were calibrated in a declining interest rate environment."[31] Thanks to this warning, some five years before the interest rate cycle turned in 2022, banks should have had ample time to stress test and to recalibrate their models to reflect customer behavior in a rising interest rate environment.

Prepayment models are particularly affected by rapid interest rate increases. Customers who have been able to "lock in" a low interest rate on *fixed rate loans* in a low interest rate environment are likely to hold them longer than expected and not repay them as quickly as they could (given certain prepayment options). It may be more attractive for customers to hold excess liquidity in bank deposits, rather than use the funds to repay the loans if the deposit account pays a higher interest rate than the fixed rate on the loan. On the other hand, *floating-rate loans* may experience a higher prepayment speed if interest rates rise rapidly, as customers may want to prepay as soon as possible.

When designing *new banking products*, paying attention to changes in customer preferences and demand, as well as observing new offerings from competing banks, can help a bank adjust its product offering. For example, once interest rates have risen sufficiently, *capital-guaranteed products* become attractive again.[32]

Finally, the size, interest rate sensitivity, and duration of a bank's *investment portfolio* may need to be adjusted if interest rates rise rapidly. In Chapter 4, we discuss an example of how a rise in interest rates affected the value of a particular bank (Silicon Valley Bank). In addition to the investment portfolio, the use of interest rate *derivatives* (as part of the ALM risk management strategy) needs to be reassessed.

In summary, a rapid rise in interest rates may force banks to fine-tune their hedging and investment strategies, which could be significantly different in a higher interest rate environment. If done properly, this could be an opportunity to increase bank profitability and reduce risk.

Notes

1. According to the ECB, Monetary financial institutions (MFIs) are "[f]inancial institutions which together form the money-issuing sector of the euro area. These include the Eurosystem, resident credit institutions (as defined in EU law) and all other resident financial institutions whose business is to receive deposits and / or close substitutes for deposits from entities other than MFIs and, for their own account (at least in economic terms), to grant credit and / or invest in securities. The latter group consists predominantly of money market funds." See https://www.ecb.europa.eu/services/glossary/html/glossm.en.html#438.

2. Data source: Deutsche Bundesbank. Downloaded from https://www.bundesbank.de/dynamic/action/de/statistiken/zeitreihen-datenbanken/zeitreihen-datenbank/723444/723444?treeAnchor=BANKEN&statisticType=BBK_ITS. Data aggregated and rounded by the author.
3. Campbell (2013).
4. Birn et al. (2023).
5. Ayadi et al. (2010).
6. Valverde et al. (2019).
7. Albertazzi et al. (2019), Campbell (2013).
8. Hoffmann et al. (2023, 14).
9. Busch et al. (2021, 289).
10. For an introductory overview of behavioral economics, we recommend Angner (2020).
11. In most cases, mortgages are not assignable, which means that a mortgage secured by a specific house cannot be transferred by a departing homeowner to the new owner of the house. Instead, the outgoing homeowner must pay off the old mortgage and the new owner must obtain a new mortgage See Campbell (2013).
12. EBA (2022, 38).
13. Backtesting consists of verifying that the internal model is consistent with a 99% confidence level.
14. If a bank were to offer a product rate that was significantly more attractive than the prevailing market rate, the bank would risk being flooded with customer business beyond what is acceptable from a risk management or business perspective; if a bank were to offer a product rate that was significantly less attractive, the bank would risk losing customer business to its competitors, or jeopardizing the customer relationship altogether.
15. Alternative data is data beyond what is typically used in the corporate decision-making process, such as traffic through corporate websites, geolocation data from smartphones, or data broadcast on social media. See Tata (2020, 123).
16. Wigglesworth and Flood (2018).
17. Gerut (2024).
18. Low, Jia Jen (2020).
19. E. g., the ISDA *2014 Collateral Agreement Negative Interest Protocol* allows parties to amend the terms of certain ISDA-published collateral agreements to reflect negative interest amounts on cash collateral.

20. Excess liquidity refers to banks' credit balances on their central bank accounts in excess of their required reserves.
21. This can be illustrated by the following example: Suppose a bank invests at $r_I + x$ and funds itself at the same rate $r_I + x$. NII would be $(r_I + x) - (r_I + x) = 0$, irrespective of the level of the indicator rate r_I. Next, we assume that investments (i. e., assets) are subject to a coupon floor and funding (i. e., liabilities) is subject to an indicator floor. NII would now be $\max(r_I + x; 0) - [\max(r_I; 0) + x]$. Here, NII is $-x$ for $r_I < -x$, r_I for $-x \leq r_I \leq 0$, and 0 for $r_I > 0$. Obviously, NII can never be positive and is negative for an indicator rate below zero.
22. Hoffmann et al. (2023, 26).
23. Grandi and Guille (2023).
24. Demiralp et al. (2021), Grandi and Guille (2023).
25. Present et al. (2023).
26. EBA (2022, 36–40).
27. In Germany, the Federal Court of Justice (Bundesgerichtshof) issued in 2023 an important decision on negative loan interest rates (BGH decision XI ZR 544/21). It was clarified that, despite the lack of a clear legal definition of "interest" in German law, interest should be understood as a remuneration for capital temporarily lent. Such remuneration cannot be negative. In the case of a loan, the borrower is obliged to provide the lender with a return. The ECB's interest rate policy does not reverse this obligation. This creates an implicit floor at 0%. However, the situation might be different if, for example, a swap contract is considered instead of a loan contract ("Darlehensvertrag").
28. Acharya et al. (eds.) (2023, 46).
29. Coulier et al. (2024, 35).
30. The European Central Bank (ECB) is required to conduct annual stress tests on supervised entities as part of its Supervisory Review and Evaluation Process (SREP), as set out in Article 100 of the Capital Requirements Directive IV (CRD IV). In 2017, the ECB conducted a test to provide the ECB banking supervisors with additional information on the interest rate sensitivity of the net interest income and the economic value of equity of the banking book positions of the largest and most significant 100+ European banks (so-called *significant institutions*, or SI). The results of the ECB's interest rate stress test feed into the SREP from a qualitative perspective. There is no direct impact on banks' capital through the Pillar 2 guidance. All participating banks have received individual feedback and are expected to

take action accordingly, in line with the set of best practices published by the ECB.

31. ECB (2017, 2).
32. Capital-guaranteed (or capital-protected) products are retail customer products, typically in the form of certificates, that limit the maximum possible loss to the customer to the loss in purchasing power of the capital invested, i. e., EUR 100 – PV (EUR 100) for an investment of EUR 100. The present value, PV, of an amount depends on the length of the discounting period and the interest rate. All other things being equal, the higher the interest rate (discount rate), the lower the PV. As interest rate rise, the customer faces more economic downside in a capital-guaranteed product, which allows the bank to offer more upside (e. g., participation in an equity index) in return. Non-interest rate risks (such as counterparty credit risk, liquidity risk or convexity risk) are not considered in this analysis.

References

Acharya, Viral V., Mathew P. Richardson, Kermit L. Schoenholtz, and Bruce Tuckman (eds.). 2023. SVB and Beyond: The Banking Stress of 2023. NYU Stern White Paper. https://www.stern.nyu.edu/experience-stern/about/departments-centers-initiatives/centers-of-research/volatility-and-risk-institute/research/svb-and-beyond-banking-stress-2023. Accessed on January 18, 2025.

Albertazzi, Ugo, Fulvia Fringuellotti, and Steven Ongena. 2019. Fixed Rate Versus Adjustable Rate Mortgages: Evidence from Euro Area Banks. ECB Working Paper Series No. 2322. https://www.ecb.europa.eu/pub/pdf/scpwps/ecb.wp2322~0ed0879d8a.en.pdf. Accessed on January 18, 2025.

Angner, Erik. 2020. *A Course in Behavioral Economics*, 3rd Edition. New York, NY: Bloomsbury Academic.

Ayadi, Rym, David T. Llewellyn, Reinhard H. Schmidt, Emrah Arbak, and Willem Pieter De Groen. 2010. Investigating Diversity in the Banking Sector in Europe: Key Developments, Performance and Role of Cooperative Banks. Centre for European Policy Studies. https://www.ceps.eu/ceps-publications/investigating-diversity-banking-sector-europe-key-developments-performance-and-role/. Accessed on January 18, 2025.

Birn, Martin, Lea Charlotte Neugebauer, and Verena Seidl. 2023. Regional Distributions of Group 1 and Group 2 Banks and Their Impact on Results in the Basel III Monitoring Reports. In: Basel III Monitoring Report February 2023. 105–108. https://www.bis.org/bcbs/publ/d546.pdf. Accessed on January 18, 2025.

Busch, Ramona, Helge C. N. Littke, Christoph Memmel, and Simon Niederauer. 2021. German Banks' Behavior in the Low Interest Rate Environment. *Financial Markets and Portfolio Management*, Vol. 36, 267–296.

Campbell, John Y. 2013. Mortgage Market Design. *Review of Finance*, Vol. 17, No. 1, January 2013, 1–33.

Coulier, Lara, Cosimo Pancaro, and Alessio Reghezza. 2024. Are Low Interest Rates Firing Back? Interest Rate Risk in the Banking Book and Bank Lending in a Rising Interest Rate Environment. Bank for International Settlements, Working Paper No. 1202, August 2024. https://www.bis.org/publ/work1202.pdf. Accessed on January 18, 2025.

Cruz-García, Paula, Juan Fernández de Guevara, and Joaquín Maudos. 2019. Determinants of Bank's Interest Margin in the Aftermath of the Crisis: The Effect of Interest Rates and the Yield CURVE Slope. *Empirical Economics*, Vol. 56, 341–365.

Demiralp, Selva, Jens Eisenschmidt, and Thomas Vlassopoulos. 2021. Negative Interest Rates, Excess Liquidity, and Retail Deposits: Banks' Reaction to Unconventional Monetary Policy in the Euro Area. *European Economic Review*, Vol. 136, 103745.

EBA. 2022. Guidelines on the Management of Interest Rate Risk and Credit Spread Risk Arising from Non-trading Book Activities, Final Report, EBA/GL/2022/14 from 20 October 2022, Mandated by Article 84 (6) of Directive 2013/36/EU (Capital Requirements Directive, CRD), European Banking Authority. https://www.eba.europa.eu/sites/default/files/document_library/Publications/Guidelines/2022/EBA-GL-2022-14%20GL%20on%20IRRBB%20and%20CSRBB/1041754/Guidelines%20on%20IRRBB%20and%20CSRBB.pdf. Accessed on January 18, 2025.

ECB. 2017. Sensitivity Analysis of IRRBB – Stress Test 2017. European Central Bank, October 2017. https://www.bankingsupervision.europa.eu/press/pr/date/2017/html/ssm.pr171009.en/ssm.pr171009_slides.en.pdf. Accessed on January 18, 2025.

Gerut, Amanda. 2024. Top-Ranked Analyst Declares JPMorgan 'The Nvidia of Banking' After It Spends $17 Billion on Tech in a Single Year. *Fortune*, May 20, 2024. https://fortune.com/2024/05/20/jpmorgan-nvidia-of-banking-tech-mike-mayo. Accessed on January 18, 2025.

Grandi, Pietro, and Marianne Guille. 2023. Banks, Deposit Rigidity and Negative Rates. *Journal of International Money and Finance*, Vol. 133, 102810.

Hoffmann, Peter, Sebastian Frontczak, and Federico Pierobon. 2023. Modelling the Duration of Retail Bank Deposits, Draft Paper Prepared for Submission to the 2023 EBA Policy Research Workshop. https://www.eba.europa.eu/sites/default/files/document_library/Calendar/Conference-Workshop/2023/12th%20Annual%20Research%20Workshop%20-%20Interest%20rate%20and%20Liquidity%20Risk%20Management,%20Regulation%20and%20the%20Macro-economic%20environment/pepers%20and%20presentations/1063514/Federico%20Pierobon.pdf. Accessed on January 18, 2025.

Low, Jia Jen. 2020. Developers Now Make Up a Quarter of Goldman Sachs' Workforce. T_HQ, February 14, 2020. https://techhq.com/2020/02/developers-now-make-up-quarter-of-goldman-sachs-workforce. Accessed on January 18, 2025.

Present, Thomas, Mathieu Simoens, and Rudi Vander Vennet. 2023. European Bank Margins at the Zero Lower Bound. *Journal of International Money and Finance*, Vol. 131, 102803.

Tata, Fidelio. 2020. *Corporate and Investment Banking: Preparing for a Career in Sales, Trading, and Research*, Cham, CH: Palgrave Macmillan.

Valverde, Santiago Carbó, Timothy Cobau, and Francisco Rodríguez Fernández. 2019. Analysing Differences in Bank Profitability: Europe Versus the US. *Funcas SEFO*, Vol. 8, No. 2 (March 2019), 5–13.

Wigglesworth, Robin, and Chris Flood. 2018. BlackRock Bulks Up Research into Artificial Intelligence: World's Biggest Investment Group to Create AI Lab in Palo Alto. *The Financial Times*, February 20, 2018. https://www.ft.com/content/4f5720ce-1552-11e8-9376-4a6390addb44. Accessed on January 18, 2025.

4

Case Study: The Collapse of Silicon Valley Bank

Silicon Valley Bank (SVB) invested heavily in debt securities during a period of low interest rates. The rise in inflation in 2021–2023 resulted in significant unrealized losses, and on March 8, 2023, SVB reported losses of USD 1.8 bn on the sale of USD 21 bn in fixed income securities. This led to a bank run, in which SVB's customers attempted to withdraw USD 142 bn in deposits. On March 10, 2023, SVB collapsed and was seized by its regulator.[1] On March 17, 2023, SVB's holding company (SVBFG) filed a voluntary petition for court-supervised reorganization under Chapter 11 of the U.S. Bankruptcy Code.

In this chapter, we examine the factors that contributed to what became the second largest bank failure in U.S. history. We begin with a brief introduction to SVB and its business model is given. We then identify some early warning signs of the problems that emerged at SVB. We then take a deep dive into SVB's balance sheet to uncover specific ALM issues, using the ALM concept and framework we discussed in the previous chapters. We conclude with a list of lessons learned from the SVB disaster.

4.1 SVB Introduction

SVB was founded in 1983 in Santa Clara, California.[2] Its focus, as its name suggests, was on clients in the innovation, entrepreneurship, and technology industries located in the Silicon Valley area of Northern California. SVB grew to offer a full range of investment banking services, including asset management, private wealth management, fund management and M&A advisory

F. Tata, *Bank Asset-Liability Management*, https://doi.org/10.1007/978-3-031-80205-8_4

services. SVB experienced a rapid influx of deposits from venture capital (VC) and technology clients during a period of exceptionally low interest rates. These deposits were largely invested in securities with longer maturities.

By 2022, SVB's assets exceeded USD 200 bn, making it the 16th largest U.S. bank. On March 6, 2023—four days before its collapse—it proudly announced on what was then Twitter (now X) "to be @Forbes' annual ranking of America's Best Banks for the 5th straight year (...)".[3]

In 2022, two correlated developments negatively impacted SVB. First, VC activity declined sharply as part of a broader pullback in technology investment. This was partly due to higher interest rates and concerns about the economy. This affected the ability of SVB to fund itself from deposits related to VC activity. The second development was the rapid rise in interest rate, which led to a write-down of fixed-income assets on SVB's balance sheet.

4.2 Early Warning Signs

With respect to risk management, there were a number of red flags during the period leading up to the collapse. Ms. Laura Izurieta resigned from her position as Chief Risk Officer (CRO) on April 29, 2022,[4] and the bank was without a CRO for eight months until Ms. Kim Olson assumed the role of CRO on December 27, 2022.[5]

A second warning sign was the low degree to which SVB's approximately USD 124 bn bond portfolio was hedged against a potential rise in interest rates. Although a large portion of these bonds were highly interest rate sensitive (30-year mortgage-backed securities), only USD 15.3 bn of the securities portfolio, or about 12.3%, was hedged with pay-fixed, receive-floating interest rate swaps at the end of 2021.[6]

A third and even bigger warning sign was that in 2022 SVB started to unwind its interest rate hedges. About USD 11 bn of the USD 15.3 bn in interest rate swap positions were unwound in the first half of 2022. Not because SVB's bond portfolio was shrinking or because the risk of an interest rate increase was decreasing, but "to juice its P&L in the short term."[7] Removing only one side of a hedge increases risk. By the end of 2022, only USD 0.5 bn worth of interest rate hedges remained, hedging just 0.4% of SVB's bond portfolio.

Finally, SVB's unstable funding from fleeting short-term deposits was a red flag all along. Bank deposits are insured by the U.S. Federal Deposit Insurance Corporation (FDIC) up to a limit of USD 250,000 per depositor. These small deposits tend to be very stable. Non-FDIC-insured deposits, on the other hand, are often made by institutional investors who "park" their liquidity for only a short period of time and are also subject to rapid withdrawal at any sign of counterparty credit risk. At the end of 2021, the SVB estimated its uninsured deposits at USD 166 bn.[8] This not only represents a large percentage of total non-maturity customer deposits (more than 88%), but also reflects an 87% increase from SVB's uninsured deposits of USD 88.6 bn a year earlier.

4.3 An ALM View on SVB's Balance Sheet

In this section, we take a forensic look at SVB's balance sheet in order to assess the quality of the bank's ALM. We start by uncovering some hidden information within the so-called held-to-maturity (HTM) positions. Second, we put on the earnings perspective hat and look at the bank's net interest income (NII). Then we switch hats and put on the economic value hat and perform a duration gap analysis. Finally, we look at behavioral assumptions about the bank's depositor withdrawal activity.

4.3.1 At a Glance: GAAP vs. Non-GAAP

A first look at SVB's year-end balance sheet for 2022 shows that equity represents approximately 5.7% of total assets (USD 12 bn out of USD 212 bn). Large portions of customer deposits (i. e., the bank's funding) are invested in available-for-sale (AFS) and held-to-maturity (HTM) assets. HTM consists of long-term mortgage-backed securities (MBS) and other bonds.[9] See left panel of Fig. 4.1.

Under U.S. Generally Accepted Accounting Principles (GAAP), securities classified as HTM are purchased with the intent and ability to be held to maturity. Classification as HTM allows these securities to be carried at amortized historical cost rather than at their volatile mark-to-market value. AFS financial investments are not held to maturity and have a readily observable market price. Gains and losses resulting from the fair value measurement of AFS investments are recognized in other comprehensive income (OCI).

A more detailed analysis shows that there is already an unrealized GAAP loss of USD 15.2 bn GAAP hidden in the HTM book.[10] A 2.7% increase in interest rates would have caused this unrealized loss of USD 15.2 bn, implying a duration of 6.25 years on the USD 95 bn HTM book. Thus,

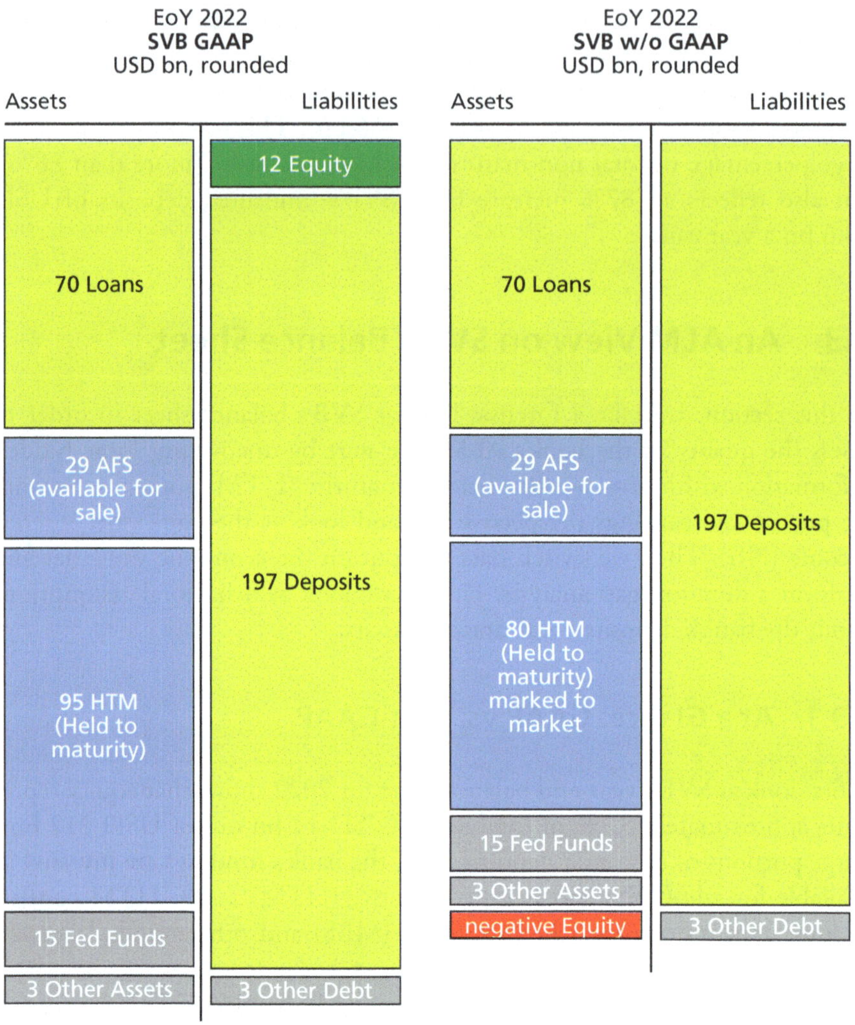

Fig. 4.1 SVB balance sheet: GAAP perspective

without the benefit of GAAP accounting, the bank's equity would have been completely wiped out by EoY 2022. See right panel of Fig. 4.1.

The AFS book can be estimated to have contributed an additional loss of approximately USD 1.7 bn on top of the unrealized loss in the HTM book.[11]

4.3.2 NII Perspective

From a net interest income (NII) perspective, the SVB appeared healthy in 2022, reporting an NII of USD 4.5 bn for the year ended December 31,

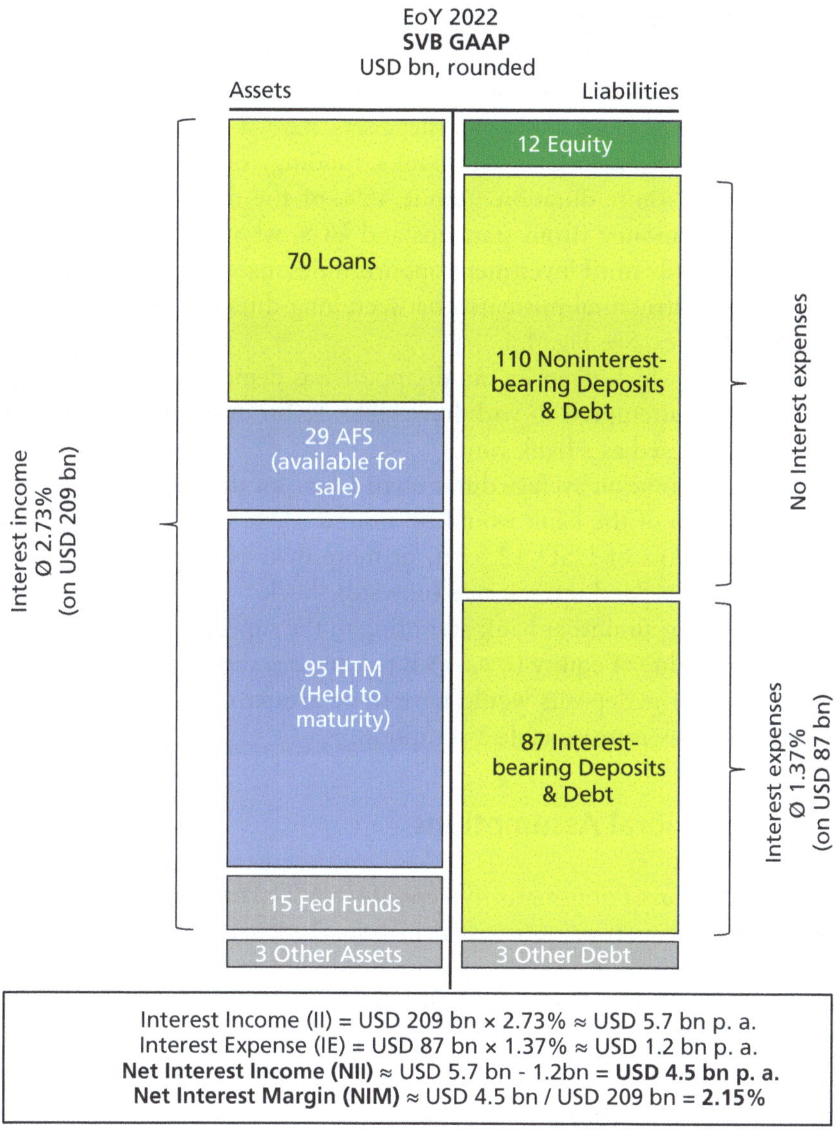

Fig. 4.2 SVB balance sheet: NII perspective

2022.[12] The NII resulted from an average interest income of 2.73% and an average interest expense of 0.57%. The net interest margin (NIM) is 2.15%.[13] See Fig. 4.2.

4.3.3 Duration Gap

Looking at the duration of the balance sheet items, the real problem of the SVB becomes clear. Some of the assets have a long duration, especially the HTM positions.[14] The bank's funding, on the other hand, is likely to have a short duration. About 45% of the deposits are early and later stage tech money (from start-ups and VCs, who typically only "park" money temporarily until investment opportunities materialize in the market). This suggests a structural mismatch between long-duration assets and short-duration liabilities. See Fig. 4.3.

The speed at which deposits can disappear was demonstrated in Q1:2023 when investors attempted to withdraw USD 42 bn in a single day in what can be characterized as a bank run.

Even if we assume an average duration of 1 year for the parked tech money, the duration gap of the bank would be around 3 years! A duration gap of 3 years implies a loss of USD 12.5 bn, or more than 100% of equity, in the event of a 200 bp Basel interest rate (upward) shock.[15]

To avoid being an outlier bank according to the supervisory outlier test on the economic value of equity (i. e., EVE risk for 2% shock < 15% of equity), the duration of the deposits would have to be greater than 3.7 years.[16] This would be a highly unreasonable assumption.

4.3.4 Behavioral Assumptions

Since the duration of non-maturity deposits (NMDs) cannot be derived from their contractual maturity (discussed in Sect. 2.4), it is necessary to model their duration based on behavioral assumptions about the extent and timing of depositors' withdrawal activity. This requires a sound understanding of the nature of a bank's customers.

SVB specialized in serving a relatively undiversified depositor base concentrated in technology startups. As SVB's 2022 annual report specifically noted, "deposits are largely obtained from commercial customers within [the] technology, life science / healthcare and private equity / venture capital industry sectors".[17] A low interest rate environment led these customers to temporarily "park" large amounts of raised capital at SVB.

When interest rates were low and SVB's depositors were flush with cash deposited at SVB, the bank invested heavily in long-term securities. Long-term assets, however, would decline in market value in the very interest rate environment in which one would expect depositors to withdraw money. And that's exactly what happened: As interest rates rose, a vicious cycle was set in

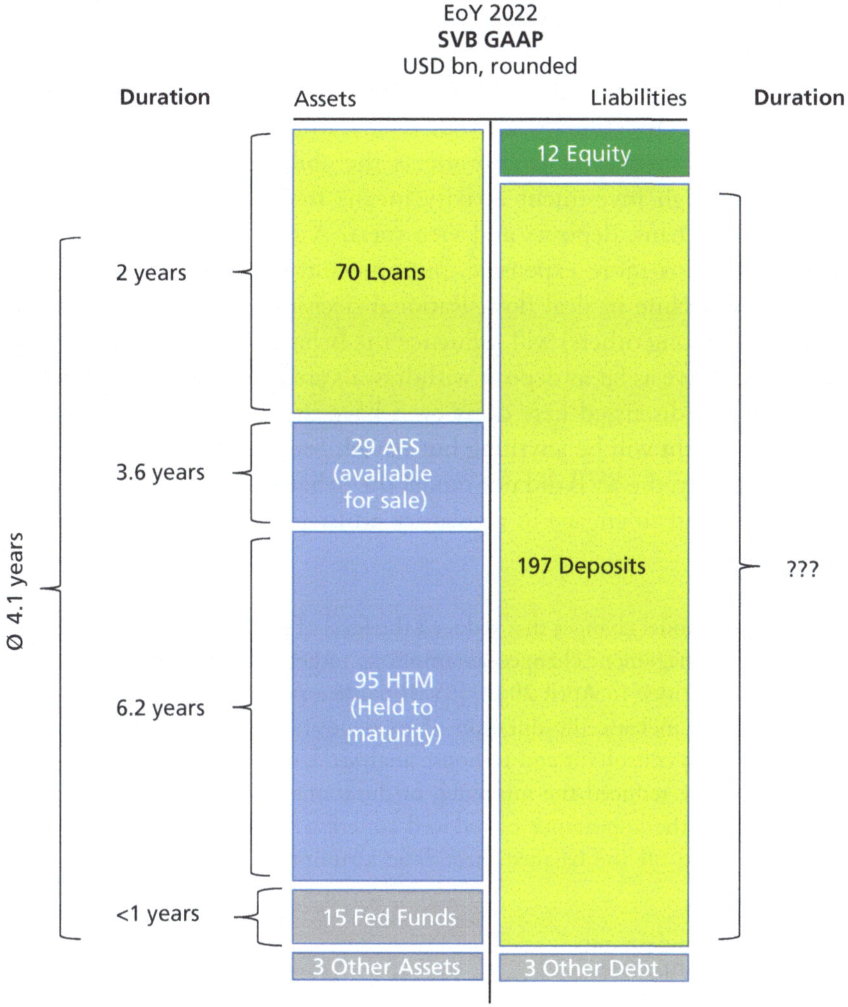

Fig. 4.3 SVB balance sheet: duration perspective

motion, with deposit withdrawals causing SVB to sell investments at a loss to raise cash. Because depositors in the startup space are tightly networked, word of SVB's losses spread quickly among depositors, and a "bad-news run" on SVB ensued.

In order to model the amount of cash that is temporarily "parked" in non-maturity deposits (NMDs) , at least two interrelated interest-dependent factors must be considered. First, the general level of interest rates (as well as their expected direction) affects how much money the investor community allocates to alternative investments, including private equity (PE) and venture capital (VC) funds. When interest rates are very low, investors tend to "chase yield" by shifting from low-risk to higher-risk investments. However, as interest rates rise, traditional investment opportunities provide sufficient returns and risk appetite for alternative investments declines. Second, the general level of interest rates also affects the ability of VC funds to invest in start-ups. High investment activity means that PE / VC funds have to withdraw their bank deposits and vice versa. A rise in interest rates makes financing startups more expensive, puts pressure on valuations and causes a temporary decline in deal flow. Rational decision making based on these two factors (among others) will influence the behavior of PE / VC funds that banks will observe as far as deposit withdrawals are concerned. Unfortunately, the two factors discussed here don't even have the same causal relationship, so modeling them will be anything but trivial. See Fig. 4.4.

Unfortunately, the SVB did not model the behavior of its depositors to best reflect reality, but to engage in regulatory arbitrage. Barr (2023) summarizes this as follows:

> [SVB] made model changes that reduced the level of risk depicted by the model (…) [and] management changed assumptions rather than the balance sheet to alter reported risks. In April 2022, [SVB] made a poorly supported change in assumption to increase the duration of its deposits based on a deposit study conducted by a consultant and in-house analysis. Under the internal models in use, the change reduced the mismatch of durations between assets and liabilities and gave the appearance of reduced [interest rate risk]; however, no risk had been taken off the balance sheet. The assumptions were unsubstantiated

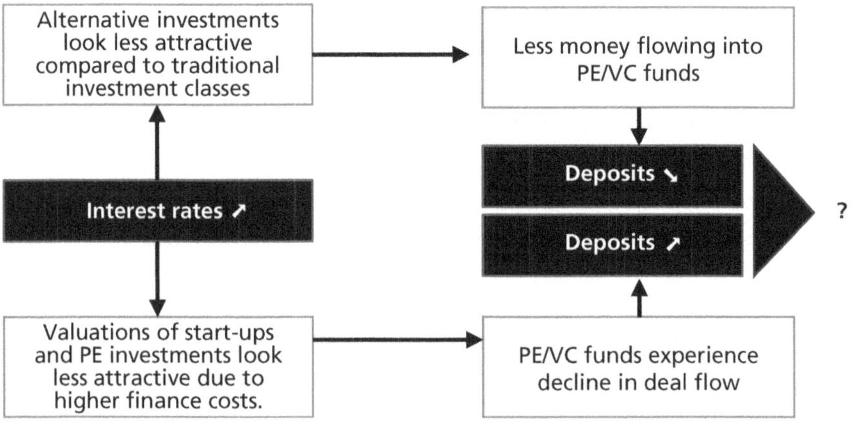

Fig. 4.4 Interest rates affecting deposit activity of PE / VC funds

> given recent deposit growth, lack of historical data, rapid increases in rates that shorten deposit duration, and the uniqueness of [SVB's] client base.[18]

4.4 Lessons Learned

The collapse of SVB was a failure on many levels. Michael S. Barr, Vice Chair for Supervision at the Federal Reserve, summed it up best in the following:

> Silicon Valley Bank (SVB) failed because of a textbook case of mismanagement by the bank. Its senior leadership failed to manage basic interest rate and liquidity risk. Its board of directors failed to oversee senior leadership and hold them accountable. And Federal Reserve supervisors failed to take forceful enough action, as detailed in the report.[19]

The main lessons may be summarized as follows:

- In certain situations, accounting allows for classifying away unrealized security losses from net income. This makes prudent ALM even more important.
- A proper governance of interest rate risk management is imperative. Flying blind for some eight months by not having a Chief Risk Office did not reflect well on SVB's board of directors and management. In this case, supervisors failed to catch the lack of governance.[20]
- The heavy concentration in SVB's customer base (mostly VC-backed technology and life sciences companies) should have received more supervisory attention. Modeling assumptions of the duration of highly correlated non-maturity deposits (NMDs) from a small group of similar depositors should have been questioned and challenged. Supervisors "identified interest rate risk deficiencies in the 2020, 2021, and 2022 Capital, Asset Quality, Management, Earnings, Liquidity, and Sensitivity to Market Risk (CAMELS) exams but did not issue supervisory findings."[21]
- Despite claims to the contrary,[22] large (and unhedged) maturity mismatches on banks' balance sheets pose a great potential danger.

Notes

1. See Brown (2023), Kim (2024, 2), Vo and Le (2023, 4).
2. For convenience, Silicon Valley Bank (SVB) and its holding company, Silicon Valley Bank Financial Group (SVBFG), will be treated synonymous.
3. SVB's Twitter account has been deleted, but its tweeds are still available at https://nypost.com/wp-content/uploads/sites/2/2023/03/NYPICHPDPICT000008239614.jpg. Accessed on January 18, 2025.
4. SVB (2023, 6).
5. SVB (2023, 74).
6. SVB (2022, 150). When interest rates rise, a pay-fixed swap gains value it receives higher floating rates, partially offsetting losses in fixed-income security positions.
7. Wigglesworth (2023).
8. SVB (2022, 82).
9. SVB (2022, 49).
10. SVB (2022, 125).
11. SVB (2022, 49).
12. SVB (2022, 7). NII accounted for approximately 72.6% of SVB's income. It consists mainly of income generated from interest rate spread differences between the interest rates SVB receives on interest-bearing assets, such as loans to customers and securities in SVB's fixed income portfolio, and the interest rates it pays on interest-bearing liabilities, such as deposits and borrowings.
13. SVB (2022, 49).
14. SVB (2022, 66).
15. Calculation: USD 209 bn $\times$ 2% $\times$ 3 [years] $\approx$ USD 12.5 bn.
16. Calculation: 4.1 [years] – { (15% $\times$ USD 12 bn) / (USD 209 bn $\times$ 2%)} $\approx$ 3.7 [years].
17. SVB (2022, 7).
18. Barr (2023, 63).
19. Barr (2023, 1).
20. According to Barr (2023, ii), "[with regard to] governance, Silicon Valley Bank was rated satisfactory in terms of management for both the holding company and the bank from 2017 through 2021, despite repeated observations of weak- ness in risk management."
21. Barr (2023, ii).
22. E. g., Drechsler et al. (2021, 1092) suggest "(…) that despite having a large maturity mismatch banks do not take on significant interest rate

risk (...) [and] that a big maturity mismatch actually insulates banks' profits from interest rate risk."

References

Barr, Michael S. 2023. Review of the Federal Reserve's Supervision and Regulation of Silicon Valley Bank, Board of Governors of the Federal Reserve System, April 28, 2023. https://www.federalreserve.gov/publications/files/svb-review-20230428.pdf. Accessed on January 18, 2025.

Brown, Eliot. 2023. Silicon Valley Bank Dropped a Hedge Against Rising Rates in 2022. *The Wall Street Journal*, 13 March 2023. https://www.wsj.com/livecoverage/stock-market-news-today-03-13-2023/card/silicon-valley-bank-dropped-a-hedge-against-rising-rates-in-2022-6MiD9ZLVY9CF8zbIM7ze. Accessed on January 18, 2025.

Drechsler, Itamar, Alexi Savov, and Philipp Schnabl. 2021. Banking on Deposits: Maturity Transformation Without Interest Rate Risk. *Journal of Finance*, Vol. 76, No. 3, 1091–1143.

Kim, Raymond. 2024. Hedging Securities and Silicon Valley Bank Idiosyncrasies. *Journal of Futures Markets*, Vol. 44, No. 4, 653–672.

SVB. 2022. Annual Report, available at: https://ir.svb.com/financials/annual-reports-and-proxies/default.aspx. Accessed on January 18, 2025.

SVB. 2023. Proxy Statement—Notice of Shareholders Meeting (Preliminary), available at: https://ir.svb.com/financials/annual-reports-and-proxies/default.aspx. Accessed on January 18, 2025.

Vo, Lai Van, and Huong Thi Thu Le. 2023. From Hero to Zero—The Case of Silicon Valley Bank. *Journal of Economics and Business*, Vol. 127, 106138.

Wigglesworth, Robin. 2023. How Crazy Was Silicon Valley Bank's Zero-Hedge Strategy? *Financial Times*, March 17, 2023. https://www.ft.com/content/f9a3adce-1559-4f66-b172-cd45a9fa09d6. Accessed on January 18, 2025.

5

Update on Regulatory and Supervisory Changes to IRRBB

Since October 2024, banks in the European Union are required to report to their supervisors the results of a new test that measures the risk of interest rate shifts on their *income* from deposits and lending activities in their banking book.

The new requirement is based on guidelines[1] and regulatory technical standards (RTSs)[2] specifying technical aspects of the revised framework for the measurement of interest rate risk arising from the banking book (IRRBB) published by the European Banking Authority (EBA) on October 20, 2022.

The EBA RTSs define two supervisory outlier tests (SOTs), one for economic value of equity (EVE) and one for net interest income (NII). While the former is just a minor update from the 2018 guidelines,[3] the latter is completely new. In addition, the RTSs detail the new standardized approach (SA) as well as the new simplified standardized approach (S-SA) for both EVE and NII.

In this chapter, we provide a brief historical overview of the European regulation and supervision of IRRBB, leading up to the most current requirements as of 2025. We then discuss the SA and the S-SA methodologies, as outlined by the RSTs, followed by the SOT on EVE and the SOT on NII. Finally, we discuss the simultaneous compliance problem presented by the two SOTs.

F. Tata, *Bank Asset-Liability Management*, https://doi.org/10.1007/978-3-031-80205-8_5

5.1 A Brief History of IRRBB Regulation

Interest rate risk arising from the banking book (IRRBB) is regulated by a number of organizations and authorities. Four layers are of particular importance: First, there is the overarching layer of supranational cooperation among global supervisors through the *Basel Committee on Banking Supervision* (BCBS). Second, at the European level, regulations and directives are adopted by the European Parliament and the Council. Third the *European Banking Authority* (EBA), as a regulatory agency of the European Union, is mandated to harmonize European banking regulation through binding technical standards and guidelines. Finally, *national authorities* play a role in transposing EU directives into national law.

The first three layers of banking regulation, with a focus on interest rate risk, are summarized in this section. Figure 5.1 provides a graphical overview of some of the milestones related to IRRBB.

5.1.1 Basel Committee on Banking Supervision (BCBS)

The Basel Committee on Banking Supervision (BCBS) was established in late 1974, partly in response to the failure of Bankhaus Herstatt in June 1974.[4] The BCBS has no formal supranational supervisory authority. Rather, it formulates broad supervisory standards and guidelines and recommends statements of best practice, with the expectation that individual regional authorities will take steps to implement them through detailed arrangements that are best suited to their own national systems.[5] As of 2016, the BCBS has 45 members from 28 jurisdictions, comprising of central banks and authorities with formal responsibility for the supervision of banking. In addition, the Committee has nine observers, including central banks, supervisory groups, international organizations and other bodies. The Committee's Secretariat is located at the Bank for International Settlements (BIS) in Basel, Switzerland.[6]

The first BCBS requirements for banks were captured in what is known as *Basel I* (titled "International Convergence of Capital Measurements and Capital Standards," also known as the *1988 Basel Accord*).[7] However, Basel I focuses is on credit risk and doesn't adequately address interest rate risk.

The history of supranational oversight of bank's interest rate risk can be traced back to 1993, when the BCBS issued a consultative proposal for measuring banks' exposure to interest rate risk[8] and, four years later, published the first version of its *Principles for the Management of Interest Rate Risk*.[9] These principles provide a framework for assessing banks' exposure

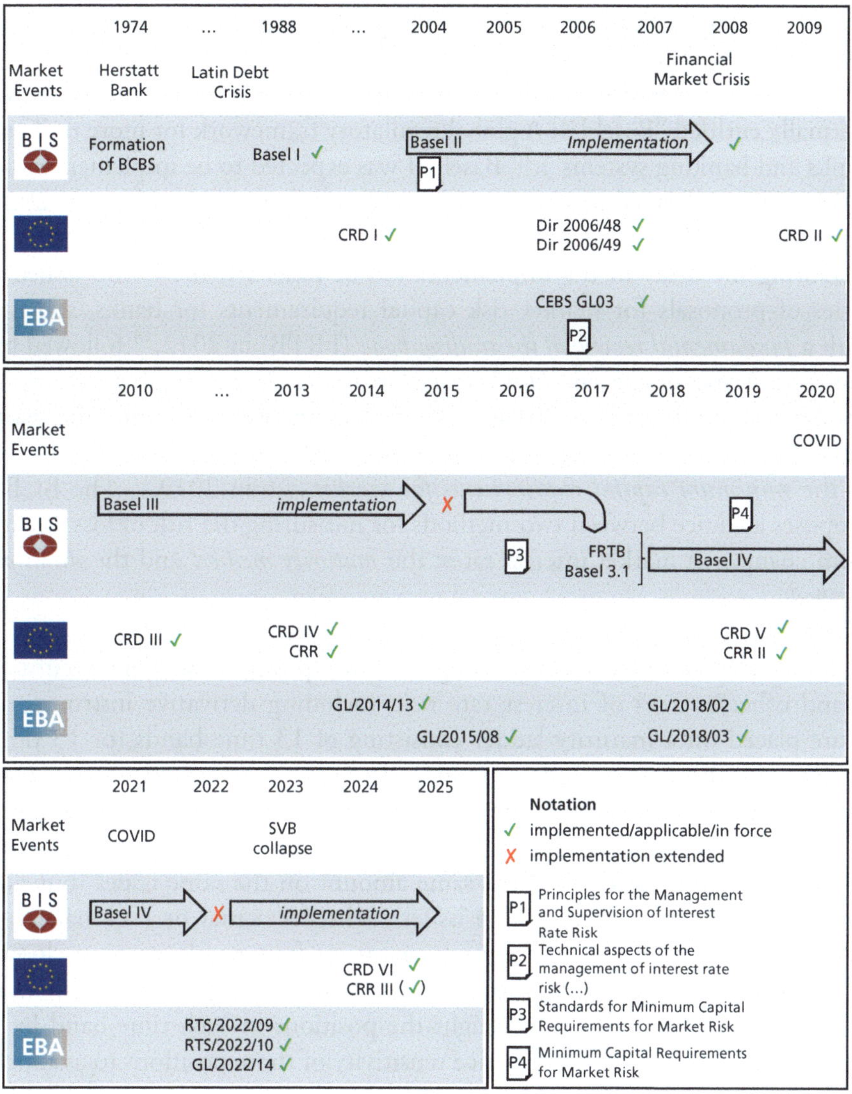

Fig. 5.1 European banking regulation timeline

to interest rate risk that incorporates both the earnings and economic value perspectives.

In July 2004, the BCBS issued an updated version of the *Principles for the Management and Supervision of Interest Rate Risk.*[10] In the same year, the BCBS issued the second Basel Accord, known as *Basel II* (entitled "International Convergence of Capital Measurement and Capital Standards: A Revised Framework").[11] In parallel, the interest rate risk framework was further developed, leading to the BCBS publication on *interest rate risk in the banking book* in 2016.[12]

In 2010, the BCBS issued the third Basel Accord, known as *Basel III* (formally entitled "Basel III: A global regulatory framework for more resilient banks and banking systems").[13] Basel III was expected to be implemented by 2015, but was delayed first to January 2022 and then again to January 2023 due to the COVID pandemic.

During the delay in the implementation of Basel III, the BCBS issued a series of proposals for market risk capital requirements for banks, starting with a *fundamental review of the trading book* (FRTB) in 2012,[14] followed by the consultative document *Fundamental review of the trading book: a revised market risk framework* in 2013,[15] which was incorporated into the *standards for minimum capital requirements for market risk* in 2016,[16] and led to the *minimum capital requirements for market risk* in 2019.[17] The BCBS proposes a choice between two methods for measuring the risk of loss arising from changes in market interest rates: the *maturity method* and the *duration method*.

- Under the *maturity method*, long or short positions in debt securities and other sources of interest rate risk, including derivative instruments, are placed on a maturity ladder consisting of 13 time bands (or 15 time bands in the case of low coupon instruments). Fixed-rate instruments are allocated according to the remaining time to maturity and variable-rate instruments according to the remaining time to the next repricing date. Opposite positions of the same amount on the same issues (but not on different issues of the same issuer), whether actual or notional, may be excluded from the interest rate maturity framework, as may closely matched swaps, forwards, futures and forward rate agreements. The first step in the calculation is to weight the positions in each time band by a factor designed to reflect the price sensitivity of those positions to assumed changes in interest rates. The weights for each time band are provided by the BCBS. The next step in the calculation is to offset the weighted longs and shorts in each time band, resulting in a single short or long position for each band.
- Under the alternative *duration method*, banks with the capability to do so use a more accurate method of measuring their overall market risk by calculating the price sensitivity of each position separately.

Improvements and additions to the Basel III framework, such as the fundamental review of the trading book, are referred to as Basel 3.1, or as Basel IV. Its implementation has been delayed and is now scheduled for January 2026.

5.1.2 European Parliament and Council

On the basis of Article 289 of the Treaty on the Functioning of the European Union, the European Parliament and the Council may adopt European regulations and directives. EU *regulations* are directly applicable because they create law that is immediately effective in all EU member states in the same way as national law, without any further action on the part of the national authorities. EU *directives*, on the other hand, must be transposed into national law by the national authorities of the EU member states.

With respect to IRRBB regulation, one set of EU directives and one set of EU regulations are particularly important: First, a series of legislative packages aimed, inter alia, at ensuring the financial soundness of banks and setting global standards for bank capital, collectively referred to as the *Capital Requirements Directives (CRD)*. Second, a body of EU regulation known as the *Capital Requirements Regulation (CRR)*.

5.1.2.1 Capital Requirements Directives (CRD)

The *Capital Requirements Directives (CRD)* establish a regulatory framework for the financial services industry in the European Union that reflects the Basel rules on capital measurement and capital standards.

The first legislative package in the CRD series, was adopted in 2000. CRD I (2000) codified previous directives in banking regulation and included measures of risk, for example in the calculation of risk-adjusted assets (in Article 42), with a focus on credit risk rather than interest rate risk.

In 2006, Directive 2006/48/EC and Directive 2006/49/EC repealed CRD I (2000) and are now commonly referred to as CDR I. An important milestone in the regulation of interest rate risk is Directive 2006/48/EC. Article 124(5) laid the groundwork for what later became the *supervisory outlier test* or standard interest rate shock. Sudden and unexpected changes in interest rates should not result in a decline of more than 20% of economic capital:

> The review and evaluation performed by competent authorities shall include the exposure of credit institutions to the interest rate risk arising from non-trading activities. Measures shall be required in the case of institutions whose economic value declines by more than 20 % of their own funds as a result

> of a sudden and unexpected change in interest rates the size of which shall be prescribed by the competent authorities and shall not differ between credit institutions.[18]

The second package, known as CRD II, followed in 2009. CRD II (2009) did not significantly address interest rate risk.

The third package, referred to as CRD III, was adopted in 2010. CRD III (2010) acknowledged interest rate risk by stating that "[t]he Commission should also be empowered to adopt delegated acts (...) in respect of measures to specify the size of sudden and unexpected changes in interest rates relevant for the purposes of the review and evaluation by the competent authorities (...) of interest rate risk arising from non-trading activities."[19]

The fourth package, known as CRD IV, was implemented in 2013. CRD IV (2013), in Article 84 (titled "Interest risk arising from non-trading book activities"), states:

> Competent authorities shall ensure that institutions implement systems to identify, evaluate and manage the risk arising from potential changes in interest rates that affect an institution's non-trading activities.[20]

More specifically, Article 98 (5) reads as follows:

> The review and evaluation performed by competent authorities shall include the exposure of institutions to the interest rate risk arising from non-trading activities. Measures shall be required at least in the case of institutions whose economic value declines by more than 20 % of their own funds as a result of a sudden and unexpected change in interest rates of 200 basis points or such change as defined in the EBA guidelines.[21]

This 200 basis point stress test is what we have already referred to in Sect. 1.2.1. as the *supervisory outlier test*, or as the *Basel interest rate shock.*

The fifth package, referred to as CRD V, was adopted in 2019 and has been in force since 2021. CRD V (2019) amends CRD IV (2013) and mandates the development of technical standards for the measurement of interest rate risk:

> In order to harmonise the calculation of the interest rate risk arising from non-trading book activities when the institutions' internal systems for measuring that risk are not satisfactory, the Commission should be empowered to adopt regulatory technical standards developed by the European Supervisory Authority (European Banking Authority) (EBA) (...). In order to improve the competent authorities' identification of those institutions which might

be subject to excessive losses in their non-trading book activities as a result of potential changes in interest rates, the Commission should be empowered to adopt regulatory technical standards developed by EBA. Those regulatory technical standards should specify: the six supervisory shock scenarios that all institutions have to apply in order to calculate changes in the economic value of equity; the common assumptions that institutions have to implement in their internal systems for the purpose of calculating the economic value of equity, and in respect of determining the potential need for specific criteria to identify the institutions for which supervisory measures might be warranted following a decrease in the net interest income attributed to changes in interest rates; and what constitutes a large decline.[22]

Article 98 of CRD IV (2013) is also amended by CRD V (2019) as follows:

The supervisory powers shall be exercised at least in the following cases:
(a) where an institution's economic value of equity (...) declines by more than 15 % of its Tier 1 capital as a result of a sudden and unexpected change in interest rates as set out in any of the six supervisory shock scenarios applied to interest rates;
(b) where an institution's net interest income (...) experiences a large decline as a result of a sudden and unexpected change in interest rates as set out in any of the two supervisory shock scenarios applied to interest rates.[23]

This was an important development in the measurement of interest rate risk under the CRD, as the economic value perspective (loss of 15% of Tier 1 capital) was complemented by the earnings perspective (decline in NII) as part of the IRRBB analysis.

The sixth (and, as of this writing, final) CRD package, referred to as CRD VI, was adopted in 2024. CRD VI (2024) further amends CRD IV (2013) with respect to non-IRRBB aspects, such as supervisory powers, sanctions, third-country branches, and environmental, social, and governance risks. While CRD VI entered into force in 2024, the deadline for transposition into national law by member states is January of 2026.

5.1.2.2 Capital Requirements Regulation (CRR)

The *Capital Requirements Regulation (CRR)* is a body of European Union legislation aimed at reducing the likelihood of bank insolvency.

The first legislative package in the CRR series, referred to as CRR I, was adopted in 2013. CRR I (2013) treated risks mostly from a credit perspective

(e. g., when dealing with credit risk mitigation in Chapter 4), rather than from an interest rate perspective.

An amendment to CRR I was adopted in 2019 and is now referred to as CRR II. CRR II (2019), in force since 2021, explicitly captures interest rate risk. For example, in Article 325bh (entitled "Requirements on risk measurement"), one of the requirements listed is:

> [T]he internal risk-measurement model shall incorporate a set of risk factors that correspond to the interest rates in each currency in which the institution has interest rate sensitive on- or off-balance-sheet positions; the institution shall model the yield curves using one of the generally accepted approaches; the yield curve shall be divided into various maturity segments to capture the variations of volatility of rates along the yield curve; for material exposures to interest-rate risk in the major currencies and markets, the yield curve shall be modeled using a minimum of six maturity segments, and the number of risk factors used to model the yield curve shall be proportionate to the nature and complexity of the institution's trading strategies, the model shall also capture the risk spread of less than perfectly correlated movements between different yield curves or different financial instruments on the same underlying issuer.[24]

In 2024, a further legislative act amending CRR I was adopted, referred to as CRR III.[25] CRR III (2024) amends previous versions of CRR regarding requirements for credit risk, CVA risk, operational risk, market risk and the output floor.

CRR III will generally be applicable from January 2025, although the European Commission has delayed the application of the market risk rules and the Fundamental Review of the Trading Book (FRTB) by one year to January 2026 through a delegated act.[26]

5.1.3 European Banking Authority (EBA)

The *European Banking Authority (EBA)* is a regulatory agency of the European Union tasked with working towards the so-called "single rulebook," which provides a single set of harmonized prudential rules to which institutions throughout the EU must adhere.[27] The EBA contributes to this by issuing *Guidelines (GL)* and *Regulatory Technical Standards (RTS).*

In October 2006, the *Committee of European Banking Supervisors* (CEBS), which was replaced in 2011 by the European Banking Authority (EBA), published *guidelines on the application of the supervisory review process under pillar 2 (CP03 revised)*[28] and, building on this, its *technical aspects of the management of interest rate risk arising from non-trading activities under the supervisory review process.*[29] CEBS (2006b) defines interest rate risk as the "current or prospective risk to both the earnings and capital of institutions arising from adverse movements in interest rates" and acknowledges that the "[c]onsideration of interest rate risk from the perspectives of both short-term earnings and economic value is important."[30] Nevertheless, this early treatment of interest rate risk still focuses on the *economic value perspective*:

> However, measurement of the impact on economic value (the present value of the bank's expected net cash flows) provides a more comprehensive view of the potential longterm effects on an institution's overall exposures. Therefore, the supervisory focus will primarily be on measuring interest rate risk in relation to economic value. However, and subject to proportionality considerations, institutions are also expected to consider interest rate risk in relation to earnings as a supplementary measure.[31]

CEBS (2006b) also proposed four measures of interest rate risk arising from the banking book (IRRBB), consistent with our definition of interest rate risk in Sect. 1.2.2: Repricing and yield curve risk (which we treated in combination as gap risk), basis risk, and option risk. Furthermore, the *standard shock*, since then also referred to as the *Basel interest rate shock* or *supervisory outlier test*, based on Article 124(5) of EU (2006), was defined:

> A standard shock could, for example, be set so that it will be broadly equivalent to the 1st and 99th percentile of observed interest rate changes (five years of observed one day movements scaled up to a 240 day year), This would currently equate approximately to a parallel 200 basis points shock for major currencies as suggested by the Basel Committee (...).[32]

In 2014, EBA (2014) issued the guideline GL/2014/13 on common procedures and methodologies for the *Supervisory Review and Evaluation Process* (SREP). SREP, as defined in CRD IV (2013), is a review process in which competent authorities review compliance with CRR I (2013) and assess banks' risks, including interest rate risk arising from non-trading activities. Outlier banks are defined as "institutions whose economic value declines by more than 20% of their own funds as a result of a sudden and unexpected change in interest rates of 200 basis points or such change as defined in the EBA guidelines."[33] In Sect. 6.5 of EBA (2014), SREP is detailed with respect to interest rate risk from non-trading activities, or IRRBB.[34]

In 2015, EBA (2015) issued the guideline GL/2015/08 on the management of interest rate risk arising from non-trading activities (IRRBB). EBA (2015) acknowledges the importance of assumptions when assessing interest rate risk for products or positions where the assumed behavioral repricing date differs significantly from the contractual repricing date, or where there is no stated contractual repricing date (non-maturity products). EBA (2015, 11) categorizes the key assumptions when assessing exposure to interest rate risk for economic value and earnings at risk (EaR, defined as the short-term sensitivity of earnings to interest rate movements) as follows:

- Behavioral assumptions for accounts with embedded customer optionality
- Behavioral assumptions for customer accounts without specific repricing dates, particularly those with no (or a very low) interest rate attached
- Banks' planning assumptions for the investment term of own equity capital

EBA (2015, 11) also illustrates cases where customers have exercisable embedded options that affect the product's interest rate repricing characteristics, such as:

- Prepayment options
- Options to extend maturity
- Options to modify interest rate characteristics

EBA (2015, 30) requires the bank to use at least one earnings-based measure and at least one economic value measure of interest rate risk for the monitoring of IRRBB.

Annex A of EBA (2015) provides a list of quantitative tools and models are listed, along with their advantages and limitations, including economic value measures (discussed in Sect. 2.1) and earnings measures (discussed in Sect. 2.2).

In 2018, the EBA issued the guidelines GL/2018/02 and GL/2018/03 on the management of interest rate risk arising from non-trading book activities. EBA (2018a) provides updated guidelines on IRRBB, while EBA (2018b) details guidelines on the revised SREP and supervisory stress testing, based on BCBS (2016a). Both are effective from 2019.

EBA (2018a, 7–8) introduces a set of *principles* that institutions should apply when calculating the *supervisory outlier test*:

- All interest rate sensitive instruments should be included
- Small trading book business should be included unless its interest rate risk is captured in another risk measure
- Common equity tier 1 (CET1) capital and other perpetual own funds without any call dates should be excluded

- Automatic and behavioral options should be included
- Pension obligations should be included unless their interest rate risk is captured in another measure
- Repayments and repricing of principal should be considered as well as any interest rate payments
- If the NPE ratio is above the materiality threshold of 2%, NPEs should be included net of provisions and should reflect the expected cash flow associated with these assets
- Instrument-specific interest rate floors should be considered
- The treatment of commercial margins and other spread components in interest payments in terms of their exclusion or inclusion into the cash flows should be in accordance with the institution's internal management and measurement approach
- A run-off balance sheet should be applied
- Lower reference rate of −100 basis points (linear function between −100 (0 year) and 0 basis points (20 + years)) is to be applied
- Material currencies are to be considered
- For exposures in various currencies, aggregation of negative and positive changes is to be applied weighting the positive changes by a factor of 50%
- One risk-free yield curve is to be applied per currency
- For non-maturity deposits (NMDs), maximum average maturity of 5 years is to be used

EBA (2018a, 8) prescribes two thresholds for measuring the change in the economic value of equity, the first stemming from Article 98 (5) of CRD IV (2013), the second from BCBS (2016b):

- The impact of parallel changes in interest rates of ± 200 basis points on a bank's own funds. If the decline in economic value is greater than 20%, the bank needs to inform the competent authority immediately
- The impact of six pre-defined shock scenarios on a bank's own funds. If the decline in economic value is greater than 15% of Tier 1 capital, the bank needs to inform the competent authority

The *six pre-defined shock scenarios* used in the second threshold are defined in Annex III of EBA (2018a):

- parallel shock up
- parallel shock down
- steepener shock (short rates down and long rates up)

- flattener shock (short rates up and long rates down)
- short rates shock up
- short rates shock down

EBA (2018a), in paragraph 115(k), also defines a maturity-dependent post-shock *interest rate floor* to be applied for each currency, starting at −100 basis points for immediate maturities and increasing by 5 basis points per year, eventually reaching 0% for maturities of 20 years and longer.

In 2022, the EBA issued two sets of regulatory technical standards, RTS/2022/09 and RTS/2022/10, and a guideline, GL/2022/14. The guideline, EBA (2022a), came into force in 2023. The technical standard specifying a standardized approach and a simplified standardized approach for assessing the risks arising from potential changes in interest rates that affect both the economic value of equity and the net interest income of an institution's non-trading book activities (hereinafter RTS/2022/09), which is based on EBA (2022b), was implemented by Commission Delegated Regulation (EU) 2024/857 and entered into force on May 14, 2024.[35] The technical standard specifying the supervisory shock scenarios, the common modeling and parametric assumptions and what constitutes a large decline (hereinafter RTS/2022/10) that is (based on EBA (2022c) was implemented by Commission Delegated Regulation (EU) 2024/856 and also entered into force on May 14, 2024.[36]

EBA (2022a), i.e. the guideline GL/2022/14, provides a regulatory framework for banks' internal measurement with respect to IRRBB, as well as a regulatory framework for the assessment and monitoring of credit spread risk arising from the banking book (CSRBB). The treatment of IRRBB is largely unchanged from the EBA 2018a, b Guidelines and is only enhanced in some areas, such as the prudent behavioral assumption for non-maturity deposits (NMDs) from non-financial counterparties.[37] What is completely new is the elaboration of the CSRBB.

RTS/2022/09 and RTS/2022/10, i.e. the technical standards, specify standardized and simplified standardized approaches for assessing the risks arising from potential changes in interest rates affecting both the economic value of equity and the net interest income of an institution's non-trading book activities, as well as supervisory shock scenarios, common modeling and parametric assumptions, and what constitutes a large decline for the purpose of calculating the economic value of equity and net interest income. Details are provided in the next two sections.

5.2 IRRBB Measures

Mandated by Article 98 of CRD IV (2013), RTS/2022/09 has developed regulatory technical standards (RTS) for a standardized approach (SA) and simplified standardized approach (S-SA) for the purpose of assessing the *risks arising from potential changes in interest rates* that affect both the Economic Value of Equity (EVE) and the Net Interest Income (NII) of an institution's non-trading book activities.

The standardized approach was developed with the goal of the most accurate representation of risk under standardized, proportionate assumptions. The simplified standardized methodology was designed for the generally less sophisticated capabilities of the small and non-complex institutions.

5.2.1 EBA Standardized Approach (SA)

RTS/2022/09 defines a *standardized approach (SA)* for the measurement of IRRBB for both EVE and for NII.

The EBA standardized approach (SA) for the Economic Value of Equity (EVE) calculates the *change in the economic value of equity* by subtracting the economic value of equity in the baseline scenario from the economic value of equity in the shock scenarios.

The *EBA standardized approach (SA)* to net interest income (NII)[38] calculates NII for the baseline scenario and for each individual interest rate shock scenario as the sum of three NII sub-components:

- The aggregation of interest payments up to and including the repricing date (i.e., NII flows that are already fixed and whose amount will not change as a result of interest rate changes); plus
- the projection of the risk-free return for each repricing cash flow between the moment of repricing up to the end of the projection horizon, in accordance with the assumption of a constant balance sheet; plus
- the projection of the commercial margin for each notional repricing cash flow between the moment of the reset of the margin (typically at the instrument's maturity) up to the end of the projection horizon, in accordance with the assumption of a constant balance sheet.

For both the SA on EVE and the SA on NII, an add-on for automatic optionality is computed. In addition, some limits are placed on behavioral assumptions about the timing and amount of the customer cash flows, e. g., for non-maturity retail and wholesale deposits, loan prepayments, term deposit redemption rates, and loan commitments.

As for the projected commercial margin component of NII (of new business production), it should be based on the commercial margin of instruments originated in the previous year.

In order to address the fundamental problem that NII calculations do not show the impact of interest rate changes that are outside of the net interest income calculation horizon (see Sect. 2.2.6), the EBA has included a component in the SA on NII that measures market value changes for these instruments. The calculation is based on a similar calculation as for EVE, but excludes instruments that are not market to market.[39] To avoid double counting, cash flows falling within the NII horizon are excluded from the calculation of market value changes.

5.2.2 EBA Simplified Standardized Approach(S-SA)

The *simplified standardized approach (S-SA)* was developed to reflect the generally less advanced capabilities of the small and non-complex bank and to meet the need for a methodology that is at least as conservative as the standardized approach (SA).[40]

Simplifications include the treatment of non-maturity core deposits and cash flows, the impact of an increase in volatility on automatic options, the granularity of commercial margins, and the calculation of interest payments up to and including the repricing date.

5.3 Supervisory Outlier Tests

As part of the Supervisory Review and Evaluation Process (SREP), Article 98 of CRD IV (2013) requires competent authorities review and assess bank's exposure to the interest rate risk arising from non-trading book activities (IRRBB). *Supervisory outlier tests (SOT)* are envisaged to enhance the ability of competent authorities' ability to identify banks that may be exposed to excessive losses in their non-trading book activities as a result of potential changes in interest rates, both from an economic value and an income perspective.

RTS/2022/10 defines specific supervisory outlier tests for EVE and on NII.

5.3.1 Supervisory Outlier Test on EVE

A *supervisory outlier test (SOT) on EVE* is envisaged to identify banks whose economic value of equity (EVE) falls by more than 15% of their Tier 1 capital under a shock scenario.

EBA (2018a), i. e., the guidelines on the management of interest rate risk arising from non-trading book activities (EBA/GL/2018/02), already laid out the EBA supervisory outlier test (SOT) with respect to the economic value of equity (EVA). RTS/2022/10 keeps the supervisory shock scenarios found in Article 98 of CRD IV (2013) and in Annex III of EBA (2018a). They are listed in Sect. 5.1.3.

RTS/2022/10 requires the change in EVE to be calculated under the assumption of a run-off balance sheet, where existing positions mature and are not replaced.

RTS/2022/10 also recalibrates the maturity dependent post-shock *interest rate floor* defined in paragraph 115(k) of EBA (2018a) to reflect the fact that in March 2022 and again in December 2020 the baseline (unshocked) interest rate moved below the floor. The new so-called *linear floor* is defined as a lower bound starting with -150 basis points for immediate maturities and increasing linearly by 3 bps per year, reaching 0% for maturities of 50 years.

5.3.2 Supervisory Outlier Test on NII

A *supervisory outlier test (SOT) on NII* is envisaged to identify banks whose one-year net interest income (NII) experiences a large decline in the context of a shock scenario. A "large decline" is defined as the ratio of the change in a bank's accounting NII[41] to its Tier 1 capital exceeding 5%.[42]

Many assumptions for the calculation of SOT on EVE and SOT on NII are harmonized, in particular those listed in Articles 3(2) to 3(4) and 3(7) to 3(10) of RTS/2022/10. However, there are two fundamental differences. Article 4 specifies that for the calculation of SOT on NII,

- *commercial margins* (and other spread components) must be included (whereas for EVE they may be excluded), and
- the change in NII must be calculated over a one-year horizon under the assumption of a *constant balance sheet*, where its total size and composition, including on- and off-balance sheet items, shall be maintained by replacing maturing or repricing cash flows with new instruments that have comparable features with regard to the currency, amount and repricing period of the instruments generating the repricing cash flows.

Currently, RTS/2022/10 NII SOT calculations do not include a linear floor.

5.4 The Simultaneous Compliance Problem

A *simultaneous compliance problem* refers to a situation where compliance with one (regulatory) constraint threatens compliance with another one. With respect to SOT, this is the case when a bank aims to become neither an outlier bank with respect to EVE nor an outlier bank with respect to NII.

If a bank is looking for the right amount and the right duration of fixed-rate assets that would be a SOT-compliant match for a large sight deposit position (modeled by the EBA standardized approach), two partially conflicting requirements must be met:

- The SOT on EVE limit imposes an upper and lower bound on the proportion of fixed-rate assets as a function of asset duration.
- The SOT on NII limit imposes a minimum amount of fixed assets.

Each requirement defines its own range of possible combinations between the share of fixed rate assets and their duration. In order to satisfy both at the same time, an optimization has to be performed. An illustrative sketch of the constraints of a linear optimization problem between SOT EVE and SOT NII requirements is shown in Fig. 5.2. Violated constraints are shown in gray, while feasible solutions are shown in white.

The zone of compliance may be very small and may move over time as a function of volume changes.

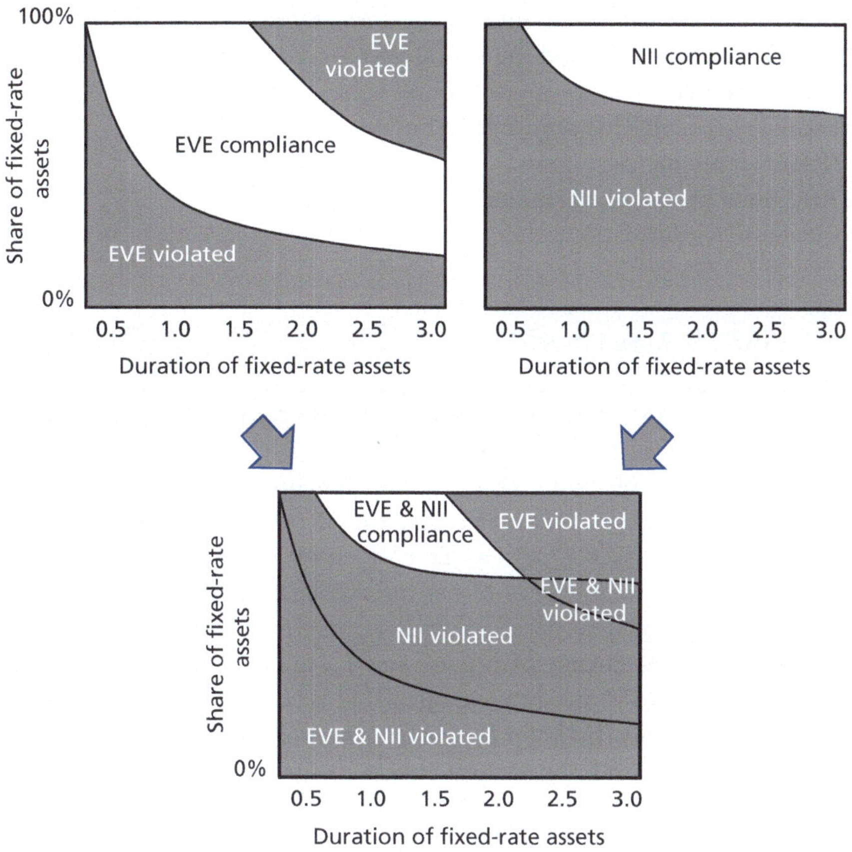

Fig. 5.2 Simultaneous compliance problem: EVE vs. NII

5.5 Supervisory Reporting of IRRBB

Supervisory reporting of interest rate risk in the banking book is detailed in Commission implementing regulation (EU) 2024/855 of 15 March 2024.[43] It details the reporting requirements for banks to provide supervisors with the data needed to monitor interest rate risk in the banking book (IRRBB) and the impact of changes in interest rates, including the interaction of the IRRBB with the bank's management of interest rate risk and the identification of outliers under both the supervisory outlier test (SOT) for economic value of equity and the SOT for net interest income.

Annex II to regulation (EU) 2024/855 contains five sets of templates:

- IRRBB assessment using supervisory outlier tests (SOTs) on economic value of equity (EVE) and the net interest income (NII), and market value (MV) changes
- Breakdown of IRRBB sensitivity estimates
- IRRBB repricing cash flows
- Behavioral modeling parameters
- Qualitative information

5.5.1 IRRBB Assessment

IRRBB is evaluated from the economic value perspective and from the income perspective. The economic value perspective focuses on the level of economic value of equity (EVE) under baseline and supervisory shock scenarios, as well as on the change of EVE (Δ EVE) and the ratio of the change of EVE to Tier 1 capital (Δ EVE ratio). The income perspective requires calculation of the level of net interest income (NII) under baseline and supervisory shock scenarios, as well as on the change of NII (Δ NII) and the ratio of the change of NII to Tier 1 capital (Δ NII ratio). Finally, the market value (MV) needs to be calculated according to a bank's internal measurement systems (IMS) for the carrying amount over a one-year horizon under the baseline and supervisory shock scenarios, as well as its change (Δ MV).

Table 5.1 provides a frame of reference for the main positions to be reported in the IRRBB assessment with reference to sections of the book where the relevant concepts are discussed.

5.5.2 Breakdown of IRRBB Sensitivity Estimates

This template requires a further breakdown of a bank's sensitivity estimates (Δ EVE, Δ NII, Δ MV) by balance sheet position and currency.

Assets include assets vis-à-vis central banks, interbank assets, loans and advances, debt securities, derivatives hedging assets and certain off-balance-sheet assets. Liabilities include liabilities to central banks, interbank liabilities, debt securities issued, non-maturity deposits (NMDs) , term deposits, derivatives hedging liabilities and certain off-balance-sheet liabilities.

Table 5.1 Reference frameworks for IRRBB assessment

Concept	*Measure*	*Calculated as*	*Detailed in Section*
EV	EVE	Level under baseline scenario	2.1
		Level under shock scenarios	
	Δ EVE	Change of EVE under "parallel shock up" scenario	
		Change of EVE under "parallel shock down" scenario	
		Change of EVE under "steepener shock" scenario	
		Change of EVE under "flattener shock" scenario	
		Change of EVE under "short rates shock up" scenario	
		Change of EVE under "short rates shock down" scenario	
	ΔEVE ratio	Ratio of the worst ΔEVE to Tier 1 capital	
NII	NII	Level under baseline scenario	2.2
		Level under shock scenarios	
	Δ NII	Change of NII under "parallel shock up" scenario	
		Change of NII under "parallel shock down" scenario	
	Δ NII ratio	Ratio of the worst Δ NII to Tier 1 capital	
MV	MV	Level under baseline scenario	2.2.6
		Level under shock scenarios	
	Δ MV	Change of MV under "parallel shock up" scenario	
		Change of MV under "parallel shock down" scenario	

5.5.3 IRRBB Repricing Cash Flows

This template requires banks to report repricing cash flows for the balance sheet items reported in the above templates. This information should be reported from an EVE perspective, taking into account the requirements and modeling assumptions specified in the EBA supervisory outlier test (SOT), and separately for each currency.

Contractual and behavioral information shall be reported, considering different forms of optionality:

- *Contractual optionality* assumes contractual repricing dates without considering behavioral assumptions. Only contractual and legal features (excluding automatic options and legal options[44]) are considered. The cash flow profile of non-maturity products (including NMDs) should be treated as short-term variable positions (shortest time bucket). Behavioral early termination and prepayment are not applied.

- *Behavioral modeling* in the baseline scenario should be consistent with the modeled repricing cash flows, which take behavioral assumptions into account where appropriate.
- *Automatic* optionality may be *explicit* from standalone instruments (including derivatives such as caps, floors and swaptions) or *embedded* in the contractual terms of other standard banking products.

5.5.4 Behavioral Modeling Parameters

In this template, *average repricing dates* are to be calculated as a weighted average of the repricing dates and the notional repricing cash flows of the positions in each relevant NMD category with a further breakdown of the part deemed to be the *core volume* (for those NMD's different to wholesale financial).

The pass-through rate (PTR), defined as the weighted average percentage of the interest rate shock assumed to be passed through to their non-maturity deposits (NMDs) under the interest rate regulatory scenarios and the NII metric specified in the EBA RTS on SOT, must be reported per NMD category. This recognizes that the rates set by the bank, known as administered rates, are only *loosely related* to market rates and that the pass-through of changes in market rates to sight deposit rates is partial (see Sect. 2.5.8 and Fig. 2.36).

Finally, *prepayment* and *early redemption risks* must be specified by providing average repricing dates and conditional prepayment and early redemption rates, respectively.

5.5.5 Qualitative Information

The fifth template collects qualitative data on the methodologies used in the IRRBB assessment based on a predefined list of options. Specific questions include:

- Which approach is used for SOT EVE and SOT NII, the Standardized Approach (SA), the Simplified Standardized Approach (S-SA), or an Internal Measurement System (IMS).

- The method used to calculate the SOT NII and the SOT EVE, i.e. repricing or duration gap analysis, a full revaluation, or a mix/other method.
- An indication of whether conditional cash flows, option risk, basis risk, loan prepayment penalty fees, pension obligations/pension plan assets, non-performing exposures, fixed rate loan commitments, risk of retail prepayments and risk of early redemption have been considered in the calculation of the NII SOT and the EVE SOT.
- An indication of whether commercial margins or other spread components have been included in the calculation of the EVE SOT.
- The method used to determine the behavioral repricing time of the non-maturity deposits (NMDs), including a replicating model.
- With respect to NMDs, relevant drivers used to identify core balances.
- Changes in the balance sheet structure since the last IRRBB reporting.
- IRRBB mitigation and hedging strategies with respect to EVE and NII.
- Indication of the risk-free yield curve used for discounting in the context of EVE and SOT EVE.

Notes

1. EBA/GL/2022/14 of October 20, 2022; see EBA (2022a). The guidelines are issued pursuant to Article 84 of CRD IV (2013).
2. EBA/RTS/2022/09 and EBA/RTS/2022/10, both from October 20, 2022; see EBA (2022b) and EBA (2022c), respectively.
3. EBA/GL/2018/02 from July 19, 2018; see EBA (2018a).
4. See https://www.bis.org/bcbs/history.htm.
5. See https://www.bis.org/publ/bcbsc101.pdf.
6. For a detailed discussion of key institutional aspects of BCBS, see Gortsos (2023, 161–181).
7. BCBS (1988).
8. BCBS (1993).
9. BCBS (1997).
10. BCBS (2004b).
11. BCBS (2004a).
12. BCBS (2016b).
13. BCBS (2010).
14. BCBS (2012).
15. BCBS (2013).

16. BCBS (2016a).
17. BCBS (2019).
18. EU (2006, 117).
19. CRD III (2010, 8).
20. CRD IV (2013, 382).
21. CRD IV (2013, 391).
22. CRD V (2019, 256).
23. CRD V (2019, 272).
24. CRR II (2019, 132–133).
25. CRR III (2024).
26. Article 1 of the proposed Commission Delegated Regulation (EU) of July 24, 2024, amending Article 520a of CRR I (2013). See https://eur-lex.europa.eu/legal-content/EN/TXT/PDF/?uri=OJ:L_202402795.
27. For a detailed discussion of key institutional aspects of EBA, see Gortsos (2023, 388–423).
28. CEBS (2006a).
29. CEBS (2006b).
30. CEBS (2006b, 4–5).
31. CEBS (2006b, 5).
32. CEBS (2006b, 11).
33. CRD IV (2013, Article 98).
34. EBA (2013, 109–119).
35. OJ L, 2024/857, 24.4.2024, ELI: http://data.europa.eu/eli/reg_del/2024/857/oj.
36. OJ L, 2024/856, 24.4.2024, ELI: http://data.europa.eu/eli/reg_del/2024/856/oj.
37. EBA (2022a, 7) introduces a five-year cap on the weighted average repricing maturity for certain retail and wholesale deposits without a specified maturity.
38. Although already mandated by Principle 8 of BCBS (2016b), EBA (2018a) has not yet addressed this NII risk measure yet. It was introduced for the first time in EBA (2022b).
39. Article 20 of EBA (2022b).
40. However, EBA (2022b) cites Article 84 Paragraph 4 of CRD IV (2013), which gives national competent authorities (NCAs) the power to use the standardized approach if they consider that the simplified standardized approach is not adequate to capture the interest rate risk arising from non-trading book activities of that institution. An NCA is a public authority or body officially recognized by national law that

is empowered to supervise institutions. Examples for NCAs are the Bundesanstalt für Finanzdienstleistungsaufsicht (BaFin) in Germany or the Österreichische Finanzmarktaufsicht (FMA) in Austria.

41. Accounting NII does not include market or fair value changes.
42. Article 5 (2) of Commission Delegated Regulation (EU) 2024/856; OJ L, 2024/856, 24.4.2024, ELI: http://data.europa.eu/eli/reg_del/2024/856/oj.
43. OJ L, 2024/855, 24.4.2024, ELI: http://data.europa.eu/eli/reg_impl/2024/855/oj.
44. Optionality dictated or imposed by national regulatory or legal arrangements.

References

BCBS. 1988. International Convergence of Capital Measures and Capital Standards. Basel Committee on Banking Supervision, July 1988. https://www.bis.org/publ/bcbs04a.pdf. Accessed on January 18, 2025.

BCBS. 1993. Measurement of Banks' Exposure to Interest Rate Risk: Consultative Proposal. Basel Committee on Banking Supervision, April 1993. https://www.bis.org/publ/bcbs11.pdf. Accessed on January 18, 2025.

BCBS. 1997. Principles for the Management of Interest Rate Risk. Basel Committee on Banking Supervision, September 1997. https://www.bis.org/publ/bcbs29a.pdf. Accessed on January 18, 2025.

BCBS. 2004a. International Convergence of Capital Measurement and Capital Standards: A Revised Framework. Basel Committee on Banking Supervision, June 2004. https://www.bis.org/publ/bcbs107.pdf. Accessed on January 18, 2025.

BCBS. 2004b. Principles for the Management and Supervision of Interest Rate Risk. Basel Committee on Banking Supervision, July 2004. https://www.bis.org/publ/bcbs108.pdf. Accessed on January 18, 2025.

BCBS. 2010. Basel III: A Global Regulatory Framework for More Resilient Banks and Banking Systems. Basel Committee on Banking Supervision, December 2010. https://www.bis.org/publ/bcbs189_dec2010.pdf. Accessed on January 18, 2025.

BCBS. 2012. Fundamental Review of the Trading Book. Basel Committee on Banking Supervision, May 2012. https://www.bis.org/publ/bcbs219.pdf. Accessed on January 18, 2025.

BCBS. 2013. Fundamental Review of the Trading Book: A Revised Market Risk Framework. Basel Committee on Banking Supervision, October 2013. https://www.bis.org/publ/bcbs265.pdf. Accessed on January 18, 2025.

BCBS. 2016a. Standards: Minimum Capital Requirements for Market Risk. Basel Committee on Banking Supervision, January 2016. https://www.bis.org/bcbs/publ/d352.pdf. Accessed on January 18, 2025.

BCBS. 2016b. Interest Rate Risk in the Banking Book. Basel Committee on Banking Supervision, April 2016. https://www.bis.org/bcbs/publ/d368.pdf. Accessed on January 18, 2025.

BCBS. 2019. Minimum Capital Requirements for Market Risk, January 2019, revised in February 2019. https://www.bis.org/bcbs/publ/d457.pdf. Accessed on January 18, 2025.

CEBS. 2006a. Guidelines on the Application of the Supervisory Review Process Under Pillar 2 (CP03 revised). Committee of European Banking Supervisors, January 25, 2006. https://www.eba.europa.eu/documents/10180/585173/9705f895-fbfa-4e39-bac9-3def3127f545/GL03.pdf. Accessed on January 18, 2025.

CEBS. 2006b. Technical Aspects of the Management of Interest Rate Risk Arising from Non-trading Activities Under the Supervisory Review Process. Committee of European Banking Supervisors, October 3, 2006. https://www.eba.europa.eu/documents/10180/16094/16458627-8682-4e68-88a0-cd34363344c3/guidelines_IRRBB_000.pdf. Accessed on January 18, 2025.

CRD I. 2000. Directive 2000/12/EC of the European Parliament and of the Council of 20 March 2000 ("Capital Requirements Directive I"). OJ L 126, 26.05.2000, pp. 1–59. ELI: http://data.europa.eu/eli/dir/2000/12/oj.

CRD II. 2009. Directive 2009/111/EC of the European Parliament and of the Council of 16 September 2009 ("Capital Requirements Directive II"). OJ L 302, 17.11.2009, pp. 97–119. ELI: http://data.europa.eu/eli/dir/2009/111/oj

CRD III. 2010. Directive 2010/76/EU of the European Parliament and of the Council of 24 November 2010 ("Capital Requirements Directive III"). OJ L 329, 14.12.2010, pp. 3–35. ELI: http://data.europa.eu/eli/dir/2010/76/oj.

CRD IV. 2013. Directive 2013/36/EU of the European Parliament and of the Council of 26 June 2013 ("Capital Requirements Directive IV"). OJ L 176, 27.6.2013, pp. 338–436. ELI: http://data.europa.eu/eli/dir/2013/36/oj.

CRD V. 2019. Directive (EU) 2019/878 of the European Parliament and of the Council of 20 May 2019 ("Capital Requirements Directive V"). OJ L 150, 7.6.2019, pp. 253–295. ELI: http://data.europa.eu/eli/dir/2019/878/oj.

CRD VI. 2024. Directive (EU) 2024/1619 of the European Parliament and of the Council of 31 May 2024 ("Capital Requirements Directive VI"). OJ L, 2024/1619, 19.6.2024, ELI: http://data.europa.eu/eli/dir/2024/1619/oj.

CRR I. 2013. Regulation (EU) 575/2013 of the European Parliament and of the Council of 26 June 2013 ("Capital Requirements Regulation I"). OJ L, 2013/575, 27.6.2013, ELI: https://eur-lex.europa.eu/eli/reg/2013/575/oj

CRR II. 2019. Regulation (EU) 2019/876 of the European Parliament and of the Council of 20 May 2019 ("Capital Requirements Regulation II"). OJ L, 2019/867, 20.5.2019, ELI: https://eur-lex.europa.eu/eli/reg/2019/876/oj.

CRR III. 2024. Regulation (EU) 2024/1623 of the European Parliament and of the Council of 31. May 2024 ("Capital Requirements Regulation III"). OJ L, 2024/1623, 31.5.2024, ELI: http://data.europa.eu/eli/reg/2024/1623/oj.

EBA. 2014. Guidelines on Common Procedures and Methodologies for the Supervisory Review and Evaluation Process (SREP), EBA/GL/2014/13 from 19 December 2014, European Banking Authority. https://www.eba.europa.eu/documents/10180/935249/4b842c7e-3294-4947-94cd-ad7f94405d66/EBA-GL-2014-13%20(Guidelines%20on%20SREP%20methodologies%20and%20processes).pdf. Accessed on January 18, 2025.

EBA. 2015. Guidelines on the Management of Interest Rate Risk Arising From Non-trading Activities, Final Report, EBA/GL/2015/08 from 22 May 2015, European Banking Authority. https://www.eba.europa.eu/sites/default/files/documents/10180/1084098/ebfa5dd5-f897-404b-aa7d-95da2f0157f0/EBA-GL-2015-08%20GL%20on%20the%20management%20of%20interest%20rate%20risk%20.pdf. Accessed on January 18, 2025.

EBA. 2018a. Guidelines on the Management of Interest Rate Risk Arising From Non-trading Book Activities, Final Report, EBA/GL/2018/02 from 18 July 2018, European Banking Authority. https://www.eba.europa.eu/sites/default/files/document_library/Guidelines%20on%20the%20management%20of%20interest%20rate%20risk%20arising%20from%20non-trading%20activities%20(EBA-GL-2018-02).pdf. Accessed on January 18, 2025.

EBA. 2018b. Guidelines on the Revised Common Procedures and Methodologies for the Supervisory Review and Evaluation Process (SREP) and Supervisory Stress Testing, Final Report, EBA/GL/2018/03 From 19 July 2018, European Banking Authority. https://www.eba.europa.eu/sites/default/files/documents/10180/2282666/6c2e3962-6b95-4753-a7dc-68070a5ba662/Revised%20Guidelines%20on%20SREP%20%28EBA-GL-2018-03%29.pdf. Accessed on January 18, 2025.

EBA. 2022a. Guidelines on the Management of Interest Rate Risk and Credit Spread Risk Arising From Non-trading Book Activities, Final Report, EBA/GL/2022/14 From 20 October 2022, Mandated by Article 84 (6) of Directive 2013/36/EU (Capital Requirements Directive, CRD), European Banking Authority. https://www.eba.europa.eu/sites/default/files/document_library/Publications/Guidelines/2022/EBA-GL-2022-14%20GL%20on%20IRRBB%20and%20CSRBB/1041754/Guidelines%20on%20IRRBB%20and%20CSRBB.pdf. Accessed on January 18, 2025.

EBA. 2022b. Draft Regulatory Technical Standards Specifying Standardised and Simplified Standardised Methodologies to Evaluate the Risks Arising From Potential Changes in Interest Rates that Affect Both the Economic Value of Equity and the Net Interest Income of an Institution's Non-trading Book Activities in Accordance with 84(5) of Directive 2013/36/EU, Final Report,

EBA/RTS/2022/09 from 20 October 2022, European Banking Authority. https://www.eba.europa.eu/sites/default/files/document_library/Publications/Draft%20Technical%20Standards/2022/EBA-RTS-2022-09%20RTS%20on%20SA/1041755/Final%20draft%20RTS%20on%20SA.pdf. Accessed on January 18, 2025.

EBA. 2022c. Draft Regulatory Technical Standards Specifying Supervisory Shock Scenarios, Common Modelling and Parametric Assumptions and What Constitutes a Large Decline for the Calculation of the Economic Value of Equity and of the Net Interest Income in Accordance with Article 98(5a) of Directive 2013/36/EU, Final Report, EBA/RTS/2022/10 From 20 October 2022, European Banking Authority. https://www.eba.europa.eu/sites/default/files/document_library/Publications/Draft%20Technical%20Standards/2022/EBA-RTS-2022-10%20RTS%20on%20SOTs/1041756/Final%20draft%20RTS%20on%20SOTs.pdf. Accessed on January 18, 2025.

EU. 2006. Directive (EU) 2006/48/EC of the European Parliament and of the Council of 14 June 2006. OJ L, 2006/177, 14.6.2006, ELI: http://data.europa.eu/eli/dir/2006/48/2014-01-01.

Gortsos, Christos V. 2023. *The European Banking Regulation Handbook, Volume I: Theory of Banking Regulation, International Standards, Evolution and Institutional Aspects of European Banking Law*. Cham, CH: Palgrave Macmillan.

6

The Future of ALM

An unprecedented wave of technological-enabled innovation and global environmental changes have accelerated change and disruption in many areas of banking. Interest rate risk management and ALM are affected in several ways:

First, emerging financial technology (FinTech) is changing the nature of banking, allowing technology-based service providers to enter the banking value chain, potentially even taking the customer relationship away from incumbent banks. This is changing the traditional banking business, resulting in a different balance sheet decomposition and thus requiring adjustments to ALM.

Second, a new class of digital assets based on blockchain technology and peer-to-peer financial networks will allow banking end users (both consumers and institutional clients) to transact *directly* with each other. These decentralized finance (DeFi) instruments don't necessarily eliminate incumbent financial institutions as intermediaries, as they will likely continue to play a role as crypto-asset service providers (CASPs). However, risk management and ALM will look different for a CASP. At the same time, crypto- and token-based assets can play a role in the ALM process, for example when a bank finances itself by issuing crypto bonds. Moreover, users of innovative instruments, such as crypto credit cards, are likely to behave very differently from less technologically inclined customers who continue to rely on more traditional banking products. The evolving of preferences and needs of digitally savvy customers, or "digital natives," should be reflected in risk management assumptions. It is prudent to recalibrate legacy ALM systems to reduce banks' exposure to changes in customer behavior.

F. Tata, *Bank Asset-Liability Management*, https://doi.org/10.1007/978-3-031-80205-8_6

Third, rapidly evolving technological advances in computing, both on a hardware and on a software level, are enabling new risk management techniques. Big data and advanced analytics (BD&AA) tools are beginning to replace basic ALM techniques. Banks, regulators, and supervisors alike will eventually need to embrace new computational capabilities.

Fourth, climate risk management is beginning to impact banks' credit risk processes and is likely to become part of their broader risk management frameworks, including FTP. Regulators and supervisors are also beginning to expect banks to incorporate climate-related risk drivers into their internal risk models.

Finally, in today's environment, banks must adapt quickly to changing customer behavior. To this end, some banks have begun to incorporate behavioral models as part of their interest rate and liquidity risk management within ALM.

6.1 FinTech

Driven by a combination of rapidly evolving information technologies, changing customer expectations and evolving regulation, FinTech (a contraction of the words *finance* and *technology*) has begun to have a fundamental impact on many aspects of the modern economy. The Financial Stability Board (FSB) defines FinTech as follows:

> FinTech is defined as technology-enabled innovation in financial services that could result in new business models, applications, processes or products with an associated material effect on the provision of financial services.[1]

FinTech activities in banking are gaining traction across a wide range of activities, including mobile payment services, lending platforms, robo-advisory, wholesale payment innovations, or digital assets, typically delivered through the use of innovative computer technologies.[2] While some market participants view these areas as mere hype or "a solution in search of a problem," others point to potential benefits such as increased efficiency, transparency, competition, resilience and financial inclusion.

As the FSB points out, "[innovation] in financial services is not a new phenomenon. Over the past few decades, innovations have included credit cards in the 1960s, debit cards and cash dispensing terminals such as automated teller machines (ATMs) and telephone banking in the 1970s and 1980s, and new financial products in the wake of deregulation of bond and capital markets in the 1990s."[3] To some extent, then, FinTech is just a new term for the ever-present change in financial markets. Nevertheless, some banks seem to be stubbornly clinging to a business model that may have worked in the past, but is increasingly outdated in the wake of technological developments of the twenty-first century.

FinTech has enabled bank customers to react much more quickly and opportunistically to changes in the interest rate environment. Whereas "sleepy" depositors used to stay put when interest rates rose, FinTech (including mobile banking) has made it less time consuming, less difficult and less stressful to switch accounts.[4] There appears to be a trend among retail bank customers (mirroring a similar trend among institutional bank customers) to become more *transactional*, and less inclined to maintain a long-term relationship with their house bank in what is known as *relationship banking*.[5]

The changing behavior of customers using FinTech innovations requires banks to rethink their ALM frameworks, especially those used to model embedded options in non-maturity deposits (NMDs). The challenge for ALM is to develop new models that reflect a heterogeneous customer base and to rely on a relatively short history when recalibrating existing models.

Tailoring banking services to less digitally sophisticated customers is also not a sustainable option for banks. The problem for banks that do not innovate is that they will eventually run out of old-school customers. We are witnessing a large transfer of wealth from *baby boomers* to younger generations, *Generation X*, *Millennials* and *Generation Z*, who make up most of the so-called digital natives.[6] In the U.S. alone, it is estimated that approximately USD 70 trillion will be transferred between generations, highlighting the need for banks to better understand the banking attitudes, habits and preferences of new generations.[7] While only 1% of *Baby Boomers* trust FinTech to securely manage their personal financial data, the figure is 3% for *Millennials* and *Generation Z*.[8]

6.2 Digital Assets

One of the megatrends shaping the world of finance is the push toward decentralization. This new form of financial activity, referred to as decentralized finance or DeFi, aims to replace central market participants with a network of decentralized entities. The most prominent case of decentralization in the financial markets comes from the field of data storage in the form of the distributed ledger technology (DLT). DLT allows information to be stored through a distributed ledger, which is a repeated digital copy of data in multiple locations, as in a blockchain.

Virtually none of the DeFi-based instruments have been tested through a full financial cycle. Asa result, there is a lack of historical data that can be used to calibrate risk management and ALM models with respect to customer behavior (e. g., prepayment, early withdrawal, switching between financial service providers).

To illustrate this, we can look at an example from the area of non-maturity deposits (NMDs): As discussed in Sect. 2.4, banks rely heavily on customer sight deposits for funding. If interest rates rise and the bank does not immediately raise the customer deposit rate, some sight deposits are expected to be withdrawn, while some customers do not immediately respond to the increase in market rates and leave their money with the bank. Thus, deposit behavior is not fully elastic to changes in interest rates, and the behavioral maturity of these overnight funds may be modeled to be significantly longer than their contractual maturity. However, if the bank were to issue blockchain-based deposit tokens,[9] smart contracts[10] could be used by users to automate a transfer of deposits on the blockchain based on rules, which could include an interest rate input. Retail customers, possibly using easy-to-use apps on their smartphones, could "pre-program" their digital deposits to be automatically sold to a third party when the deposit rate becomes unattractive,[11] while the third party, acting rationally, would then likely trigger a withdrawal of funds from the bank. It would be naïve for a bank to assume that the behavior of its deposit base would remain unchanged if deposits were tokenized.

6.3 Big Data and Advanced Analytics

As early as 2020, the European Banking Authority (EBA) predicted the following:

> The growing use of Big Data and Advance Analytics (BD&AA), including Machine Learning, across the industry will rapidly evolve in the next few years.[12]

The EBA defines *Big Data* as "large volumes of different types of data, produced at high speed from many and varied sources (e. g. the internet of things, sensors, social media and financial market data collection), which are processed, often in real time, by IT tools (powerful processors, software and algorithms)" and *Advanced Analytics* as techniques that "include predictive and prescriptive analytical techniques, often using AI [artificial intelligence] and ML [machine learning] in particular, and are used to understand and recommend actions based on the analysis of high volumes of data from multiple sources, internal or external to the institution."[13]

Artificial intelligence (AI) can be defined as the mental ability like that of (human) intelligence performed by machines. Machine learning (ML) involves building a computer system that automatically improves with experience.[14] Novel risk management and stress testing techniques inspired by deep reinforcement learning have already entered the field of finance, such as Deep Hedging, Deep Treasury or Deep ALM.[15]

As banks collect a wealth of data from thousands and millions of end customers, it makes sense to gain insights that can be used for risk management and ALM. While the computing power of the past did not allow for detailed analysis of each individual customer, today's massive computing power, cheap data storage capacity, and advances in artificial intelligence and machine learning make it possible to assess risk in real time and at customer-level granularity. In the same way that social media platforms deliver individualized content to billions of users, banks could, for example, model the expected duration of each individual sight deposit in real time, based on each individual customer's behavior as observed by the bank. In an ideal world, the bank anticipates a customer's withdrawal before it happens and proactively makes the necessary ALM adjustments.[16]

Auditability is an important issue when it comes to the use of artificial intelligence and machine learning in ALM. As part of model governance, supervisors expect that when validating IRRBB measurement methodologies, "institution should document and explain model specification choices as part of the validation process."[17] The FSB suggests that "[in] some cases, firms may be simulating the outcomes of AI models in traditional models or restrict themselves to a smaller set of AI approaches that do not suffer from 'black box' problems."[18]

With machine learning models, the risks of data set uniformity, model herding (the inadvertent use of similar algorithms), procyclicality, and network interconnectedness could compound.[19] Regulators and supervisors need to focus on banks' governance of big data[20] analytics. This is highlighted by the FSB:

> Big data analytics are driving transformation across industries with the ability to conduct extensive analytics rapidly and enhance risk identification and assessment. Similar to the use of algorithms in other domains, such as securities trading, the complexity and opacity of some big data analytics models makes

> it difficult for authorities to assess the robustness of the models or new unforeseen risks in market behaviour, and to determine whether market participants are fully in control of their systems.[21]

At the same time, regulators and supervisors may (eventually) need to use AI and machine learning tools themselves, e. g., to identify outlier banks or better assess systemic risks.[22] According to Araujo et al. (2024), "AI systems could act as 'co- pilots' to human supervisory teams by learning from a combination of regulatory data, prior supervisory actions and broader market developments."[23]

6.4 Climate Risk Management

Climate change is an issue in all sectors of the economy. On the one hand, society as a whole aims to reduce greenhouse gas emissions[24]; on the other hand, every company has to start managing climate-related risks as part of its business model.

In the banking sector, efforts to integrate the management of climate risk (also known as carbon risk) into existing risk management frameworks are still at an early stage. At present, the focus is primarily on communication issues, such as ethical concerns about potential *greenwashing*[25] and the use of *green bank financing* projects.[26]

Climate risk impacts banks' earnings and capital through several transition channels. These include:

- Counterparty credit risk channel: The bank's customers and capital market counterparties may be affected by climate change. This affects their credit quality and should be reflected in credit risk management.
- Funding channel: Banks' funding channels (such as bond issuance) may be affected by their perceived climate risk. This affects their cost of funding.
- Investment channel: Banks' return on investment in assets (e. g., their securities portfolio) may be affected by climate risk. This affects not only the expected return on assets, but also the realized return after climate events have occurred.
- Regulatory channel: Regulators and supervisors are pushing banks to assess climate risks and to maintain capital and liquidity buffers. This affects, among other things, banks' regulatory cost of capital.

An example of an area where climate risk management is likely to become an integral part of treasury and ALM in the future is the FTP process. Certain climate events (flooding, extreme heat, etc.) can lead to adverse customer behavior (reduction in loan payments, withdrawal of deposits, increased use of credit facilities), and ideally the FTP rate should penalize business that leads to a concentration of these risks.

Regulators and supervisors are beginning to take climate risk more seriously. In 2022, the ECB conducted a *climate risk stress test* to assess how well banks are set up to manage climate-related risks in different scenarios, assessing physical risks such as heat waves, droughts and floods, as well as short- and long-term risks arising from the transition to a greener economy.[27] The stress test shows that while some progress has been made since 2020, "banks do not yet sufficiently incorporate climate risk into their stress-testing frameworks and internal models."[28]

In its General Principles on Climate and Environmental Risk, the ECB already expects banks to incorporate climate-related risk drivers into their internal risk models:

> Institutions should assess the materiality of all risks in the life cycle of their internal models (…), including climate- related and environmental risks. Where climate-related and environmental risks drivers are found to be relevant and material, institutions should include such risk drivers in their internal models approved for use for the calculation of own funds requirements for credit and market risk.[29]

6.5 Behavioral Modeling

In Sect. 3.3, we discussed how the field of behavioral economics can be used to better understand a bank's *customer base* and the *behavior of other banks*. Banks are currently still in the process of fully embracing behavioral modeling as part of their interest rate and liquidity risk management within ALM.

A common approach to behavioral modeling in ALM is to *segment* a bank's customer pool into more granular buckets according to customer-specific factors, such as socioeconomic status, borrowing history, geography, net income, or physical age.[30] Soulellis (2017, 123) details several key differentiators that can be used to model differentiated deposit balance behavior:

- The amount of originating incoming balance
- Whether or not a promotional or introductory deposit rate was given
- The physical age of the customer

- The depth and age of the customer's relationship with the bank
- The origination channel when opening the deposit (e. g., online vs. in a branch).

After segmenting the customer base, multiple behavioral models are individually calibrated to the different observed behaviors within each pool. On an ongoing basis, these models need to be adjusted, calibrated and back-tested to reflect changes in market factors (interest rates, etc.), macroeconomic events, new banking products, differences in customer sophistication, changes in competitor strategy and the evolution of the bank's balance sheet.

Regulators and supervisors have only recently begun to focus on the behavioral aspects of banks' IRRBB and ALM. The collapse of Silicon Valley Bank in 2023 (discussed in Chapter 4) has added to the sense of urgency to do so:

> Moreover, supervisors (…) have developed approaches based in behavioral science that incorporate data on institutional attitudes and norms related to risk factors, such as complacency, overconfidence, short-term focus, and lack of effective challenge that can reveal institutional blind spots and contribute to vulnerabilities like those seen at SVB.[31]

Notes

1. FSB (2017, 7).
2. These include artificial intelligence (AI), machine learning, could computing, distributed ledger technology (DLT), cryptography, natural language processing (NLP), and biometrics.
3. FSB (2017, 10) with reference to Dermine (2016).
4. Acharya et al. (eds.) (2023, 47).
5. From the customer's perspective, a strong and lasting banking relationship can be valuable because, as Ongena and Smith (2001, 449) point out, "banks will be more willing to make unprofitable loans to customers during difficult financial times when they trust losses will be recouped over the course of a long relationship." On the other hand, banks may be tempted to lock in customers and to extract monopoly rents.
6. *Digital natives* are consumers who have grown up with digital technology. *Generation Z* is widely referred to as the generational cohort born between 1995 and 2010, following *Millennials* (born between the early 1980s and the late 1990s), following *Generation X* (born between

the mid-1960 and early 1980s), and *Baby Boomers* (born between the 1940s and the 1960s).

7. MX Technologies (2021, 5).
8. MX Technologies (2021, 16).
9. Deposit tokens are the equivalent of existing commercial bank deposits, but that are recorded on a blockchain. This allows them to be transferred from a seller's digital wallet to a buyer's digital wallet.
10. Rule-based algorithms that execute transactions on the blockchain, often in real time, without the need for intervention by the parties involved.
11. While deposit rates are typically below market rates because bank customers derive a benefit from the transaction and payment services provided by the bank, customers could search the market for the bank that charges the lowest spread between deposit rates and fair value market rates and move their funds accordingly.
12. EBA press release dated January 13, 2020: "EBA Report Identifies Key Challenges in the Roll Out of Big Data and Advanced Analytics"; see https://www.eba.europa.eu/publications-and-media/press-releases/eba-report-identifies-key-challenges-roll-out-big-data-and.
13. EBA/REP/2020/01; see EBA (2020, 11).
14. Jordan and Mitchell (2015, 255).
15. See, for example, Buehler et al. (2019), Englisch et al. (2023), and Krabichler et al. (2024).
16. While this sounds like *science fiction* in the banking world, it is worth noting that this kind of data mining and monetization of information is at the very heart of the largest and most valuable technology companies, often referred to as Big Tech. These include Alphabet (Google), Amazon, Apple, Meta (formerly Facebook), Microsoft, Netflix, Baidu and Alibaba.
17. EBA/GL/2022/14; see EBA (2022, 33).
18. FSB (2017, 56).
19. See Aldasoro (2024, 2).
20. A term referring to the massive amount of data that is generated by increasingly powerful and inexpensive digital tools, information systems, storage, data sensors, and other IT hardware and software.
21. FSB (2017, 2).
22. This could potentially lead to a technology race between regulators and supervisors on the one hand, and private sector institutions on the other hand. Whether regulators and supervisors will be able to keep up in terms of up-skilling their staff and making the necessary

IT investments remains to be seen, as Goldman Sachs estimates that global private sector investment in AI will approach USD 200 bn by 2025; see Goldman Sachs (2023).

23. Araujo et al. (2024, 5).
24. Best reflected in the so-called *Paris Agreement*, a legally binding international treaty on climate change. It was adopted in 2015 by 196 parties at the UN Climate Change Conference (COP21) in Paris and entered into force in November 2016. Its overall goal is to keep the global average temperature increase well below 2 °C above pre-industrial levels, and to pursue efforts to limit the temperature increase to 1.5 °C above pre-industrial levels.
25. Greenwashing refers to potentially deceptive and misleading claims (e. g., in advertising) about *green* and *sustainable* business practices.
26. Green bank financing is bank-led financing of primarily private investments in green energy and climate transition. McKinsey (2022) estimates that in the U.S. alone, some USD 27 trillion in climate investments may be needed to achieve net-zero greenhouse gas emissions by 2050.
27. The European Central Bank (ECB) is required to conduct annual stress tests on supervised entities as part of its Supervisory Review and Evaluation Process (SREP) as set out in Article 100 of the Capital Requirements Directive IV (CRD IV). In 2022, the ECB conducted a climate risk stress test on the largest and most significant 100+ European banks (so-called *significant institutions*, or SI). The results of the ECB's climate stress test feed into the SREP from a qualitative perspective. There is no direct impact on banks' capital through the Pillar 2 guidance. All participating banks have received individual feedback and are expected to take action accordingly, in line with the set of best practices published by the ECB.
28. ECB (2022, 53).
29. ECB (2024, 13).
30. The process of customer segmentation and clustering can be facilitated by classification algorithms, often using of big data and advanced analytics, including machine learning, deep learning or neural network computing.
31. Barr (2023, 97).

References

Acharya, Viral V, Mathew P. Richardson, Kermit L. Schoenholtz, and Bruce Tuckman (eds.). 2023. SVB and Beyond: The Banking Stress of 2023. NYU Stern White Paper. https://www.stern.nyu.edu/experience-stern/about/departments-centers-initiatives/centers-of-research/volatility-and-risk-institute/research/svb-and-beyond-banking-stress-2023. Accessed on January 18, 2025.

Aldasoro, Iñaki, Leonardo Gambacorta, Anton Korinek, Vatsala Shreeti, and Merlin Stein. 2024. Intelligent Financial System: How AI Is Transforming Finance, BIS Working Papers No. 1194, June 2024. https://www.bis.org/publ/work1194.pdf. Accessed on January 18, 2025.

Araujo, Douglas, Sebastian Doerr, Leonardo Gambacorta, and Bruno Tissot. 2024. Artificial Intelligence in Central Banking. Bank for International Settlements, Bulletin No. 84, 23 January 2024. https://www.bis.org/publ/bisbull84.pdf. Accessed on January 18, 2025.

Barr, Michael S. 2023. Review of the Federal Reserve's Supervision and Regulation of Silicon Valley Bank, Board of Governors of the Federal Reserve System, April 28, 2023. https://www.federalreserve.gov/publications/files/svb-review-20230428.pdf. Accessed on January 18, 2025.

Buehler, Hans, Lukas Gonon, Josef Teichmann, and Ben Wood. 2019. Deep Hedging. *Quantitative Finance* Vol. 19, No. 8, 1271–1291. https://doi.org/10.1080/14697688.2019.1571683.

Dermine, Jean. 2016. Digital Banking and Market Disruption: A Sense of déjà vu? Financial Stability Review, Banque de France, April 2016, No. 20, 17–24. https://publications.banque-france.fr/sites/default/files/medias/documents/financial-stability-review-20_2016-04.pdf. Accessed on January 18, 2025.

EBA. 2020. EBA Report on Big Data and Advanced Analytics. EBA/REP/2020/01 From January 2020. European Banking Authority. https://www.eba.europa.eu/sites/default/files/document_library//Final%20Report%20on%20Big%20Data%20and%20Advanced%20Analytics.pdf. Accessed on January 18, 2025.

EBA. 2022. Guidelines on the Management of Interest Rate Risk and Credit Spread Risk Arising From Non-trading Book Activities, EBA/GL/2022/14 From 20 October 2022, Mandated by Article 84 (6) of Directive 2013/36/EU (Capital Requirements Directive, CRD), European Banking Authority. https://www.eba.europa.eu/sites/default/files/document_library/Publications/Guidelines/2022/EBA-GL-2022-14%20GL%20on%20IRRBB%20and%20CSRBB/1041754/Guidelines%20on%20IRRBB%20and%20CSRBB.pdf. Accessed on January 18, 2025.

ECB. 2022. 2022 Climate Risk Stress Test. European Central Bank, Juli 2022. https://www.bankingsupervision.europa.eu/ecb/pub/pdf/ssm.climate_stress_test_report.20220708~2e3cc0999f.en.pdf. Accessed on January 18, 2025.

ECB. 2024. ECB Guide to Internal Models. European Central Bank, February 2024. https://www.bankingsupervision.europa.eu/ecb/pub/pdf/ssm.supervisory_guides202402_internalmodels.en.pdf. Accessed on January 18, 2025.

Englisch, Holger, Thomas Krabichler, Konrad J. Müller, and Marc Schwarz. 2023. Deep Treasury Management for Banks. *Artificial Intelligence* Vol. 6. https://doi.org/10.3389/frai.2023.1120297.

FSB. 2017. Financial Stability Implications From Fintech: Supervisory and Regulatory Issues That Merit Authorities' Attention, Financial Stability Board. https://www.fsb.org/wp-content/uploads/R270617.pdf. Accessed on January 18, 2025.

Goldman Sachs. 2023. AI Investment Forecast to Approach $200 Billion Globally by 2025. https://www.goldmansachs.com/intelligence/pages/ai-investment-forecast-to-approach-200-billion-globally-by-2025.html. Accessed on January 18, 2025.

Jordan, Michael, and Tom Mitchell. 2015. Machine Learning: Trends, Perspectives, and Prospects. *Science* Vol. 349, No. 6245, 255–260.

Krabichler, Thomas, and Josef Teichmann. 2024. A Case Study for Unlocking the Potential of Deep Learning in Asset-Liability-Management. *Frontiers in Artificial Intelligence* Vol. 6. https://doi.org/10.3389/frai.2023.1177702.

McKinsey. 2022. Navigating America's Net-Zero Frontier: A Guide for Business Leaders. https://www.mckinsey.com/~/media/mckinsey/business%20functions/sustainability/our%20insights/navigating%20americas%20net%20zero%20frontier%20a%20guide%20for%20business%20leaders/navigating-americas-net-zero-frontier-a-guide-for-business-leaders-vf.pdf. Accessed on January 18, 2025.

MX Technologies. 2021. Modern Banking Experiences for Gen Z & Millennials. https://cms.mx.com/assets/9ec3dc6f-e3ee-4209-98c7-d59601ae6941. Accessed on January 18, 2025.

Ongena, Steven, and David C. Smith. 2001. The Duration of Bank Relationships. *Journal of Financial Economics*, Vol. 61, No. 3 (September), 449–475.

Soulellis, George. 2017. The Modelling of Non-maturity Deposits. In: Bohn, Andreas, and Marije Elkenbracht-Huizing (eds.): *The Handbook of ALM in Banking*, Second Edition, Risk Books, 109–145.

Correction to: Bank Asset-Liability Management

Correction to:
F. Tata, *Bank Asset-Liability Management*,
https://doi.org/10.1007/978-3-031-80205-8

The original version of this book was inadvertently published with formatting issues primarily related to tables and missing paragraphs in Chapters 2 and 3, which have now been updated. The book and the chapters have been updated with the changes.

The updated versions of these chapters can be found at
https://doi.org/10.1007/978-3-031-80205-8_2
https://doi.org/10.1007/978-3-031-80205-8_3

F. Tata, *Bank Asset-Liability Management*, https://doi.org/10.1007/978-3-031-80205-8_7

Index

F. Tata, *Bank Asset-Liability Management*, https://doi.org/10.1007/978-3-031-80205-8

N

O

R

The manufacturer's authorised representative in the EU is Springer Nature Customer Service Centre GmbH, Europaplatz 3, 69115 Heidelberg, Germany. If you have any concerns regarding our products, please contact ProductSafety@springernature.com

Printed and bound by CPI Group (UK) Ltd, Croydon, CR0 4YY
30/09/2026
02225567-0009